HYTHE LIBRARY
01303 267111

12/07.

Staplehurst Library
(01580 WITHDRAWN

7/08

05. 08.

20. SEP 08

11/10/08

14. NOV 08

KT-419-897

Mrs Brad

20. DEC 08

15. MAY 09.

−2 JUN 2009

23 JULY

16 FEB 2010

− 8 WITHDRAWN

Please return on or before the latest date above.
You can renew online at *www.kent.gov.uk/libs*
or by telephone 08458 247 200

C153183016

MISS CHOPSTICKS

MISS CHOPSTICKS

Xinran

Translated from Chinese by Esther Tyldesley

CHIVERS

British Library Cataloguing in Publication Data available

This Large Print edition published by BBC Audiobooks Ltd, Bath, 2007.
Published by arrangement with Random House.

U.K. Hardcover ISBN 978 1 405 64236 1
U.K. Softcover   ISBN 978 1 405 64237 8

Maps by Reginald Piggott

Printed and bound in Great Britain by
Antony Rowe Ltd., Chippenham, Wiltshire

For PanPan

My son, my best friend, the powerhouse
behind my motherhood

A NOTE ON CHINESE NAMES

In Chinese, the surname comes before the given name, e.g. 'Li Zhongguo', who, in this book, is the eldest son in the Li family. 'Zhongguo' is the Pinyin way of writing the Chinese character that represents Mr Li's name 李. Pinyin is a language system that uses the roman alphabet to represent the sounds of Standard Mandarin. However, in Chinese, different characters can have the same sound. 忠 (pronounced *zhong*), which means 'loyalty', sounds exactly the same as 中 (also pronounced *zhong*), which means 'middle' or 'central'. For this reason, the Chinese often hasten to give the meaning of their name when introducing themselves, to avoid confusion. For example, in chapter eleven of *Miss Chopsticks*, 'Li Zhongjia', the second brother in the Li family, is asked by the policeman how to write his name: 'Li as in the fruit tree? Zhong as in loyalty? Jia as in family?'

Names are further complicated by the fact that a lot of Chinese are called one thing at home, and another on their official registration documents. This is why, in chapter four, the managers at the Dragon Water-Culture Centre are so surprised to find that Five doesn't have any other name but 'Five', which sounds like a family nickname.

TRANSLATOR'S NOTE

Translating anything from Chinese into English is never an easy task. The two languages are so different, both structurally and grammatically; individual words often do not have an exact match; what seems pithy and concise in one language can seem clumsy and tedious in the other. I have heard translating between the two compared to capturing a cloud and putting it in a box: you will never quite get it all in—and by the time you are through, the result, though not without its own merits, will no longer be exactly the same shape.

This was particularly true when trying to convey a sense of Xinran's Nanjing, a city with a distinctive regional culture, centuries of history and its own very special cuisine. As a native of Nanjing, Xinran has brought her home city vividly to life in this book. However, her passing references to the things that make Nanjing unique often assume a certain knowledge in the reader, and take a lot of explaining in English. Fortunately for me, Xinran was always happy to help answer my queries. What are *Yangchun* noodles? What was it the Red Guards did with the fine paper from the houses of the courtesans? Surely that thing Nanjing girls love to eat couldn't really be a boiled egg with a feather-covered embryo inside . . . or could it? But finding answers to my questions was only the beginning of my work: how could I incorporate what Xinran had told me into the text, while at the same time keeping her lightness of touch and not drowning the reader in information?

Another problem was the shape of the Chinese language. There are not many different sounds in Mandarin, providing endless opportunities for puns, and allowing the Chinese to express a great deal of sly humour in very few syllables. Preserving these flashes of brief, offhand wit is always one of the hardest challenges for a translator, and was particularly so in this book, which is full of such humour. A related challenge was Chinese's great wealth of proverbs, folk sayings and four-character set phrases handed down from the classical language. Xinran's text is richly studded with these idioms, which are highly condensed and contain more information in four or five characters than a long English sentence. Include every detail and you end up with a ponderous, inelegant English style; leave them out and the language becomes sparse, dull, and quite unlike the lively original. How, too, could I convey to the reader the ideas behind the political slogans with which the characters jokingly pepper their conversation without embarking on digressions to explain Chinese politics?

A further issue for this book was its use of register and dialect. In a country bigger than continental Europe, dialects vary hugely from region to region, to the point where some dialects could arguably be classed as different languages altogether (the incident in the dormitory where girls from different provinces of China cannot understand each other is no exaggeration). On top of this, north China is as different from the south as the east is from the west, or Germany from Spain. All of this is reflected in the way people talk. Because the heroines of *Miss Chopsticks* come from a poor, country village, their way of expressing themselves, and the logic behind their thinking, is completely different from that of their city employers. What's more, the fact that, unlike her sisters, Six has been to school for several years means that she speaks and thinks in yet another register. Trying to give all the characters in this book individual voices, retaining their liveliness and local colour without slipping into parody, was far from simple!

No translation can ever live up to the variety and beauty of the original. Still, I hope that when you open the box that is this book, you will find enough of Xinran's beautiful cloud— the sense of place; her empathy with the resourcefulness and courage of three young women so far from home they seem to have entered another time; the moments of

poignancy, and the flashes of subtle sarcasm—
to give you a sense of what I found when I first
took up *Miss Chopsticks* and began to read.

Esther Tyldesley, Edinburgh, February 2007

CONTENTS

INTRODUCTION

Before I came to England in 1997, I worked as a radio presenter in Nanjing. My programme *Words on the Night Breeze* was a talk show that discussed women's issues and, in order to research items for the programme, I frequently travelled to many corners of China. Once, in a small village in the northern province of Shanxi, I heard about a woman who had committed suicide by drinking pesticide because she couldn't give birth to a boy—or, as the Chinese put it, she couldn't 'lay eggs'. Virtually no one in the village would attend her funeral, and I asked her husband what he felt about this. 'You can't blame them,' he said, without a trace of rancour. 'They don't want her bad luck to rub off on them. Besides, it's her fault that she only managed to give birth to a handful of chopsticks and no roof-beam.' I was struck by this way of referring to girls and boys. I had never heard it before, but it seemed to epitomise the manner in which the Chinese view the differences between men and women. While men are believed to be the strong providers, who hold up the roof of the household, women are merely fragile, workaday tools, to be used and then discarded. The thought made me feel melancholy, but, as

I was standing there pondering the man's words, I heard one of his daughters pipe up from nearby, 'I'll show the people in this village who's a chopstick and who's a roof-beam.'

In the course of my work as a journalist, I met many 'chopsticks'—girls from poor villages who lived lives of drudgery in arranged marriages. At first my encounters with them were limited largely to my visits to the countryside. However, as China began to reform its economy during the 1980s, and peasants were allowed to seek work in the cities, these 'chopstick' girls began to be found working as waitresses and cleaners in city restaurants, shops and hotels. City people would often overlook them, almost as if they weren't there, but I always tried to engage them in conversation, and to find out their stories. And I thought about them a lot when I first arrived in London.

In order to survive financially in those early days in England, I worked for a short time as a shop cleaner and waitress. Western people looked through me in the same way as city people looked through 'chopstick' girls in China, and I felt that I understood better what their life must be like. I was inspired by the self-belief and determination that drove them to make a place for themselves away from their homes and relatives. As I've said, that period of my life was brief, and, after working as a teacher, I was able in 2002 to publish my first book, *The Good Women of China*. Since then I have returned frequently to my homeland and have watched the extraordinary changes that are taking place in China as it surges into the twenty-first century. Whenever I visit, I see hundreds of chopstick girls becoming part of the structure that holds up the roof of China, in the same way that China itself, which was closed to its neighbours for so long, is now becoming part of the framework that holds up the world.

For a long time now I have wanted to write down some of the stories of the girls that I have met. I've felt that, if I didn't capture these lives for myself, my son, and for others, I would regret it deeply. Of all the girls I have talked to, there are three particularly close to my heart, and whose stories seem to speak for so many others. In order to protect their identities, I have written this book as if they were sisters who all worked in Nanjing, even though, in real life, they are not related to each other and I only met one of them in Nanjing—the other two came from Beijing and Shanghai.

It has given me great pleasure to write about Nanjing, the place I love best in China. Situated on the lower reaches of the Yangzi River, it is a city of huge importance in Chinese history and culture. It was the capital of six dynasties and, when the Republic of

China was founded on 29 December 1911, with Sun Yatsen as its provisional President, Nanjing became its capital too. Evidence of its long history is everywhere—in the beautiful Confucius Temple, situated near the Qinhuai river, and in the great city wall, which was built between 1366 and 1386 by Emperor Zhu Yuanzhang after he founded the Ming Dynasty. This wall was constructed with such skill and was so strong that it still exists almost in its entirety, and is the oldest standing city wall in the world. Of course, modern Nanjing has spread beyond its boundaries and, of the thirteen original gates, only two are still standing. But, walking along the top of the wall, as I liked to do when I lived and worked in the city, it is possible to look down at the ancient trees and the old moat, and imagine oneself back in time. Nanjing is renowned for its plum blossom and, in spring, I loved to watch the first pink buds open against the backdrop of dark-green cedars which are a feature of the city. Outside the walls, parks had been created where, throughout the day, you could watch Nanjingers relaxing amidst the trees. The morning was the time for old people to exercise and play chess; later in the day women would come to chat, sew and prepare vegetables; in the early evening, men would stop by on their way back from work until their wives or children called them home for dinner.

4

In 2002, I revisited one of my favourite haunts: the section of wall that lies in the south of the city. I was astounded to find it transformed. Hundreds of buildings had sprung up outside the wall, like bamboo shoots after rain, and there was a large street market. It was then that I thought that perhaps the story of my chopstick girls should begin here, close to the Zhonghua Gate that has stood for six hundred years and witnessed so much joy and pain.

1

UNDER THE BIG WILLOW

Beside Nanjing's ancient moat, there is a big old willow tree much loved by the people who live nearby. Beneath its shady branches, men play chess and local women peel vegetables or scour cooking pots while they sit and chat to each other, occasionally glancing across the water at the crumbling city wall with its magisterial gate, which has survived since the Ming dynasty. These days it's not easy to spot the willow tree amidst the hubbub. The local street market, which sells everything from fruit and vegetables to animals and bicycles, has become so popular that crowds of people throng the narrow lanes of stalls and shops. And a new job centre has been built not far away, which attracts queues of migrant workers wanting to take part in China's boom.

It wasn't always like this. In the late nineties, these streets close to the southernmost gate in the city wall were far sleepier. There was no ring road, few people had cars and, if you wanted to get somewhere fast, you had to endure a bone-shaking ride in a makeshift taxi that was actually one of the three-wheeled tractors mass-produced for agriculture. Yet, even then, the traffic must have seemed extraordinary to someone newly arrived from the countryside. To people brought up with a peasant lifestyle, who had never seen cars, tall buildings or telephones, and who were often illiterate, the city, with its looming wall, was a huge and daunting prospect. Fortunately for them, the men and women under the big willow were always happy to help a stranger, and would give them the nod about friends and acquaintances who had a job to offer. Little by little, the big willow gained a reputation for being the place to go if you were looking for work, and the market beside it grew ever bigger, much to the delight of the local government officials who got more rent from the stall holders, and the annoyance of the local residents who complained about the noise and the dirt.

This story starts in 2001, when the market was neither big nor small, and the men and women under the willow were good at finding people jobs but not yet overwhelmed by the task. It begins on a cold, February morning when a nineteen-year-old girl called Sanniu, which means 'Three' in Chinese, found herself standing beside the big willow tree, bewildered by the coming and going around her. Three was running away from home because her parents planned to marry her to the crippled son of a local government official. She had been lucky. Her Uncle Two had been sympathetic to her plight and had agreed to help her leave their small village in Anhui Province. He worked on the building sites of Zhuhai, a prosperous city on the southern coast of China, and only ever came back to the village at New Year, when they celebrated Spring Festival. As soon as he had arrived home that year, he had seen what was in store for Three and promised secretly he would take her with him when he returned to his job at the end of the holiday.

Uncle Two was the second brother in the Li family; Three's father was the first. Both brothers were dogged by the misfortune of having families of girls. In fact, Three was the third daughter of six. Her father had been so disappointed by his lack of sons that he had never given his children real names, and so they became known by the order in which they had been born.

It was one thing to help Three escape from the village, but quite another to know what to do with her. Uncle Two had racked his brains until he remembered his friend, Gousheng, who came from Nanjing. Gousheng was one of the migrant workers who worked with him on the building sites and Uncle Two often spent the night at his home in Nanjing in order to break the long journey between Anhui and Zhuhai. He had a warm-hearted, capable wife who sold tofu from a tiny shop, and would be just the person to give Three advice.

What Uncle Two didn't know—and which

would prove to be very useful—was that Gousheng's wife was one of the best-known traders in her area, and that her shop was situated not far from the old willow. Everyone in the neighbourhood called her the Tofu Lady and used to joke that her personality was hotter than the chilli oil she served, and her voice bigger than her minuscule shop.

Fortunately for Three, the Tofu Lady had also refused to marry the man her parents had chosen for her. In the early nineties, she had been living in Shanxi, a poor, dry province in northen China, and had eloped with her childhood sweetheart, Gousheng, rather than marry the son of a neighbouring family in exchange for a wife for her older brother. She and Gousheng had taken the bus to Xuzhou, the furthest destination their local bus station had been able to offer. But even there, they felt worried that their parents might find them, so they gritted their teeth and paid tens of yuan for train tickets as far south as they could go: all the way to Nanjing. In Nanjing they were forced to recognise that dreams must give way to reality. They had just enough money for three nights in the city's cheapest guesthouse; after that they were penniless. On the fourth day, Gousheng had joined a labour gang that was going to work down south, while the Tofu Lady found a menial job in a small takeaway restaurant selling stinky tofu fritters: a great Nanjing speciality not unlike deep-fried blue cheese.

From then on, life was hard. Gousheng came back to Nanjing only for the Spring Festival holiday, when many of the migrant workers returned home for a month. But, even then, the couple had to be secretive about their relationship. With no authorisation from their village they could not obtain a marriage certificate, and cohabitation was still against the law. If anyone asked, they said they had lost their certificate and were getting a new one, while all the time secretly searching for someone who would make them a fake. A few years passed, and they managed to save some money. It was just enough for the Tofu Lady to bribe the Nanjing police to authorise their marriage, and to obtain the necessary permission to set up her own little tofu shop.

In fact this so-called shop was really no more than a hole in the wall. It had a front open to the elements and a few rickety wooden tables set out on the road. Inside, the entire establishment consisted of a wok of oil for deep-frying, a stove made from an oil drum, an old school desk she had picked up somewhere, etched all over with mathematical equations and sums, and a bench that could seat one person comfortably but was cramped for two. There was a bottle of soy sauce, a small jar of chilli oil and a few cheap disposable bowls and chopsticks.

Although the locals made jokes about the

Tofu Lady, they also acknowledged that her heart was warmer than her wok of boiling oil. She never took money from children who wanted a snack and she couldn't abide seeing girls from poor families picked on. If a country girl in search of a job stopped at the shop to ask her way to the big willow, the Tofu Lady would force her to sit down and eat several bamboo skewers of stinky tofu before she went on her way—without pausing to enquire whether or not the girl was partial to this particular delicacy. Rumour has it that, if a country girl had experienced this once, the next time she came to visit she would bring along a steamed bun or a pancake so as to avoid having to accept any tofu, the strong smell of which hung like a cloud over the whole area.

Three and Uncle Two, however, relished the tofu they ate when they eventually found their way to the Tofu Lady's shop on that February morning. They had got up before dawn to catch the long-distance bus, and were so hungry that they wolfed down several skewers of it. They had barely finished when the Tofu Lady banked up her fire, asked the owner of the breakfast stall next door to keep an eye on things, and, without taking off her apron, marched Three and her uncle over to the big willow to see if any of the chess players there had connections that could set the frightened country girl on the right track.

They arrived in the middle of an argument. A group of chess fanatics were engaged in a heated, red-faced debate about whether one of them should have moved his knight, while four old ladies who were sorting vegetables a little distance away looked on in amusement.

'Hey,' shouted the Tofu Lady, her loud voice easily making itself heard above the shouting, 'haven't you lot had enough of bickering about your games? Why not do a good turn for once and give this girl a helping hand?'

The men all turned round at once.

'So, Tofu Lady,' one of them shouted, 'who's your maiden in distress today? At this rate, you might as well turn that tiny snack bar of yours into a job centre. You could call it the "International Centre for Village and City Integration".'

'Yeah,' said another, 'the government may tell us that our businesses should be "International", but we're already ahead of the game here. In six months, your pokey little lane will be covered in signs for Foreign/Chinese Joint-Funded Companies and Global Ventures. You'll have everything but the United Nations!'

The people under the tree burst into loud laughter, but their teasing didn't bother the Tofu Lady. It was her philosophy that if you didn't have the money to amuse yourself, you needed a bit of idle chatter to spice up your life, otherwise you'd go mad from boredom. She turned to a man who was standing slightly apart from the others.

'Mr Guan Buyu, I heard that girl you helped the other day has gone on to great things in the department store. You may rather watch chess than play it, but when it comes to people, they're pawns in your hands. So, hurry up and think of something for our Three here. Aren't you the one who's always saying, "You should seize the moment when a life's at stake, for gratitude is eternal"?'

The man standing next to Guan Buyu nudged him and chuckled. 'Who'd have thought the Tofu Lady was so quick off the mark? These days as soon as she opens her mouth, logic and philosophy come pouring out!'

'If I am, it's all thanks to your training,' said the Tofu Lady, smiling. 'This big tree seems to have become a kind of school for philosophers, like the ancients had. But come on, let's hear your ideas. Country girls are like plants trying to grow through cracks in stone: they need a bit of nurturing.'

'Yes, do stop trying to be clever all of you,' shouted someone. 'If you know of something for the girl, let's hear it. The sooner we get rid of the Tofu Lady, the sooner we can get back to the chess match. What's the fun of a game half played?'

At this, the suggestions came thick and fast.

14

'I've heard that Ma Dahao has opened an International Interior Decorating Materials Centre. Perhaps they're in need of workers there?'

'Think before you speak! It takes brute strength to move that kind of gear about. She might be strong for a girl, but she only comes up to my shoulder. How could she work alongside male porters?'

'Then how about the Good Luck Dumpling Restaurant? Uncle Wang, you're their neighbour. Sound them out for her.'

'Can't be done. You've only to look at this girl to know she's from a poor village where they eat only sweet-potato flour and rice. How will she know how to stuff dumplings? The boss of the Good Luck is looking for people who can make thirty dumplings a minute. I can't pass a pawn off as a knight!'

It was at this point that Guan Buyu stepped forward.

'Little sister,' he said to Three in an avuncular manner, 'why don't you tell us what you have an aptitude for and then we might be able to think of something for you.'

Three, who had been standing there, stunned by the incomprehensible conversation that was flying about her ears, was thrown into confusion. She had no idea what the man meant by 'aptitude' but made a guess.

'I love to eat eels when I can get them. My mother always says that eels the size of a pen are the best: longer and they're too old, shorter and there's nothing to eat on them . . .'

Yet another gale of laughter followed. The Tofu Lady put her arm round Three's shoulders, and whispered, '*Aptitude* is not the same as *appetite*. It's an educated person's word for the thing that you're good at. Tell them what it is you do well.'

Three blushed a deep red. She thought of all the warnings about language Uncle Two had given her as they travelled through the night. 'City people never use crude language,' he had said, but he hadn't explained what kind of language they did use. She took a deep breath.

'Mother says that, when I arrange vegetables in the baskets for her to take to the market, they look very pretty and catch people's eyes so she gets a good price. And I can look after children. I took care of my three younger sisters . . .'

'You've got three more, younger, sisters?' someone broke in.

'Yes, and two older ones. My father is very unhappy that my mother gave birth to six chopsticks one after another . . .'

The red-faced man who had protested at the idea of Three working at the Interior Decorating Centre looked at her in surprise.

'That's the first I've heard of people giving birth to chopsticks. What on earth do you mean?'

16

Three blushed an even deeper red and looked over at her uncle as she whispered her reply, terrified of saying something wrong.

'In my village, girls are called "chopsticks" and boys "roof-beams". They all say that girls are no good because a chopstick can't support a roof.'

But hardly anyone was listening to her answer because they were all debating the fact that she belonged to a family of six children.

'How is it there's no one in charge of the Birth-control Policy where you come from?'

'I . . . I don't know.'

'Doesn't your Production Brigade keep an eye on you?'

'I s'pose . . . I'm not sure . . .'

'We've heard that, in the countryside, they tear down houses and smash the furniture to punish families who have a second child. How come your Production Brigade hasn't done anything about your family?'

'I don't know. Two of my father's younger brothers are the Production Brigade Heads, and I've never seen them breaking up anyone's stuff or pulling down anyone's house . . .'

'Oh, so that's it! You've got an influential family. Well, if they're so important, why have you left to look for work?'

'I . . .'

Three was lost for words.

'Oh, for heaven's sake,' broke in the Tofu Lady, 'leave the poor girl alone. It's bad

17

enough that she's had to leave her home without you lot giving her the third degree. Her uncle's just told me her story. Listen, then you'll change your tune. It's like this. Those two powerful uncles of hers have got everyone eating out of the palms of their hands. They've already turned a blind eye to the Birth-control Policy, and now they're trying to curry favour with the Head of their area by organising a marriage between Three here and his crippled son. Her eldest sister was married at seventeen to the regional Head's widowed uncle—fifty, if he was a day . . . It makes me speechless with rage that these young girls' lives should be in the hands of such bastards, just because they have money or power . . .'

The Tofu Lady's outburst was followed by silence as everyone stood and looked at Three in pity.

As for Three, she was utterly bemused. No one in her village would ever dare to talk about local Heads, or even ordinary men like that. And certainly no man would listen to a woman in the way that the chess players here were listening to the Tofu Lady. Uncle Two had been right: city women really did have the nerve to talk to men as if they were their equals.

At this moment, one of the women who was sorting her vegetables a little way off stepped forward with a basket of spring greens.

'Girl, you said you could arrange vegetables,

18

didn't you? Come and arrange this lot for me. Show us city-folk what you can do!'

Three glanced nervously over at the Tofu Lady, then, receiving a nod of encouragement, squatted down and began arranging the leaves. They were the first growth of early spring and varied in size and colour because of the difference in temperature between the cold nights and strong daytime sun. Everyone watched as Three swiftly picked out the yellow or withered leaves and made little piles according to size. In less than two minutes a basket of jumbled green leaves had been transformed. Some had been gathered into little cabbage-like clusters, others made to form open flowers with green petals around a white centre. There were fans and feathers, but, best of all was a cunning little tree-shape, like a bonsai. The crowd of onlookers was struck dumb with astonishment.

Then, as if she had been holding her breath till that moment, the Tofu Lady gave a great shout of glee.

'Well I'm blowed, the girl's an artist! A phoenix raised in a hencoop! What a shame my tofu only comes on bamboo sticks, otherwise I'd get this girl in to create displays for my shop. She'd make me rich.'

'You know, that's a good idea,' said the man called Guan Buyu. 'Why doesn't she go and work in the restaurant my brother's just setting up? He needs help attracting customers.

19

'Miss Three here might be perfect for him.'

'Well, Mr Guan,' said the Tofu Lady in admiration, 'I think you've found the solution. Didn't I say that you were a master strategist when it came to people? All the same—let's get the bad stuff out of the way—if you let anyone pick on this clever girl, I'll fry you in my wok!'

'Don't worry, Tofu Lady,' laughed Guan Buyu, 'my younger brother's wife will look after her. She's forever leaping to the defence of country girls. They'll get along fine.'

*   *   *

And so it was that Three went to work at 'The Happy Fool', a fast-food restaurant that had been started that year by Mr Guan Buyu's younger brother, Guan Buyan and his wife, Wang Tong. On her days off, she often went back to the big willow by the old city wall to visit the kind people who had shown her the sunlit road now stretching ahead of her. And sometimes she even gave advice to a country girl who had come, like her, to ask for help. She remembered her mother's words: 'If someone saves your life with a mouthful of water, digging a well will not be enough to repay their goodness.'

But, despite all her good fortune, she couldn't feel entirely happy while she was separated from her mother and her little

20

village in Anhui. Her first year of work in the city passed quickly and, as Spring Festival approached, Three spent many sleepless nights trying to decide whether she should return to her village for the holiday, and thinking of ways to avoid the beating she was sure her father had in store for her. In the end, it was Wang Tong, the proprietress of the Happy Fool, who suggested a solution. Why not ask the chess-players and vegetable-ladies under the willow tree to pose for photographs with her? Then Uncle Two could go back to the village first, taking the pictures with him, and tell everyone that the people in the photos were high-up officials (far more important than the regional Head) who had offered Three their support.

The plan worked like a dream. When Three arrived home, all the villagers rushed out of their houses shouting, 'Three's back, the girl who was in the photos with all those high-up officials', 'Look how pale and clear her complexion is—just like a pretty girl in a picture' and 'What soft hands! She must be living the good life down there in Nanjing . . .'

Her mother who, for a year, had imagined the most terrible fate for her daughter, stood there with tears rolling down her face. Beside her was Three's father, his face set in a frown. But he didn't say anything. And when, later, he saw the bundle of hundred-yuan notes that she had managed to save in the course of the year, his eyes moistened and his mouth turned up at the corners: this was more than the whole family could save from two years of working in the fields.

In the days that followed, Three's mother was beside herself with happiness, bustling about her daughters and chatting to the village girls who dropped by to hear Three's stories of city life. Three's younger sisters, Four, Five and Six, were so entranced that they did their housework in a dream and, almost without noticing, tidied the storeroom, which hadn't been cleaned for years, until every pot was in its place and the oldest, rustiest tool was gleaming. Four, who was deaf and dumb and relied entirely on the family's gestures to understand them, could sense the excitement and did everything she could to follow what the girls were saying. Five and Six were delighted with their sister's happiness. Although they worried that she still showed no interest in marriage and was in danger of living up to her reputation for having a heart of stone, they saw that city life suited her. It seemed to them that she was a seed that had grown into a cauliflower, a silkworm who had become a butterfly.

2

A NEW YEAR AND A NEW LIFE

Li Zhongguo, known in the village as Li Brother One, was a man who never smiled. Although he was the eldest of the Li brothers, the fact that he had six daughters meant that he could never hold up his head like a true man, but instead had to bow to his younger brothers and accept a lower status in the family. In the village, too, anyone could easily silence him by calling him 'chopstick man'. His six daughters were a great burden to him and he worried all the time about finding them husbands. Who, after all, would dare to marry the daughters of a man who could not 'plant eggs'? Everyone thought that the Li girls carried within them their father's bad fate. This was why no matchmaker crossed the threshold of his house until Li Brother Three who was high up in the village Production Brigade, arranged for the eldest daughter, One, to be married to the widowed uncle of the regional Head, a man a good decade older than her father, who lived in the local town. Finally, Li Zhongguo could look his fellow villagers in the eye and know that none of them would dare to make fun of him any more now that he had such powerful relations. Nevertheless, five unmarried daughters remained and, once again, he was obliged to call upon the help of his influential younger brothers. It was his youngest brother who acted as matchmaker for his second daughter. Li Brother Four was just starting to make a name for himself and he arranged for Two to be married to the son of the regional Head. The groom was high-ranking but paralysed from the waist down, having suffered an accident in childhood.

Though the stoical Two did not utter a word of complaint about her father's decision, the day after the bride-gifts arrived, Li Zhongguo found his wife clasping the dead body of her daughter in her arms. Two had been fished out of the well that morning. It was just before Spring Festival and the weather was freezing. She was wearing nothing but her underwear, her clothes carefully put away to be passed on to her sisters.

Agony clutched at Li Zhongguo's heart, and his head, which he had just started to raise, was lowered once more. When people came from the the local town to say that Three could fill the gap left by her sister, he was thrown into confusion and didn't know what to do. He knew that he must send her, but at night his wife would whisper that, if he did, she would follow her second daughter into the well. After days of anxiety, his decision was made for him when Uncle Two spirited Three away in the night. There was nothing left for Li Zhongguo to do but accept that all his hopes of becoming a 'man of standing' were nothing more than dust in the wind, and his family line would end with him.

But now that Three had found a job in the city with a handsome salary, her father found that he commanded a certain respect. For nearly fifteen years now, peasants had been allowed to leave their villages to find work, and thousands of men, who had not been able to make anything of their lives at home, had packed their bags and gone off to the city. Although they did menial jobs for low pay, working on building sites and acting as night watchmen, the money they brought home was still far more than they could ever hope to earn in the fields. In some villages, so many men left that the women and children had to take charge of the farming themselves. However, it was far more unusual for women to leave. Although the men who came back to the village for Spring Festival talked of how more and more country girls were finding their way to the city, it seemed they often worked in shameful professions. Sometimes they earned money with their bodies, or else they were shut up in factories doing unskilled labour, where you had to ask permission to go to the toilet and got your pay docked for doing so. It was truly unheard-of for a girl like Three to be posing for photographs in broad daylight with so many city folk, and a great credit to the father.

As the Spring Festival holiday reached an end and Three began to pack her bags in order to return to Nanjing, all the girls in the village clamoured to go with her. Uncle Two's daughters chattered around him like magpies and Three's younger sisters looked at Li Zhongguo with pleading eyes. Uncle Two, who was the family's authority on city life, was troubled by all the commotion. Three was not ready to take people back with her, he said, and they should wait until she had carved out a proper life for herself in Nanjing.

*   *   *

The next Spring Festival, Three brought back even more money, making people even more envious. For the whole of the holiday, her good fortune was the sole topic of conversation in the village. From family kitchens to the Production Brigade office, all anyone could talk about was who should go to the city with her. Of course, the older generation didn't begin to imagine that a 'chopstick' could ever become a 'roof-beam', but those banknotes Three had brought home were the genuine article: why not let a chopstick earn money?

Li Zhongguo was more cautious. Chopsticks can easily snap, and if something should happen to one of his daughters, it would bring great shame. On the other hand, he knew in his heart that Three's success had won back a lot of respect for his family—or, as the Chinese call it, 'face'. Even his wife, who was usually terrified of everyone, had the confidence to speak. And when he thought of his dead second daughter and his accusing, tearful eldest daughter, his resolve hardened: he couldn't let the girls endure the sufferings of the peasant life.

The question remained: who should go? It was obvious that Four, who was deaf and dumb, couldn't accompany her sister. That left Five and Six. Five had a reputation in the village for being ugly and stupid, while Six was the only girl in the area to have finished middle school. If an ugly girl is away from home, her parents have little to worry about. As for educated girls, Li Zhongguo had heard that they landed the plum jobs. He decided to send them both.

So it was that, two days later, Uncle Two led Three, Five and Six out of the village before the first glimmer of daybreak had appeared above the horizon. He wanted to catch the Tofu Lady before crowds of people arrived looking for jobs, and it was better to spend the night travelling than in an expensive city guesthouse. During the two hours it took to walk through the fields to the bus station, Uncle Two issued warning after warning to the

27

girls, terrified that their innocence might make them prey to bad men: never smile at a man or listen to his compliments; remember that he had never heard of a city man making a proper wife out of a country girl. He continued his lecture during the three-hour bus journey, telling them everything he knew about city customs: how you had to wash every day after work and clean your teeth morning and night; how a man couldn't go out into the street without a shirt or a woman without her trousers; how women painted their faces and wore perfume; and how, when you went to a public toilet, you had to take paper, and sometimes money so you could get in.

Three dozed through Uncle Two's lecture, her head lolling every time the bus went over a bump, but Five and Six listened wide-eyed as their uncle described to them a world that they could hardly imagine.

'Don't nod your head when going into a shop, otherwise the attendants will force their goods on you and you'll end up paying through the nose for them. Don't go into shops where there aren't many people or goods: those are for rich people. And you can't spit on the ground or wipe off snot on walls or trees . . .'

When they arrived in Nanjing, it took them half an hour to walk from the bus station to the Tofu Lady's shop, Five and Six staring around them in astonishment at the cars, the people and the big buildings. Throughout their walk, Uncle Two's lecture did not stop: 'Lower your head and say "Hello" when you enter a building and don't forget to turn back and say "Goodbye" when you leave. Always bow when thanking people . . .' By the time he saw the Tofu Lady, his throat was dry and hoarse, and he had hardly any voice left to speak.

Although Three had met the Tofu Lady many times since she had started working at the Happy Fool, it had always been at the big willow, never at her shop. She was astonished by the change. The basic hole-in-the-wall, greasy and black from deep-frying, had been transformed into one of many standardised units, and the lane had become a designated 'food street' in the market, with shops selling all manner of delicacies. Gone was the school desk with its graffiti, and the bench onto which everyone had squeezed. Gone, too, was the oil-drum stove. In their place were four small, red-painted tables, a proper cooker and a glass-fronted cabinet to hold the disposable bowls and chopsticks. There were pretty pictures on the walls illustrating the well-known stories of 'The Eight Immortals Crossing the Sea' and 'The Goddess of Heaven Scattering Flowers', and a picture of a plump baby boy with a carp in his arms, symbolising abundance (Three felt bad that such a lively fish had been given to an ignorant baby to play with). Most puzzling to Three was a picture of a blond, blue-eyed Western child eating a skewer of stinky tofu fritters and giving the thumbs-up. Had Three's reading been good enough to decipher the slogan underneath, she would have known that it said 'Tofu Lady's world-famous stinky tofu fritters!' The Tofu Lady was extremely proud of this 'international' advertisment, which she said she had got from a student at one of the vocational colleges in exchange for twenty bamboo skewers of tofu. The student had simply pasted over the ice lolly in the child's hand.

Uncle Two pushed a couple of tables together and piled them with the gifts they had brought. The Tofu Lady started to peel off the wrappings, all the while trying politely to refuse his generosity.

'There you go again, bringing me things! Didn't I tell you not to bother? You're wasting your energy—you won't make me like you any more than I already do, you know. Anyway, it's not like it used to be: if you've got the money you can buy this sort of thing in every big city in China, you don't need to go to the countryside for it . . . *Aiya*, this year's sticky rice! This will be wonderful in an eight-treasures pudding. The stuff you buy in the city's always a year old. And money chillis? I've not seen chillis like this for years, with so much oil they look golden. Did your family grow them? Look at this powdered lotus root, you can't get it this pure anywhere in the city;

30

they all cut it with powdered chalk! And I've been telling everyone about your dried sweet potatoes.That lovely sweet taste stays in your mouth for hours, and they're delicious all year round, steamed, fried or boiled. What's this? Some of those little grass carp the fishermen used to feed to the pigs until they discovered they could change the name to 'whitebait' and made big money! *Aiya*, you're treating me with so much respect it's embarrassing. I know they say a drop of kindness should be repaid with a river of gratitude, but that doesn't mean you have to bring me big presents every single time, or pay tribute every year! I'm really doing well out of you lot!

'Now, who have you got with you this time? Are these two looking for work too? Well you don't need me to wave the flag this time. Three's a clever girl who knows what's what, and money's really growing on trees at that big willow these days. Three, you must have seen—it's really busy there: hordes of people looking for work or workers. And our Mr Guan has just opened an office by the tree— an International Business Affairs Office, specially to help people like you find companies to work in! These intellectuals are quick off the mark, aren't they? He didn't have to invest any money, he just got the local government to set him up . . .

'Hey, girls, am I boring you with all this talk? All right, all right, I'll fry you up some tofu. When you've finished you'd best hurry over and find yourselves a good spot next to Mr Guan's office. I won't go with you today. It's just after the holidays and business is good, I can't get away. Besides, they've got a whole system going under that tree now. Newcomers can figure out what's what in two minutes, and Three knows everyone there anyway, so she can sort you out. You'd best let your uncle tell you a thing or two about how to answer people's questions. Oh, and whatever you do, don't forget to tell any potential employer that you've got brothers in the city. There are some dirty old men with funny ideas around here. Those ...'

Uncle Two was concerned that the Tofu Lady's good-natured advice would terrify his two nieces who knew very little about men, so he hurriedly interrupted her.

'Thank you, but please don't worry about feeding us. It's safer if we go and bag ourselves a place now—besides I've got to catch the noon train.'

'That's too bad! Listen, take some tofu with you then. I'll put some seasonings on now. It won't be very crisp, but the main thing is you won't go hungry! Take five sticks each, that'll keep you going till lunch. Oh, and if you two girls don't find a boss today for any reason, come and squeeze in with me for the night. Don't waste your precious money getting ripped off in those thieving guesthouses.'

By the time they had thanked the Tofu Lady, and found their way to the big willow tree, it was already ten o'clock, and there were lots of people milling around. It was easy to spot the ones who were looking for work. They were standing about with their luggage, their faces frostbitten from field work, the girls dressed in the bright colours that country girls wear—cherry pink, bright green, orange and sky blue. The employers were obvious too. They had well-made clothes in subdued colours and wandered through the crowd with a relaxed expression on their faces, looking people up and down.

Since the start of their journey, Five had simply followed her uncle and older sister wherever they led her, her mouth open and her eyes wide in amazement. Because she couldn't read, the fact that there were signs everywhere saying things she couldn't even guess at bewildered her further. Six, however, was far more anxious to take control of her own destiny. After all, she was the only sister to have spent more than a short time in school. She was determined to prove that her education had been worth all the sacrifices the family had made. When she saw how many people were looking for jobs, she was filled with fear that her dream of a new life in the city would end before it had begun.

'We're too late, aren't we?' she asked anxiously. 'No one will want us now, will they?'

Uncle Two tried to reassure her. 'Don't worry. Those city bosses all have big business dinners late in the evening, and then the nightclubs keep them busy till the cock crows. They haven't turned up yet. The bigger the boss, the later he comes.'

Meanwhile, Three had found some acquaintances.

'Uncle Wang, Uncle Li,' she called out, 'are you still arguing over that chess game? And how are you, Auntie Luo? Who's selling the best vegetables today?'

The group of old people by the willow tree smiled in recognition.

'Oh, it's young Three! Are you here looking for new staff for your Happy Fool?'

'Introduce us to your sisters. Are they looking for work? You must take them to see Mr Guan. You can always trust the people you know. His business is doing so well he doesn't need to turn up before ten-thirty, however long the queue is.'

'Oh, I don't think Mr Guan will make young Three queue! Good luck comes to good people.'

Three was very touched by their kind words. Two years of working in a restaurant where customers sometimes looked down on her for her country ways had made her deeply aware that polite words should always be treasured. There weren't many city people who would be so considerate to a migrant worker. Shrewd

34

Six, on the other hand, was paying more attention to their faces than their words: she had noticed that the old men and women looked exactly the same as the 'high officials' in Three's photographs.

'Hey, girls, looking for work?' Two middle-aged women, one fat, one thin, dressed in white uniforms with two red bars on the sleeves and collar, were making their way towards the three sisters.

'Yes, yes, these two are,' said Three, pushing her sisters forward. 'We're sisters from the same village. I've already got a job but this sister is very good at housework—she can cook, or do anything around the home—and my youngest sister is the cleverest girl in our village. She's the only one to finish middle school, and she can speak some foreign English too!'

'We don't need secretaries, we just want an honest, simple girl who'll stay at her post and do the work.'

The women's uniforms had the words 'Dragon Water-Culture Centre' printed on the left breast. Neither Three nor Uncle Two had any idea what this meant, but they didn't dare to ask in case they were laughed at.

They saw the two women muttering in each others' ears. Three strained to hear what they were saying, but all she could make out were a few broken phrases: '. . . not too pretty, she'll be headhunted . . . too confident and she'll

35

make trouble . . .'

Finally, they seemed to come to a decision.

'Miss,' the fat woman said to Five, 'have you worked in the city before?'

Five was dumbstruck. She had never been called 'Miss' by anyone, let alone been spoken to in such an amiable manner. Embarrassed by her silence, Uncle Two jumped in to apologise.

'I'm sorry, ladies, this girl's never been away from home before and she's not much of a talker anyway. Please don't mind . . . Come on, Five, these Managers are speaking to you.'

The thin woman gave him a disapproving look.

'Listen, sir, we don't need you to play the big man here. Women can speak for themselves in this city.'

'That's right,' added the fat woman turning to Five with a kind look on her face. 'Miss, if you want to find a job, you're going to have to do the talking yourself, you hear?'

Poor Uncle Two stepped back in confusion. In his village, people called him a 'weak seed', barely a man at all, and yet now in the city they were accusing him of being a 'big man'.

Five summoned all the courage she possessed to answer their question.

'I . . . I've never been away from home, not even to the other villages, because the fields and the market are only two *li* away from where I live. But, even though I haven't been to the city, I'm a very good worker . . .'

'Well said,' approved the fat woman. 'Now tell us, what'll you do if you miss home?'

'Cry, I s'pose,' answered Five.

Three tugged at her. 'What's the good of crying? Tell them you'll get used to it.'

'I'll-get-used-to-it,' Five repeated mechanically.

Both women spluttered with laughter and exchanged a glance, apparently thoroughly satisfied with Five's honesty.

'So, what wage are you looking for?' the thin woman asked.

'I . . . don't know . . .'

Five looked beseechingly at Uncle Two, but now that the two women had taken him to task, he didn't dare raise his head to look at them. By this point, Three was getting anxious. She realised that she had forgotten to talk to her sisters about what salary to ask for, and she was terrified that Five would lose this opportunity. With all her advantages, Six would have no difficulty finding work, but Five, inferior in appearance, education and intelligence, was another matter. The two women appeared to be genuine (only big companies supplied uniforms like that), and Five couldn't afford to let this piece of good fortune pass her by.

'Well, this is what we are offering,' said the thin lady. 'You'll start on an unskilled worker's salary. Food and lodgings are included, as well as tips. How does that sound? Shall we go and sort out the contract now, or would you rather go and see what else is available?'

'Will you give me two minutes to explain all this to my sister,' begged Three.

The two women glanced at their watches. 'Don't worry, we'll come back for you later. If your sister decides she wants to take the job, then don't leave.' They began to walk away.

'OK, I'll take it!' said Five, spreading her arms to block the women's path. She guessed that they were going to look around to see if there was anyone else suitable, and if they found someone better, they wouldn't come back for her. Five had lost out to her sisters too many times to stand by and watch this job being taken away.

'Are you sure? In that case, we'll ask the office to draw up a contract straightaway. They can make a copy for your friends here too, so that they know where to find you, and can help you find a representative if you have any complaints. We have over a hundred workers at our Dragon Water-Culture Centre. This is our registration number.'

The thin woman began opening a big folder.

'You might also like to know,' added the thin woman, 'that Mr Guan is our guarantor.'

Three's face lit up at this information. 'That's wonderful. Mr Guan found me my job too. I've been working at his younger brother's restaurant for two years now, we were just waiting for him.'

At this moment, the group of people queuing by the office began calling out 'Mr Guan is here!' Seeing the number of people who seemed to know who he was, Three kicked herself for thinking that she could use her acquaintance with him to jump the queue. Reluctantly she told Uncle Two to wait under the willow tree and pulled Six to the back of the long line of job-seekers. Five was led by the two white-coated women to the queue for registration, which only had three or four people in it. Three was prepared for a long wait, but as Guan Buyu passed by on his way to his office, he stopped at the place where Three stood and gave her a smile.

'Is that Three? What are you doing here? Come into my office. There's something I've been wanting to talk to you about.'

Filled with pride, Three dragged Six by the hand and followed Mr Guan through the crowd and into the lobby of his impressive office. The lobby had two desks, one for registering job-seekers and one for sorting out contracts, and Three expected Mr Guan to sit down at one of these. Instead he led her through to the inner office where there was a desk that seemed the size of a bed, and a high-backed chair that dwarfed even the tall Mr Guan. Although the office was small, three of its walls were covered in books.

Three immediately noticed on the desk the gift that she had asked the Tofu Lady to pass on to Guan Buyu—a piece of brightly coloured brocade. Because she didn't understand silk, she had asked someone to buy it for her from the well-known old silk shop, Rui Fu Xiang, and it had cost her half a month's wages. Her mother often said that if you fail to repay a debt you know you owe, you will be paid back in bad luck!

Guan Buyu picked up the piece of brocade.

'Three, my sister-in-law says you've been doing so brilliantly at the restaurant, you've become her right-hand woman. I'm delighted. This is exactly what this office is for: helping you girls from the countryside find your feet in the city. But I don't like to see you imitating city people's bad habits and spending money on presents. I know this brocade is no use to your family, so I won't return it. But take this money for your mother instead, and when you want to thank me in future, thank me by being a good person and doing good deeds, do you hear? Now then, tell me, is this a friend you've brought with you?'

'This is my younger sister Six. Another sister, Five, came with us, but she's already in the queue for contracts with two women in white uniforms from some water place.'

'Well, that's excellent. The Li family is clearly very lucky. I'll be interested to hear how Five gets on.'

Throughout this conversation, Six had been entranced by the fact that Mr Guan seemed to

40

be able to twist around on his chair without moving his body. When he suddenly span round to face in the opposite direction, she gave a gasp of shock.

'What's the matter?' he asked.

'I'm sorry,' mumbled Six, embarrassed at having drawn attention to herself. 'It's just that I . . . I've never seen anyone turning round while sitting down.'

Guan Buyu gave a loud bark of laughter and looked a little closer at the girl standing next to Three.

'Tell me about yourself, Six. What is it that you dream of doing?'

Six did not hesitate. 'To work in a library,' she blurted out. 'My teacher said that cities have a place where you can look at books, touch books, be with books all the time. It would be so great if I could work in a place like that.' Six's eyes shone with her yearning for books.

'Goodness,' said Guan Buyu in surprise. 'You're the first person from the countryside to want work as a librarian! How odd that, when so few city people have ever thought of such a profession, I should find a country girl with an affinity for books.'

Mr Guan appeared to be muttering to himself and Six was worried that she had said the wrong thing, but suddenly he swung round on his chair and gave her a huge smile.

'Six, I can't find you a library to work in

right now, and besides that kind of job requires a very particular kind of training. However, I've got a friend who's about to open a very special teahouse where the customers will be able to borrow books to read while they drink their tea. If you're willing, I could propose you as a waitress. That way you will be working surrounded by books, and will perhaps get a foot on a ladder that will help you find other work with books later on. What do you say?'

Six felt her cheeks turn red in excitement. 'Really? Oh yes! I would love a job like that, Mr Guan!'

'Then take this note to the contracts people and they will draw up an agreement for you to sign.'

Guan Buyu stood up and offered his hand to Six: 'I'm very pleased to meet you, Six. Now, off you go with your sister and promise me you will do good work and read good books.'

In all Six's seventeen years she had never before shaken hands with a man, but she knew from her books that she ought to do so as naturally as she could. 'Thank you,' she whispered. 'I promise I will be a good person, read good books and do good deeds.'

It was with huge excitement that the three sisters burst out of the doors of the job centre to find their waiting uncle. Uncle Two, who had been squatting next to their pile of luggage, watching the spectacle of the market and the crowds of people chatting and haggling over prices, was completely taken aback by his nieces' good fortune. He had never dreamed Five and Six would have found jobs by lunchtime and he was delighted for them. But he was also anxious. It was time for him to go and catch his train, and the two girls had been told to wait until their new employers could come to collect them. Would they be safe? He wouldn't see them again until they all returned to the village for Spring Festival.

Three told him not to worry. Then she reached up to the big willow and broke off a twig. Carefully pinching off the new shoots, she drew out the core so that, in her hand, there remained only a tube of willow bark. She pulled off a piece of the outer bark at one end to reveal the softer layer of bark beneath. In this way she made a mouthpiece for a spring willow-whistle of the kind their mother had taught them to make when they were children. Putting the willow-whistle to her lips, she gave a quick toot and passed it to Uncle Two.

'If you ever miss us, blow this,' she said. She hoped it would bring her uncle the luck of the big willow.

3

THE HAPPY FOOL

Three didn't make it back to the Happy Fool restaurant until later in the afternoon. She had waited until Five had gone off with her new employers and then she had started to walk back to the restaurant, which was in the bustling area of Nanjing close to the Confucius Temple. Preparations for the evening meal were already well under way when she arrived and Three had no time to take her luggage to her lodgings two streets away. Instead she put on her uniform and got straight down to work, pausing only to greet her employers, Guan Buyan and his wife, Wang Tong, whose little business had become her second home.

The Guan brothers, Buyu and Buyan, had no history of involvement in business. In fact, to be more precise, they belonged to a family who had, like many Chinese, looked down their noses at business people for generations (believing the old saying 'Only the crooked engage in trade') and had considered themselves to be intellectuals. Their elderly father had never worked outside an institute of higher education in his life. Even during the Cultural Revolution, when intellectuals were condemned as 'passers-on of useless knowledge', he retained a post in the university—albeit cleaning the toilets. His wife suffered paroxysms of anxiety at the time about his refusal to bow down to the peasant leaders. He was young and strong-willed, and he knew that, because the peasants were illiterate, he could use his cleverness to make a mockery of them behind their backs. Like everyone, he wrote the required Letter of Resolution, saying that he espoused the aims of the Cultural Revolution, and pasted it up on the wall of his workplace. However, his had a double meaning.

Because some Chinese characters are pronounced in the same way, the language offers many opportunities for puns. For example, the sound of Five's name, Wu'mei, means either the number 'five', 五妹, or the adjective 'charming' 妩媚 . Old Guan made clever use of this possibility for misunderstanding when he wrote his Letter of Resolution. If you were listening to someone reading it out, and couldn't see the characters, it could mean this:

I resolve every day to clean away shit, to brush the white-tiled floor and not to forget the teachings of our peasant leaders.

But if you were looking at the characters, you could also take it to mean the following:

Every day I must clean away History, get rid of the professional class and follow the dirty feet of our peasant leaders.

The peasant who had been put in charge of the university couldn't read, of course. When he saw that people were laughing at Old Guan's Letter of Resolution, he was perturbed and asked for it to be read out to him. Fortunately, he couldn't hear anything amiss because he had no concept of what a pun was. Old Guan was safe, and was saved the punishment of being sent to poverty-stricken North Jiangsu to plant sweet potatoes. However, his wife was so traumatised by the experience that, by way of a warning to their first-born son, she changed his name from Yu (meaning 'Speak') to Buyu ('Don't speak'), and when she became pregnant with their second son, she decided he would be called Buyan ('Be silent'). Sadly, she lost so much blood during childbirth that she died before she had a chance to name him herself.

During the Cultural Revolution, each urban family was required to send their children to the countryside in order to be 're-educated' by the peasants, who, it was believed, understood life better than any academic. Fortunately, Guan Buyu managed to finish junior middle school before he was sent off to the fields so when, in 1977, the Cultural Revolution came to an end and China reinstated university examinations, he passed without difficulty. After taking his degree, he stayed on at the university to teach, and although he did not make it to the level of Professor, he was nonetheless a recognised expert in sociology within the university.

His younger brother, Guan Buyan had not fared so well. After failing the university entrance exam, he had to resign himself to a lowly job as a bookseller for the government-run bookselling chain Xinhua. Their father was deeply disappointed that his second son would not bring honour to his ancestors, but took comfort in the fact that Buyan's work was still within the sphere of culture, and that his marriage was stable whereas Buyu and his wife were on the verge of separation.

But Buyan's life was to be turned upside down by the government's introduction of the Open Policy. This policy included three major reforms that would have a huge impact on people's lives in the 1980s. Peasants were allowed to leave their land to seek work elsewhere; permission was given to trade with foreigners (although at first only to companies in the specially designated Economic Zones in the south); and anyone at all was allowed to set up their own business. Educated people were immediately suspicious. To them, this was just another political movement by a different name, and it was better not to get involved. After all, the first pig to get fat is the first one to find itself on the table. But matters developed in a most unexpected way: poverty gives rise to a desire for change, and those who had nothing to lose—the peasants and the urban unemployed—began hawking goods from little stalls. Their risk-taking paid off, and before anyone noticed, people who had once held the lowest status in society were suddenly the heads of 'ten-thousand-yuan households'—a terrible shock to those state workers whose monthly wage was less than a hundred yuan.

It was only in the early 1990s that city people really began to wake up to the fact that ignorant yokels had taken over the streets outside their own front doors. Still, when all was said and done, they had the advantage. Peasants had only limited education and experience, and they didn't really have the vision for anything major. With the freedom to choose one's own career and the opening up of the market causing every household to rush to modernise their home and buy new electrical goods, a shockwave of consumerism rapidly spread across China. Before long, even the educated couldn't ignore the huge sea of opportunity that stretched out before them. In fact, it became the fashion to 'jump into the sea' of commerce and, even people who didn't know how to run a business, let alone how to keep accounts, took the plunge, often using the government as a safety net by winning government contracts or having a government functionary as a manager or consultant. Those without such connections simply opened up shop in their own homes. There was a saying at the time: 'Out of nine hundred million people, eight hundred million are in business and another hundred million are waiting to open for business.' Countless people drowned in this sea of commerce, but since the people on the shore could not see those who had failed and sunk, all they witnessed were the successful bosses returning in triumph. Those who came late to the race were taking an even bigger gamble, especially as they often leapt into the sea with decades' worth of their friends' and relatives' savings. All this continued until 2000, when the tidal wave of people setting up private businesses started to recede from the densely populated east of China.

The Guan family had been among those who believed that this mad rush to go into business would lead to social chaos, and that the emphasis on short-term success and instant benefit would have a very bad influence on national morality. So those close to them were extremely surprised when, in 2001, at a time when the shores of commerce were littered with shipwrecks, the Guan family's younger son decided to scrape together the capital to open a fast-food restaurant—especially since he planned to open up right alongside the

American giants McDonald's and Kentucky Fried Chicken. For a time, Guan Buyan's acquaintances talked of nothing else.

'I suppose that, after twenty years of standing enviously on the sidelines, the family's finally cracked,' said one friend. 'But they're in for a shock if they think opening a restaurant is like running a Xinhua bookshop. Because the government owns every single Xinhua bookshop in the country, the employees simply obey orders about which books to stock. What's more, those bookshops will never be short of customers while there are all those work units buying up hundreds of copies of a particular book to distribute to their staff. But fast-food restaurants are another matter . . . Ten years ago there was a whole forest of them, the streets were full of the smell of cooking. Now the surviving places are all either part of a chain or Westernised. If you want to attract customers you've got to call your restaurant something like "N Donald's" or "Kentucky Duck" to attract customers. But Guan Buyan's planning to call his "The Happy Fool". He'll never get anywhere with a common old name like that.'

Another concerned friend went to talk to Guan Buyan's older brother.

'What's come over Guan Buyan, trying to build a business out of the last few drops of opportunity? You're older than him, why don't you try to talk him out of it?'

But in this matter, as in chess, Guan Buyu remained true to his name: silent and watchful. Although the brothers had never discussed the matter in detail, it was plain to him that his younger brother was not simply chasing after fashion, or taking a risk just for sake of it, he was actually having problems at work.

Guan Buyu was cleverer than his younger brother. Though he taught sociology at the university, his eyes and ears were everywhere and he knew how to seize an opportunity. It took only a couple of evenings and a few drinks with local officials to find himself invited to be an employment consultant. He was allowed to open an office by the big willow tree and given a remit to dispense advice and help to peasants and laid-off city workers looking for jobs. In this way, he earned a nice bit of additional income. If he hadn't been in the throes of a divorce from his wife, he would have been extremely contented.

Guan Buyan, on the other hand, was not as outgoing or ambitious as his brother and knew that he could never measure up to him. He had planned to pass his days quietly in the Xinhua bookshop, asking no more of life than for a bit of food in his bowl. It had never occurred to him that his job would be in jeopardy from the new reforms, but not long after he got married in 1998, even the state-owned media began to totter. Until then, fewer than five hundred publishers had served a population of over 1.3 billion, but now they were decentralising and splitting up. This inevitably led to reforms at every level of the quasi-military publishing industry, including the government-run bookshops. Guan Buyan saw redundancy looming and decided to jump before he was pushed. Chinese people need to 'keep face' as a tree needs to keep its bark, and luckily there was still time for Guan Buyan to get himself a reputation for being 'in search of better things', rather than on the shelf.

He went home to talk things through with his wife, who worked in a printing factory. At first Wang Tong was reluctant. All her life she had loved books and she wasn't sure she wanted to join the uncultured ranks of small traders. Nor could she see herself as the boss-lady of a restaurant, all slavish smiles and servility to those above her, all frowns and severity to those below. However, when Guan Buyan explained the gravity of the situation, she reconsidered. They had only been married two years and had no child, why not try to turn their fortunes around by starting a business? After all, how could a man who couldn't keep himself become a father in the future?

Guan Buyan's plan was to open a fast-food restaurant on a very small scale, since a small boat is easier to steer. This meant that he would not need many staff or a fancy shopfront and, if he chose a good location, close to a commercial or tourist centre, he might just be able to survive, or even expand. As the saying goes: the belly can do without clothing but not without food.

The name came to him before anything else. His father had always told him that his dead mother had been determinedly cheerful, even when faced with the worst. 'Don't be sad,' she would say, 'if there's nothing to be cheerful about, look for happiness, for only those who fool themselves can be truly happy.' He decided that he would call his restaurant 'The Happy Fool' after the mother he had known only from a photograph copied from her work-unit card. All the other photographs of her had been destroyed during the Cultural Revolution because of their connotations with the 'past'. There was no wedding photograph because the embroidered wedding gown had been considered 'feudalist', no graduation picture because the clothes she had been wearing were 'capitalist', and the group photograph that had been taken when some Soviet experts visited her workplace was said to be 'revisionist' now that China had fallen out with the USSR.

By a great stroke of luck, a family friend knew of a small shop to rent on Red Guard Lane, near to the Confucius Temple. It was an area where the streets were always full of shoppers and tourists, so Guan Buyan took the place immediately, even though it meant being neighbours with Kentucky Fried Chicken. It wasn't his intention to become a 'people's hero' among fast-food restaurateurs, but he had been reared on the slogans of Mao Zedong and so it was natural that he should create a slogan for his shop. On its first day of business the Happy Fool was emblazoned with the words, 'Don't Let McDonald's and Kentucky Fried Chicken Destroy Our Chinese Taste for Freshness.'

Few people know the history of Red Guard Lane, or the fact that, before the Communist Party came to power in 1949, it had a very different name. Then it was known as Face Powder Lane, after the pink rouge that its many courtesans applied to their cheeks, and it was famous throughout the Yangzi delta for its large number of sophisticated brothels inhabited by artistic women who could sing and dance. Clients would be welcomed into the courtyards with lines of verse recited by the strapping fellows on the gates, and when choosing a young lady, would be required to guess her name from a fragment of Tang or Song dynasty poetry. In this way, rough working men who had never touched a calligraphy brush or read the classics would be prevented from entering its perfumed rooms.

In the early 1950s, Face Powder Lane became Red Guard Lane, and the reformed prostitutes earned their living by writing lucky couplets for doorways, or copying correspondence for the illiterate. Then came the ten years of the Cultural Revolution, and the few remaining women were forced to undergo Political Criticisms and physical punishment. By the end of the seventies, the street had become 'one hundred per cent Red' and all the houses had been taken over by worker and peasant functionaries. These people converted the slabs of famous Anhui ink (which the prostitutes had hidden under the floorboards) into props for the legs of wonky beds, and turned the wolf-hair calligraphy brushes that had been treasured for generations into bottle washers. High-quality rice paper that had once borne beautiful poetry was used 'to resolve the outgoing problems of the masses'—that is, as toilet paper—while the silk on which the courtesans would paint their delicate pictures was stuffed into the split-crotch trousers of babies and toddlers to serve as makeshift nappies. Incense burners from the Ming dynasty became crocks for storing rice and beans; writing tables with secret, mirror-lined drawers were transformed into hen-coops or shelving. As for the rest of the furniture, it served—along with the manuals on the art of love, the erotic drawings and the diagrams showing how men could conserve their sexual energy—as firewood; it was said that one long opium couch could last for fourteen meals. In short, anything the worker and peasant functionaries had not seen before was labelled 'feudalist, capitalist and revisionist', and destroyed. The Red Guards had no idea that the beautifully decorated, tiny porcelain shoes (which they imagined to be a form of punishment for the prostitutes, who would be forced to have their feet jammed inside them) were in fact the famous 'golden-lily drinking cups' that were used to serve spirits and wine to the clients at the brothels. The only things they left untouched were the alcove beds, carved with dragons and phoenixes, on which countless prostitutes and their clients had slept. After a comfortable night in one of these, workers and peasants, who had previously slept on wooden planks or on the floor, could be heard to exclaim angrily, 'No wonder those vile women weakened the wills of their clients. Just sleeping on those beds turns your bones to jelly.' But, even so, they couldn't quite bring themselves to chop these 'beds of sin' into firewood. Instead they reformed them by stuffing pictures of Chairman Mao into the frames at the bedhead that had once contained erotic art.

Nanjingers said that Red Guard Lane was the most revolutionary street in the whole city, and it is perhaps because it was so thoroughly reformed that its history was completely forgotten until recently. It was only at the end of the 1990s, by which time almost all the streets and alleys with some claim to past fame had been rediscovered and registered by the city officials as historic Chinese sites, that people began to recall old Face Powder Lane, which had flourished over a hundred generations and several dynasties. Or perhaps it wasn't a lack of historical knowledge, but a fear of its bad reputation. Whatever the reason, when the American giant Kentucky Fried Chicken decided it wanted to open a branch on this street, the city officials were surprised. If the Yanks are so clever, they muttered behind closed doors, why didn't they want the prime territory on Sun Yatsen Avenue?

Who knows. Perhaps the Americans had got wind of the colourful history of Red Guard Lane and gave it a greater value than the locals.

The Happy Fool restaurant stood right next to Kentucky Fried Chicken, and was dwarfed by its American neighbour's huge sign. The shopfront was fewer than five paces wide and its sole adornment was a tray hanging in the middle of the window with a display of the food on offer. Nevertheless, passersby always stopped to look in the window, and very often what they saw made them pop in to have something to eat.

This food display had been dreamt up by Guan Buyan when he saw how Three was able to turn a basketful of vegetables into a work of art. Early every morning his wife, Wang Tong, would go to the nearby farmers' market and choose the freshest vegetables, and every day Three would create a new arrangement for the tray hanging in the window. It wasn't a fancy tray, but it had a rosewood border, and was suspended from two brocade ties with elaborate Chinese knots which hung down on either side. Below it, written in neat green letters was Guan Buyan's slogan: 'Don't Let McDonald's and Kentucky Fried Chicken Destroy Our Chinese Taste for Freshness.'

Nanjingers are known across China for their love of fresh fruit and vegetables, but even in this city it was rare to find a grand hotel that used such fresh produce, let alone a fast-food restaurant. Soon people who lived close to the Happy Fool began to visit it, not to eat, but to see what vegetables they should be buying for their own tables. One woman from northern China, who rented lodgings in Red Guard Lane, used to come and look in the window every single day before she went to the market.

Three's talents were also employed inside. Instead of the glitzy photos of mountains and rivers that decorated the walls of other restaurants, the Happy Fool had rows of paper plates hanging from plastic hooks, to which Three attached single leaves or vegetable hearts. She also filled glasses with sliced-open fruit. Quite often, a number of the brightly coloured plastic tables would be occupied by parents using Three's displays to teach their children about the natural world. The children's naive questions would have everyone sitting nearby in fits of laughter. And so it was that the Happy Fool became a place that truly made ordinary people happy.

In the early days of running the restaurant, Wang Tong had been daunted by the task that lay before her. There is a saying in Chinese that 'a horse can run itself to death before it reaches the mountain it has been running to', and Wang Tong was forced to recognise that, if she was going to survive, she would have to be realistic about her aspirations. However, she had good instincts. She knew immediately that, with a mixed clientele, a kitchen only two metres wide and very little storage space, the restaurant should serve only dishes that could be cooked fast and where the ingredients could easily be replenished by a quick twenty-minute trip to the local market. The delicately flavoured stir-fries traditional to Nanjing were perfect for this, unlike slow-cooked northern food, which wasted time and heat, and leached colour and freshness from the vegetables. She also had the idea of introducing cold dishes that were not native to the area because they were easy to make and store, and suited Nanjing's hot southern climate.

Nanjing women love eating and shopping for food just as much as they like buying clothes and jewellery, and Wang Tong was typical in this respect. She understood all the nuances of the local cooking. For example, when people from outside Nanjing eat salt-water duck, what they are interested in is the fact that it is a Nanjing speciality. Nanjingers, on the other hand, are most particular about how the brine is made and the breed of duck. There is a Nanjing saying that 'every part of a duck or goose is a treasure'. From the down in quilts and jackets to the blood and intestines used in the delicious 'Duck Blood Soup', every scrap of the bird is put to good use. The stock is even used to fill the delicious steamed 'soup' dumplings which Nanjingers love to eat for either breakfast or lunch.

Nanjingers also like edible wild plants, and they are very proud of their 'Eight Dry Fresh Things' and 'Eight Watery Fresh Things'. The Dry Eight consist of purslane, Hen's Head, malantou, wild celery, rocambole, Chinese wolfberry greens, shepherd's purse and reeds. The Watery Eight include shrimps, snails, lotus root, fish, water caltrop and wild rice stems. When food-lovers go to any Nanjing restaurant, no meal is complete without a dish of fresh reeds, gathered from the banks of the river and fried with dried stinky tofu. Another favourite are the fresh buds of the Chinese toon tree, plucked before the Festival of Pure Brightness, which can be fried with egg, eaten cold with tofu, or made into soup with chysanthemum flowers and toon-tree leaves. Nanjingers adore these little dishes of wild food which give them a taste of nature and help them to feel in tune with the seasons.

Wang Tong was courageous in her choices at the market. She didn't only buy local produce, but piled her basket with 'imported' vegetables that came either from abroad or from different parts of China. Often the market-stall holder had no idea what to call these vegetables and adopted the name their peasant-growers had given them. So it was that Wang Tong came back with things called 'Yankee Smiles' (pale green cucumbers) or 'George Bush's Nose' (a kind of melon or courgette, pointed at the base and going out to a bell at the top). Clients at the restaurant loved discussing what these vegetables should really be called and even Old Guan, Guan Buyan's father, couldn't resist bringing out his botanical dictionaries. Sometimes, Wang Tong put up a 'Wanted' poster, calling on scholars and experts for the name of a plant. She made a number of interesting new acquaintances in this way and joked to Three that, with her help, she hoped to turn the Happy Fool into the first Chinese museum of vegetables.

Wang Tong's other good idea was to charge just a little bit more for the dishes they served.

'We won't get customers by undercutting prices,' she said. 'We've got to have some markup for "freshness", but we can't rob them blind either. We'll add just five fen to our prices. It's only a sixth of the price of a box of matches and people who want to eat at our restaurant won't make a fuss. Those who don't want to eat with us would complain about our prices even if we only charged half a yuan a dish.'

Some of her friends worried that it would be difficult for customers to find this kind of small change. As the cost of living increased in the late nineties, the value of the fen had become so small that it had practically disappeared. With the new millennium, some people were starting to treat five-fen coins as collectable items. But Wang Tong wasn't too concerned. She said that she would simply make sure she got in a good stock of five-fen coins from the bank each week to give as change. And since the extra five fen added to the price of each dish was hardly going to make them a huge profit, she would donate it to children in the countryside. After all, a city person would hardly bother to pick up a five-fen coin if they saw it in the street, but it could make a huge difference to a peasant child. Guan Buyan thought that this was a good idea, so he begged an old-fashioned metal biscuit tin from his father, and stuck a slip of paper to it which read: 'We respectfully ask you to contribute your five-fen change to help poor children who have not been to school. We will report back to you on their progress. Thank you.'

It was this tin that had caused a hitch on their opening day. On the advice of his elder brother, Guan Buyan had invited thirty party officials for a meal in the restaurant in order to ensure that they would regard his business venture favourably in future. Since the Happy Fool was so tiny, it was of negligible interest to these officials, most of them simply stayed long enough to say a few polite words and pick up the two bottles of spirits that Guan Buyan was offering as a gift. However, one man from the local administration offices took more of a look round. His eyes immediately fell on the five-fen biscuit tin with its request for contributions.

'Don't you know that only registered religious organisations are allowed to make collections for charity?' he asked sternly.

Wang Tong's heart flew into her mouth. 'But hasn't the government called for citizens to help "eradicate poverty"?' she asked in a nervous voice, looking over at her husband.

The official wasn't to be swayed. 'The Government has asked for contributions of clothing and money for poor people,' he said even more fiercely, 'not for you to collect other people's cash!'

'This isn't . . .'

Guan Buyan restrained his wife. 'This Leader is right,' he said. 'When the business is up and running, we can send money to the countryside ourselves.'

'Quite correct, you can't break the law, not even in a good cause,' said the official, and took an extra bottle of spirits with him when he left.

That was the end of the five-fen collection tin, but Guan Buyan's wife continued to collect the extra fen each week, and to put them into a special account. She had wanted to find a way to help people in the countryside ever since she had visited the village where her elder sister, Ling, had spent the Cultural Revolution. Because city families had been allowed to keep one of their children with them provided they sent the others to the countryside, Wang Tong had had a very different experience of the Cultural Revolution from her sister. However, she couldn't forget Ling's stories of how the inhabitants of Guanyun, a village in the north of Jiangsu Province, was so poor that even a postage stamp was considered a great luxury. Ling had talked of how the local postman had befriended the young city people, who had no way of communicating with their parents except by letter. He showed them how to steam open letters from their parents, place a new one inside, then return the original envelope to the sender, so that they didn't need to buy the stamps they couldn't afford. She spoke of how this man had, in a way, saved the lives of many of them who, without the comfort of communication with the outside world, might have taken their lives.

Wang Tong had found her sister's accounts of village life, with its starvation diet of sweet potatoes barely credible. After all, she had never read such things in the newspapers. Determined to see the village with her own eyes, she persuaded her sister to return to Guanyun, a few years after the Cultural Revolution had ended, to show her where she had lived. Wang Tong was horrified by what she saw. There was a girl of fifteen with no trousers to wear even though the autumn winds had begun to blow, and children wailing for a small piece of sweet potato. The family they stayed with were in despair over the fact that a ten-yuan note that they had carefully stored in an earthenware crock buried beneath the kitchen stove—their entire savings for the year—had been chewed by rats. Ling spent the evening try to piece together the damaged note by the light of a dim lamp, so that she could take it to a bank in town and change it for one of the new ten-yuan notes before the family lost their savings in a different way when the old notes were phased out. When Ling presented their hosts with a new ten-yuan note, the whole family almost got to their knees in gratitude. Wang Tong wept. She didn't understand why life was so poor and so hard in a village that was only a short distance north of Nanjing. From then on, she would collect the paper that the printing factory where she worked threw away, and staple it into little booklets which she would send to the family in Guanyun. She hoped that the children, who had no school to go to, could at least use it to draw pictures.

Because Wang Tong understood where Three had come from she was particularly moved to see how this young girl could transform the Happy Fool with the skills she had learned in the countryside. She loved to watch her customers making the circuit of her restaurant discussing the displays, especially the parents and children, and she tried hard to increase her own knowledge about what produce was best in which season. Three's ambition and skill were an inspiration to her and she no longer felt that it was unworthy to engage in trade, nor that one should simply accept one's lot in silence. On the contrary, she was filled with such energy that she could feel her slow, measured personality, which had used to make her older sister jump up and down with frustration, becoming more and more outgoing.

For her part, Three was amused to see how city people clustered around wild plants that grew all over the place like weeds where she came from in order to debate their special properties. However, when she heard some of them discuss how it was good to find mud on vegetables because it showed they were fresh, or that insect holes were a sign that harmful pesticides hadn't been used, she felt sad. She thought of how carefully her mother prepared vegetables for market, always pinching off any

66

damaged leaves and washing away the mud. She would say that, in this way, every fen people paid would go into their mouths.

As she began her third year in Nanjing, Three felt that, finally, she was beginning to understand the ways of the city. With only two years of schooling under her belt, she had struggled in the beginning. She had needed all her concentration to follow what Guan Buyan and his wife were saying, and customers often laughed at her. Determined to avoid this humiliation, she made a point of observing and copying other people's behaviour, but there was so much to learn. The men who worked in the south and returned to the village at Spring Festival had never mentioned that there were so many forms of address in the city! Chairman, Inspector, Officer . . . the list seemed endless. A journalist friend of Guan Buyan's had once told her that it would be better to claim that pigs could fly than to get an official's title wrong. Trivial cases were fined, but more serious ones could result in you losing your job. Three was so scared when she heard this that she would quail whenever she saw a man with a protruding gut walk into the restaurant, afraid that if she used a lower form of address than his actual status it would cause trouble for the business.

Although Guan Buyan and Wang Tong, with their city education, had little idea of quite how terrifying everything was to Three, they did their best to help her settle in. Guan Buyan would try to explain everything very slowly, and would warn her endlessly about potential problems, no matter how small; Wang Tong was more easy-going than her husband, treating Three more like a little sister who needed help, and never mocking her for asking foolish questions or making mistakes. True, the couple's tolerance had been tested the first time Three came to their house. The only toilets Three had ever known were holes in the ground, so she had been bemused by the porcelain in her employers' bathroom. After spending several minutes pondering what to do, desperation overcame her and she jumped up on to the seat and squatted down. Not knowing where the flush was either, she simply closed the bathroom door and hoped for the best. That night when the Guans arrived back at their small apartment after the evening shift, they were struck by the bad smell. Opening the bathroom door, they discovered two dirty footprints on the toilet seat and a large turd in the bowl. Guan Buyan's reaction was one of anger. How could Wang Tong not have shown the girl how to use a toilet? But Wang Tong was more forgiving. She simply gave the toilet a good clean and, the next time Three came to her home, showed her how to sit on the seat. It was only then that Three realised how much she had embarrassed herself on her first visit.

4

THE WATER DRAGON

Five's new employers were great talkers. They didn't stop chatting from the moment they left the job centre to the moment they got off the bus that had taken them into the heart of Nanjing. This put Five at her ease. She realised that city women gossiped just as much as country women. However, it didn't make her any the wiser about her new job because she couldn't understand a word they were saying. When they first got on the bus, she listened carefully to their conversation, but realising it wasn't going to help her, she gave up. Instead she stood on tiptoe and craned her neck so that she could look out over the heads of the other passengers at the city streets.

Many of the buildings reminded her of the tall houses she had seen in Uncle Three's photographs of the local town. They were covered in porcelain tiles on the front, but the brick on the side walls was left bare. These Nanjing buildings looked newer though, and were cleaner and prettier. Even the best brick building in her village would look shabby next to them. There were lots of people hurrying about on the streets and Five spotted many women. They were all carrying bags of different shapes and sizes, and their faces were thickly daubed with paint like the actresses from the opera group who sometimes came from the town to perform in the village. Uncle Two had told her how city women had soft and delicate skin, but Five could hardly see a single face that had been left without paint. The old ladies were an exception to this but they shocked Five still further with their figure-hugging clothes. Aunt Two said that dressing like that in middle age was disgusting. In fact, Aunt Two never had a good word to say about city people. She had made one trip to visit Uncle Two in Zhuhai and had come back full of criticism. Uncle Two, on the other hand, never said anything against the city: it was as if they had both been to different places.

Five was surprised not to see any children playing on the streets. In her village there were always runny-nosed little children dashing around. In summer, the smaller children were outside from dawn to dusk while the older boys and girls helped the adults in the fields. When the colder days of late autumn and winter came, and there was not so much work in the fields, the older boys would join in the noisy games, played with sticks and clods of earth; of course, winter was the season when peasant women did needlework, and the girls had to stay in and learn from their mothers how to keep house and practise handicrafts. This was why Five had almost no memory of

70

playing.

As the bus made its way through the crowded streets, Five was puzzled by the large glass doors—or were they windows?—with very thin men and women behind them, standing absolutely still. What were they doing? And why were so many people standing about watching them? Perhaps she, too, would be able to go and watch when she had the time . . .

When they got off the bus, the fat woman led Five down the street while the thin woman bustled off in another direction after speaking more incomprehensible words.

'Now tell me,' said the fat woman, 'why did you give your name as Five when you were registering just now? Why didn't your village issue you with papers in your official name?'

'Official name?' Five began to panic, thinking the woman might be about to take the job away.

'The name you use for work and study. Didn't you say you'd been to school?'

'No.'

The woman looked surprised so Five tried to explain.

'The teacher told my dad I was too stupid, and he should take me home to work. He said that trying to teach me would be a waste of money.'

'So you must have been at school for a little bit . . .'

71

'A week and a half.'

'Only a week and a half? Really?'

'Really, I'm not having you on, honestly. Ask my sister if you don't believe me . . .'

'Don't worry, I believe you. So you can't read . . .'

Five didn't understand why the fat woman looked so thoughtful.

'Is Five a bad name?' she asked.

'No, no . . . Five's fine as a name, but . . .' The fat woman seemed confused about how to explain things. 'Look,' she said, 'let's say that Five's your name for when you are at home, but here you're going to need another name, if that's all right with you. Don't worry, I daresay that in a minute when we register, Manager Shui or one of his people will give you a work-name.'

'What's a work-name?' Poor Five could not believe that one person could have so many names. Nobody in the village had ever so much as mentioned official names and work-names . . .

'A work-name is a name for you to use while you're working at the Dragon Water-Culture Centre. Well, Five, here we are. This side door is for us, the employees. The customers go through that big door in the dragon's mouth . . .'

Five let out a 'Wa!' of surprise as her gaze followed the fat lady's pointing finger. There was a beautiful dragon crouched by the side of

72

the road, its scales all the colours of the rainbow and a big pearl in its mouth. It was several metres long, and inside the pearl was a door big enough for five people to walk through side by side. But, before she could take in any more, the fat lady ushered her through the iron side door and into a blast of hot air.

Five raised her hands to her face in alarm. She was standing in a place full of steam, with a great roaring sound all around her, and the strange smell of herbs. The fat lady took Five's arm kindly and led her through a maze of hot, noisy corridors, uttering strange words like 'pump room' and 'medicine preparation' and telling her that it would soon become quieter. Sure enough, once they had gone a little further and walked through a metal door, the roaring disappeared and all Five could hear was the sound of water running through the pipes that were fixed to the walls and ceiling.

'It's like the Water Dragon's Palace, don't you think?' said the fat lady.

Five looked around her in bemusement. She had heard old people tell stories about the Water Dragon's Palace, but they had talked about shrimp soldiers, crab generals and an army of water creatures doing battle in the waves. They had never mentioned anything about pipes, pumps or medicine. Never in all her life had she thought she might end up in a city people's Water Dragon Palace and she wanted to tell the fat lady that she couldn't swim. What if she drowned here? Her mother always said that people who couldn't swim (and that was most of the girls in the village) shouldn't go near the local pond because the water ghosts had eaten all the soggy drowned bodies they wanted and were always eager for a taste of a little dry duckling who had never gone near water. She remembered a childhood friend, Hehua, who had slipped into the pond while washing clothes.

But before she had time to tell the fat lady she couldn't swim, a shout made Five jump.

'Back so soon, Banyue? Did you have any luck today? I remember how last week you froze for a whole day without finding anyone. So this is the new assistant. Hello there!' A middle-aged lady wearing a white uniform with green bars at the collar and sleeves greeted them hurriedly.

'Her name's Five. Five, this is Ping from the Pool of Mental Cultivation—she's very nice. Yes, that's right, Ping. Manager Shui keeps telling me to find assistants who will stay, but these days it's as if decent girls have oil under their feet they leave so quickly. Vocational school certificates and a smattering of English are all very well, but as soon as one arrives, another goes off to be a "personal secretary". We've virtually become a headhunting company! It seems like education and practicality are fire and water—they can't be mixed. Anyway, see you later, Ping . . .'

*　　　*　　　*

The first thing that struck Five when she was
introduced to Manager Shui was the size of his
stomach. It was so enormous it seemed to Five
that you could keep a piglet inside it. What
made a man's belly grow so big? She thought
about the fattest man in her village. They
called him Bao Daye, meaning 'Old Mister
Treasure', not because it was his real name,
but because of his great learning. He was the
most widely travelled man in the whole village
and had even been to the far north-east of
China where the trees were tall, people were
giants and the horses were strong. It was said
that, up there, even their pancakes were like
the lid of a barrel. Five had always believed
that Bao Daye kept all his learning in his fat
tummy, and that was why he was always able to
answer questions and tell stories. Clearly
Manager Shui must have a belly full of
learning too and deserved her utmost respect.
She felt her shoulders start to hunch forward
in an involuntary bow, though she really
wanted to stand up straight.

'Pleased to meet you, Miss Five,' said
Manager Shui in a jolly voice. 'I'm not a great
one for "Manager this" and "Manager that" all
the time, but since my staff all call me
Manager Shui, you'd better go along with

75

them. Now, Five, tell me a bit about yourself. I don't believe this form holds the story of your life! What do you say? Will five minutes be enough, I . . . Hold on, sorry . . . Hello . . .'

Manager Shui pulled a beeping thing out of his pocket and walked into an inner room with it, squeezing his stomach through the narrow doorframe. Five could hear him laughing behind the closed door and guessed that he must be talking on the telephone even though she hadn't seen him holding a receiver like the one in the village Production Brigade office. Three had told her that city people all had phones they could carry about so that they could talk to family and friends wherever they went, or even read jokes on it or use it as a clock. She felt proud of herself for working out what was going on.

Manager Shui stayed talking in the inner room for a long time, so Five took the opportunity to look around the huge office. It was much bigger than the Production Brigade office with several tables, two hard seats and three chairs of different sizes wrapped in red cloth. On the largest table, which gleamed with polish, were a telephone—the kind her uncles used—and something that Five had never seen before: a glass window in a plastic frame with little fish swimming across it. She felt rather nervous of this so she turned to look at the smaller tables, on which stood some brightly coloured statues that were far more familiar to her. There were the Eight Immortals Crossing the Sea, Lao Shou Xing, God of Longevity, carved in yellow wood with a long floating beard, twinkling eyes and a branch of heavenly peaches, and Five's favourite goddess, Guanyin, the great Bodhisattva of Mercy. How clever Guanyin must be to have men kneeling at her feet! Five remembered how, after a few bowls of spirits, her father would curse her mother for being a hen who couldn't lay eggs and brought shame on the Li family's firstborn son. At those times, her mother would always kneel before the family's statue of Guanyin and burn a stick of incense. By the time the stick was half gone, her father would have stopped shouting and walked off with a sigh. Once, Five had returned home to pick up some farming tools and found her father praying for sons in front of Guanyin. She often thought that, if not for Guanyin, the house would be so full of quarrels that no one would get a moment's peace, not even the dogs and chickens.

Another of Manager Shui's small tables held a terracotta figure that Five guessed must be Chairman Mao because it had a face like the pictures hanging in the village houses. The old people said that apart from Guanyin, Chairman Mao was kindest to the people in the countryside. Her grandfather had talked about how Chairman Mao had made the revolutionaries in the village burn all the IOUs that the peasants had given to the big landlord. If it weren't for him, her family would have had to sell their house to pay back all the money they owed the landlords, and would have starved. But was Manager Shui's statue really Chairman Mao? The face was right, but the figure was wearing the grass sandals of a peasant and holding a straw hat in his hands, and she had never seen Chairman Mao looking like that.

Five jumped when the telephone on the polished desk started ringing. Manager Shui came out of the inner room, still talking into his portable phone.

'Uh-huh . . . you're right, but you know how people are these days. They grab power and then abuse it. I don't think . . . Wait a moment, someone's on the other line . . .'

Manager Shui picked up the big phone in his other hand. 'Hello, Miss Lin, who's calling? . . . Tell him I won't be in till after eight. If he wants me he can come to the Foot Massage room, I'll be there.'

He put down the big phone and was just about to carry on talking into the moving phone when he noticed that Five was still waiting for him.

'Look, my friend,' he said to the person on the other end of the line, 'come here for a bathe. It'll be much nicer to talk with our jackets off . . . What, you think I'm abusing my power to push my friends around? . . . OK,

OK, just let me know when you're on your way and I'll make sure there's a quiet room for you. That's settled then. I'll be waiting!'

Manager Shui put the phone back into his pocket and brought his train of thought back to the office with visible effort.

'Sorry, sorry, remind me who you are . . . It's Five, isn't it? That's right, the new assistant! Well now, Five, is that what your family call you? Is there something else you'd prefer to be called? No? Never mind, I like calling you Five.'

Without giving Five time to reply, Manager Shui pressed a small bell on the desk, and a thin girl came in like the ones Five had seen standing behind the big glass windows. She was dressed entirely in green, and her clothes were extremely eye-catching. Five's heart began to beat faster just looking at her and she didn't even dare to lift her head to look this green person in the eye.

'Miss Lin, this is Five, who's just come to join us. Will you take her to see Engineer Wu in the pump room, please. Also, it's my reading hour next, but if Director Chen from the City Political Bureau calls, please put him through.'

'Certainly, Manager Shui. No calls between one and two, unless it's the City Government Director. Come on now, Five, let's go and see Engineer Wu.'

Five followed the green girl out of the

office, keeping her head lowered. Then, to her distress, instead of leading her silently down the corridor, the green girl started asking her questions. Five was terrified she would give a stupid answer and kept her eyes glued to the floor.

'Five, where are you from?' asked the green girl kindly.

'Chuzhou Prefecture, Anhui Province,' Five said in a voice as faint as a mosquito.

'Have you ever been to Nanjing before?'

'No,' she whispered.

The green girl tried again.

'Five, what kind of flowers do you like?'

'Flowers?' Five was puzzled, but she still did not dare to raise her head, keeping her eyes fixed on the two pretty legs walking along beside her.

'Flowers from your garden, or flowers that grow nearby your house? What sort do you like the best?'

'Sweet-potato flowers,' Five answered without hesitation.

'Sweet-potato flowers? What are those like? I've never seen a sweet-potato flower.'

The green high-heeled shoes came to a stop. Five had only ever seen one pair of high-heeled shoes in her life. Uncle Three had bought them in the local town for his wife and they had been the talk of the village for quite some time, until Aunt Three said they hurt her feet and she wasn't going to wear them any more. But the green girl's shoes were much higher.Weren't they uncomfortable?

'Come on, Five. Tell me what a sweet-potato flower looks like.'

'Oh, I . . .' Five had no idea how to describe a sweet-potato flower. Surely they were so common that everyone knew what they looked like? As always, she fell back on her mother's words: 'Some are as big as a hundred-day-old baby's fist, but then you find tiny ones, like a woman's thumbnail. When they are open, they are the shape of a funnel, and the fields look like a green sky filled with stars.'

The high heels started walking again. 'Well, Five, you're full of surprises. I've never heard of a "green sky". That must look very beautiful. So, tell me some more about yourself. If someone invites you out to eat, what kind of food do you like?'

Five didn't know how to reply to this question at all. She had never in her life been invited to a table where there were guests, and her father had always said that girls couldn't take part in banquets.

The green girl didn't seem to mind that Five wasn't answering and launched into other questions.

'Perhaps you like karaoke? Or films? Why don't you look up? I think we must be about the same age.'

Five tried her hardest to raise her head but she still felt very uncomfortable at the idea of looking directly at such an elegant person.

'You're very lucky to have found a job here, Five,' the girl continued. 'I've worked in a lot of companies, but our Manager Shui's the most cultivated manager I've had, and the most honest and fair. You can spend three years in most companies without laying eyes on the boss, but Manager Shui is always chatting to the staff. There's lots to learn here, whether you've got an education or not. You'll pick up some very useful skills . . . Now, I'm going to introduce you to Engineer Wu. His full name's Wu Dali, but everyone calls him Engineer Wu because he's in charge of the pump room and the plumbing. He doesn't talk much, but he's an honest man, and very good with technical things. If there's any problem with the machinery, he knows what it is just by listening to it, or looking at the water in the pools. Manager Shui says he's a complete treasure and is worth half the company, so no one dares to disobey Engineer Wu's orders.'

Although Five had some difficulty keeping up with what the green girl was saying, she managed to form a picture in her head of a tall, imposing man. But when she was led in front of Engineer Wu, she realised she could not have been more wrong. In fact he was what the people in the village called 'half a yard': no taller than Five, and very skinny. His flesh barely covered his bones and, every time he moved, you could see the muscles rippling under his skin.

'Hello,' he said, in a voice that seemed far too kind to be a man's, 'you must be Miss Five! Don't worry if you feel all at sea right now. Anyone chosen by Banyue will be able to learn quickly. Use your eyes to watch and your mouth to ask, and in just a few days you'll know all about what happens inside the Water Dragon's Palace.'

For the first time since she had entered this strange place, Five relaxed. Engineer Wu spoke in a way she could actually follow. She even had the courage to raise her head a little and look properly at the difficult-to-understand green girl. How beautiful she was! Just like the pictures of film stars Three had brought home at New Year. Village women said a beautiful woman had a face like a full moon, a mouth like a cherry and lips like thin willow leaves, but the ones in Three's pictures all had pointed chins, hollow cheeks, big mouths, and lips full enough to fry dinner on. Five remembered hiding in the storeroom every day to look at herself in a mirror she'd sneaked into her pocket. She knew she wasn't beautiful by village standards but perhaps she had a 'city' kind of beauty. Despite days of gazing into the mirror, she couldn't decide what to think of her appearance, but she knew that no one else in the village measured up to Three's pictures either. Even Six, whom everyone said was so pretty, had lips that were too thin. But this green girl had everything . . .

Engineer Wu gently tapped Five on the shoulder.

'Five, are you all right?'

'I'm . . . I'm fine. It's just that she's so pretty!' The words slipped out before Five could stop them and seemed to embarrass the green girl, who whispered a few words in Engineer Wu's ear and swayed off down the corridor. Five watched her until she disappeared round a corner and then sighed.

'Why didn't I look at her earlier?'

'What was that?' Engineer Wu asked.

'Nothing,' Five whispered, trying to implant the green girl's beautiful face in her memory. 'Nothing . . .'

Engineer Wu seemed to be a very patient person because he didn't speak again until he was certain that he had Five's full attention.

'Now, Five, let's go and get some lunch. We'll have to start work in a while and, while we're eating, I'll tell you a bit about the Water Dragon's Palace.'

Five felt anxiety welling up inside her.

'How can I work if I don't know anything?' she cried. All her life she had thought herself clumsy. It took her ages to learn how to do new things. She remembered how, the first time Three came back from the city, she had tried to teach her to arrange vegetables. A day and a half went by and Three kept yelling, 'How could our mother have given birth to two

84

such different people? Why can't you see you'll damage the produce if you handle it like that!' Her father had been sitting nearby, and had rebuked Three, knocking his pipe out on the stove. 'Stop laying into Five just because she's a bit slower than you. Don't think that, just because you've spent a bit of time in the city, you can tell your sister what to do.' Three had cried all night because of this reprimand, and Five had felt it was all her fault. Now this Engineer Wu thought he could explain her job in a few words! What if she didn't understand? Three said that countryside people were naturally more stupid than city people, and she was the stupidest girl in the village . . .

*   *   *

When Engineer Wu took Five to the workers' canteen to eat lunch, he made sure to sit her in a corner facing the wall so that she had her back to the endless stream of employees coming to get their lunch. He could see that she was having difficulty coping with the stress of meeting new people, and was struggling to communicate. He knew that, without a careful handling of the situation, it would be easy to destroy her confidence. The Dragon Water-Culture Centre was a relatively new business and even Nanjingers had taken a while to get to understand how it worked. He was going to have to find a way to explain things to Five slowly and clearly otherwise she would never get to grips with city life.

Engineer Wu's understanding of the countryside came from his mother, who had been born in a village in Sichuan. As a young woman she had come to work in the city with her husband, but she never managed to shake off her feeling of inferiority. Even in later life, when she was helping take care of old people who lived alone, she would refer to herself as 'stupid', and rarely laughed, joked or went for a stroll in the streets with friends. Engineer Wu, who had grown up with his mother's silence, felt a great deal of sympathy for country girls like Five who came from male-run villages where they received little love or attention. To him they were like blades of grass growing in the cracks between stones: they wanted to see the sunlight and find a space to breathe, but the wind and rain hammered down on them. It was all too easy for these girls to be utterly crushed by men and to feel that they were worthless. Although their ignorance gave them courage to leave their homes, this same ignorance could very quickly become a source of fear and self-loathing when they realised how little they knew. He had known girls who had committed suicide because, after living the circumscribed way of life in the countryside, that hadn't changed for centuries, they found it impossible to adapt to the pressures of modern life in a city, or deal with its freedoms. He was determined that this shouldn't be Five's fate.

'Here's your lunch,' he said to her, placing a tray down in front of her. 'Eat up.'

Five looked at the food and remembered the first time her father's fist had struck her head: 'You've done no work,' he had shouted. 'How can you eat?' It had not been a hard blow, but it had been strong enough to bash into Five's four-year-old head the belief that you can't eat before you've completed your tasks.

'I'm not hungry,' she said.

'You may really not be hungry, but this is the big city. All workers eat at mealtimes, or else you have to go hungry until the next meal: there's no stove to keep your food warm here. Hurry up and finish it. This is a part of the wages you'll be earning from today. Just make sure you do your work properly afterwards.'

'All right, I'll eat.' Five gave a nod and started to wolf down her food. In a few minutes the big tray of fried rice and vegetable soup was empty, consumed by Five with great slurping noises. Engineer Wu smiled. By the looks of things, she would have fainted if she hadn't had something to eat soon, and her healthy appetite was a good sign. The man who had taught him his trade had once said that people who liked big meals, ate quickly and weren't picky about their food, made hard, capable workers. This was why in ancient times artisans choosing apprentices always held a meal called 'Welcoming Meal to Greet the Master' as a practical test of their skill.

When Engineer Wu had finished eating he put his tray on an empty table to his left, and took out several pieces of paper from an inner pocket of his orange boilersuit. Selecting a blank piece of paper, he plucked a pen from his top pocket and drew a diagram.

'Take a look at this, Five. What do you see: a body, a head with eyes, nose, mouth, ears, whiskers and horns, claws, and a tail? OK, what is it?'

'A dragon,' exclaimed Five, delighted by the skill of Engineer Wu's drawing.

'Now, Five, listen carefully. The dragon's head is for thinking and organising and that's called the office. Manager Shui works with his assistants in the office, telling everyone what to do. The tail of the dragon is used to store the herbs that will be brewed into medicine for the pools. It is also where the pumps and boilers are kept—that hot and noisy place that you saw when you came in. In this dragon's belly are all the guts: the pools, the treatment rooms, and the relaxation rooms. Pump-room workers and assistants like you are the dragon's feet and claws; if any part of the dragon's body hurts or itches we'll be there to soothe or scratch it, because customers will only be happy if there is no problem anywhere on the dragon's body. That's the only way we can turn a profit!'

'But what are the pools for?' Five asked in confusion.

'We fill the pools with medicinal herbs,' Engineer Wu explained patiently. 'Bathing in these waters can cure illnesses or stop you getting ill.'

Five seemed completely taken aback.

'But aren't you supposed to drink medicine?' she asked. 'Not just wash in it . . . In our village, we all drink the medicine from the doctor. It's really bitter, but my dad says that if medicine's not bitter it won't work!'

'This isn't a hospital. We do occasionally give the customers some herbal medicine to drink to sort out internal problems but it's not usually that bitter . . .'

'But I don't know anything about medicine!' The more Five heard, the more alarmed she became.

'You're an assistant, Five, not a medic. You will accompany Auntie Wang on her rounds. If anybody runs out of something, has a message to send or an urgent task they need done, you'll help them.'

'Will I have to wear a uniform?'

'Everyone here has to wear a uniform. Each uniform has coloured bars on the sleeves and collar to help clients understand what job that person does; gold for the doctors, silver for the technicians, green for the medicine pool managers, fiery red for the office workers and earthy yellow for the patrol team run by Auntie Wang. So, you'll be yellow.'

'But you and the green girl aren't wearing white clothes with tabs,' Five protested.

'That's because we're different. Ms Lin is often out on business and so it would be inappropriate for her to wear a uniform. I wear orange to help people find me if a machine needs fixing.'

'Do I have to be able to swim?'

Engineer Wu laughed.

'No, walking on the ground is fine! OK, let's go and see Auntie Wang. She's got a quick temper but a soft heart. She'll show you the ropes in no time.'

*   *   *

Later Five would remember that first meeting with Auntie Wang as being the first time anyone had praised her. Auntie Wang's kindness had given her the courage to think that she might be able to survive in the Water Dragon's Palace after all.

She heard the woman's laugh before she saw her. Then Engineer Wu led her into the patrol-team office and she was overwhelmed by an enthusiastic welcome.

'Here she is, here she is, great stuff. Thank you, Engineer Wu. Now, tell me, did your mother see great things for you when she named you Charming? Perhaps she knew that one day you'd come to our Water Centre, a place which practises beauty therapy. You'll go far here—we wizened old things need a little bit of charm to keep us young! What's that, Engineer Wu? Her name actually means Five. Well, that's even better! We haven't got any fifth daughters working here yet. That makes you even more special, Five, because you'll have learned a lot of clever tricks from your older sisters.'

Faced with this woman who was to be her boss, Five suddenly remembered the polite words Three had taught her to say.

'I'm a country girl,' she blurted out, 'I'm no good at anything. Please be so kind as to look after me.'

'Look at that, what a nicely spoken young woman!' exclaimed Auntie Wang. 'Now don't you go looking down on yourself. City people differ from country people, just as tall people differ from small people, but everyone has their virtues. Short people raise their heads to look at people and so they see people's eyes turning up when they smile and happy jaws; tall people look down on people so all they see are bald heads and long faces. Don't believe me? You stand on a stool some time and look down on those tall people. You'll see how different happy faces can look from a new angle. Ha! I'm sure you're going to be one of those clever countryside girls. Now come along with me so that I can show you where you'll be

91

sleeping tonight. Every little bird needs a nest . . .'

And with that, Auntie Wang led Five on a winding route through doors and corridors until they came to a big room in which six or seven girls were busy folding up quilts and arranging them underneath a number of sofas that were pushed against the wall.

Five was surprised to hear Auntie Wang's laughing voice transform itself into a serious, professional tone.

'This is our new assistant, everyone. She's called Five and will be sleeping in Bed Ten. She's not yet twenty, and it's her first time in the city, so everyone keep an eye out for her. Remember what Manager Shui is always saying: helping others is like helping oneself, and doing ill to others is bound to come back to haunt you one day. You girls should look after each other when you're together, just like sisters, and then your days will be happy. Good, Five, put your things in the box under your bed, let Mei Mei from Bed One show you where the bathroom is, then wait for me here. I'll be back shortly.'

Five watched with anxiety as Auntie Wang bustled out of the room but Mei Mei seemed kind enough. She was a tall girl with pale, delicate features and a gentle voice.

'We have to fold up our beds so they can be used as foot massage couches during the day,' she explained. 'The timetable here takes a bit of getting used to. You can stay in bed till eleven-thirty every day because business hours are 1 p.m. to midnight and we can't go to bed until all the clients have left. There's a meal at twelve-noon before we start work, then we eat supper in different sittings from six to eight. After we shut up shop, they come round with a snack, which is mostly food that clients haven't ordered and which won't keep till the next day. Some girls decide to miss supper so they can have this nice food later in the evening but it's a risk: sometimes there are so many clients there's nothing left, and then they're sorry. This is the shared bathroom. You can use my shower gel and shampoo if you want. And ask me if you need anything else. I'm a foot masseur so you'll always find me in this room.'

Five was about to thank Mei Mei when she heard Auntie Wang returning down the corridor.

'Oh yes, she'll be good, this one. Not like the last girl. How was a crazy old bat like me supposed to keep up with a vocational school graduate? This Five, you can see at a glance she's a stayer . . . Ah yes indeed, aren't we lucky . . .'

Auntie Wang came back into the room.

'Now, Five, have you got yourself sorted out? I hope you could hear what Mei Mei was saying. The little thing always speaks in such a quiet voice that we all grow long ears listening to her talk. Come with me and we'll get to work.'

Auntie Wang gave Five a clean uniform and spent the next hour showing her how the medicines were arranged in the storeroom. Five felt as if she was beginning to find her feet until a message came that Auntie Wang was wanted in the Pool of Mental Cultivation. Five followed her boss through a door only to be confronted with a pool full of men and women in tight, revealing swimming costumes laughing and chatting together.

She immediately blushed a fiery shade of red, averted her eyes and fled. A bemused Auntie Wang called after her to stop, but no amount of shouting could call her back.

5

THE BOOK TASTER'S TEAHOUSE

Six had been left all alone at Mr Guan's job centre when Five had left. Three had gone back to work, and the man from the teahouse who was coming to collect her had telephoned to say he had got stuck in a traffic jam. To her relief, Mr Guan had suggested she come into his office to wait. All his staff were so busy they didn't have time to look after her, he said, but she could spend the time looking at his books.

Books were precious to Six. There were none in her village and she hadn't owned one until she had started attending the middle school an hour's walk from the village, and been given a textbook. After that she would sometimes go to her teachers' houses to look at their books, since the school didn't have a library. But, until now, she had never seen a collection of books as large as Guan Buyu's. The shelves in his office were filled, from floor to ceiling, with hundreds of volumes and, for a moment, Six had no idea where to start. In the end she decided to pick the one with the most eye-catching spine to look at first. Pulling out a book with a painting of a woman's face on the spine, she saw that it was a novel called *Jane*

Eyre by an English writer called Charlotte Brontë. It looked quite long and complicated so she put it back and continued browsing. The next volume to catch her attention was a book with the title *Sexual Love—A Basic Human Need* written in red. She was astonished to see that a man like Guan Buyu had something like this on his shelves. Her teacher had warned her that books with the word 'sex' in the title were dirty, and that she should steer clear of them if she didn't want to end up in prison. Looking away rapidly, Six cast her eye further along the shelf until she noticed something called *My Books*. Attracted by the title, she took it down and discovered that it was written by a French student who had come to study in China in the fifties. In it the student had listed all the books that he liked best and written descriptions of them. Without quite knowing why, Six didn't put this book back but kept it in her hand as she looked along the other shelves. *Ulysses—A Reader's Guide, Rodin's Art, On Plato, Nietzsche* . . . There were rows and rows of books on subjects she had never heard of, as well as many volumes called things like *Zen and Enlightenment, The Study of Daoism*, and *The Hundred Scholars of Early Confucianism*. She was struck by how many books had the word 'beauty' in the title, or had titles that mixed the Chinese character for 'study' with the character for 'beauty' (which she later

96

learned meant 'Aesthetics'): *Thoughts on Aesthetics, Analysis of Western Aesthetics, Communication and Aesthetics* . . . What was a city man doing openly reading books on such a female subject? Perhaps there was more respect for the idea of beauty in the city. Six thought sadly about the girls who had been to primary school with her and were now all married. If they tried to make themselves look beautiful, they became a laughing stock. It simply wasn't done. Maybe now that she had escaped her village, she would have a little more time for beauty . . .

Six lost all track of time as she stood in front of Guan Buyu's bookshelves. She was neither hungry nor thirsty, but drunk on the knowledge around her.

'Six, have you still not seen enough?' said Mr Guan, poking his head around the door. 'It looks like you're *really* fond of books! How much of what's here can you understand? You'll be able to read lots of books at Shu Tian's teahouse. You'll have to tip me off if any interesting new titles come in. I go there often myself. But I'm afraid I'm going to have to throw you out of my office now: your lift's here. Shu Tian says he's three hours late because there was a traffic jam. Honestly . . . In the days when no one had cars, they used to blame their alarm clocks for not going off, but now traffic jams are eveyone's favourite excuse for being late. People really are lamentable:

instead of owning up to their faults, they treat other people like idiots who'll believe their lies. Ah, the baseness of human nature! Come on, let's go. If you like that book you've got in your hand, you can borrow it. Just make a note of it here so I won't forget who's got it.'

It seemed that Guan Buyu often lent books to people because he had a little noticeboard on the wall with lots of pieces of paper pinned to it giving the titles of books. When Six had written her note, he added it to the board. She felt a sense of pride that her own handwriting had joined the words of so many scholars—and in such a grand office too! Then she pocketed the book and followed Guan Buyu.

Outside stood a man who looked like a teacher. He had glasses as thick as the bottoms of soy sauce bottles and a traditional Chinese black jacket that fastened down the front. He walked up to her, bowed politely and shook her hand.

'Pleased to meet you. I am Shu Tian.'

'My name is Six. Please be so kind as to look after me.' This was the first time in Six's life she'd introduced herself so formally.

'Mr Shu is the boss of the Book Taster's Teahouse,' Guan Buyu explained. 'I'm sure you're going to enjoy working there, but if you're worried about anything, don't hesitate to come and find me here by the big willow. You must treat this place as your own home, is that clear?' Then he turned to his friend. 'Six is a real bookworm, Old Shu. You did her a favour by coming three hours late: she got the chance to go through my bookshelves. She may be young, but she's got the makings of a great reader.'

'Thank you, Old Guan. You always know how to find the right person for the job. The last thing my teahouse needs is a good worker who doesn't like books. The place would be like a prison to them. And her youth isn't a problem at all. I'll make sure I look after her. Come on, Six, let's go.'

With a last nod of gratitude to Mr Guan, Six followed Thick Glasses down the street to his waiting car.

Six had never been in a car before. In fact she had only ever been in a bus four times: once to travel to the local town and back to represent her school in an essay competition, once when she had gone with Aunt Two to visit Uncle Three (his son had given them a lift back on his tractor), and the fourth time to come to Nanjing. As soon as Thick Glasses turned the ignition key, sweat broke out on Six's palms. The ramshackle car juddered and roared like a tractor, then set off at such a pace that it seemed to Six they were in danger of hitting every pedestrian who crossed the road. She managed to stop herself from crying out loud—she didn't want Mr Thick Glasses to think country people were cowards—but she opened her eyes wide, breathing in great gulps of air, and very soon she realised she had got the hiccups.

'Six, here's some water. Take ten sips and you'll be fine.'

Thick Glasses took one hand off the steering wheel to hold out a bottle.

'I'm fine—hic—I know how to stop—hic—hiccups . . . You just have to pinch the nail of the fourth finger hard—hic—and you're fine . . .'

Six pinched with all her might, but somehow it didn't work. How strange. At home she always managed to stop her hiccups like this . . .

'Quick, take a few sips of water. It hurts just listening to you.'

Six couldn't see how she was going to manage to hold the bottle of water. She had put her meagre luggage on the back seat of the car, but the book she had borrowed from Mr Guan was still clasped between her legs and she was clinging tightly to the seatbelt with both hands, not daring to take her eyes off the street or the people rushing towards her. It was as if she herself were driving, and she was afraid that if she were to close her eyes for an instant, the car would hit something.

A pedestrian suddenly stepped into the middle of the road, and Thick Glasses braked sharply. Six could not suppress a cry of terror, and for the first time her driver noticed that she had both eyes screwed shut and beads of sweat dripping down her forehead. Out of consideration, he decided to turn into a small side lane, but he had barely twisted the steering wheel when someone in the car behind shouted, 'Hey, you in front, don't you know how to use your indicator? Go home and walk, if you don't know how to drive!' Shu Tian braked for a moment in confusion, which only encouraged the man in the car behind to lean out of his window and continue his harangue. 'This road isn't your private property, you know! There are rules . . . Look at that heap you're in. No one's driving Xialis these days. I suppose you want to have an accident so you can collect the insurance money and buy yourself a decent car . . .'

Six could vaguely hear the voice shouting, but she had no idea what it was saying. She was barely even aware that they were now going down a quieter road. It was not until Thick Glasses had tapped her on the shoulder several times that she opened her eyes. She saw that he was now driving much more slowly, breathed a sigh of relief, and felt a wave of exhaustion sweep over her.

But her trials were not over. Before long, they got stuck behind an old lady who was tottering down the middle of the road with her walking stick, an empty basket on her arm. The old lady glanced behind her at the car, then continued as she was, ambling unhurriedly down the lane. Thick Glasses gave

101

a quick toot of his horn, at which the old lady jumped, turned round and, eyes full of rage, jabbed at the bonnet of the car with her walking stick.

'Impatient, are we? Think this old lady's too slow? Go and drive on the main road if you're such a big shot. I've seen your sort before. Running around with young girls and siphoning off public money for your dirty practices like you're above the law of the land. Do you have no shame—flaunting your filthy behaviour like that?!'

The more the old lady cursed the angrier she got, and the more confused Six became. Thick Glasses's face went from pale to red and back again. The little lane, which had been almost deserted, was suddenly filled with a crowd of people, who clustered around the car and peered in through the windows. It was just the same in the village: whenever there was a family argument, people flocked to watch. But it had never occurred to Six that, on her first day in the big city, she'd be cursed in public. Not knowing how big Nanjing was, Six was thrown into despair by the idea that, from now on, she would be recognised and gossiped about wherever she went. She shot a look at Thick Glasses. Why wasn't he defending her? But he merely gave a helpless gesture.

'There's nothing I can do, Six. A good man doesn't fight women. And, anyway, a bookish intellectual is no match for a toothless old lady. We'll just have to wait until she gets it out of her system.'

Just then, a man walked from out of the crowd.

'All right, old woman. That's enough. I saw the whole thing and this guy hasn't done anything wrong. You were wandering right down the middle of the road. What was he supposed to do? Crawl along behind you? Besides, not everybody who drives a car is necessarily a bent official. Look at his thick glasses. Does he seem like a wicked man? And how many officials drive knackered old Xialis? You should think carefully before you accuse an honest person falsely. Come on now, be off with you. They say, "Good health underlies Revolution". Save your good health and righteous indignation for someone who's really corrupt.'

'Thank you, kind sir!' shouted Thick Glasses, raising his bottom from the seat to bow in a way that made Six smile, even though she was still shaking with fear. Their saviour led the old lady away and Thick Glasses set off down the lane again, sighing with relief.

They drove along back lanes for another twenty minutes before returning to the main street and pulling up in front of a small row of shops, of which one was a beautiful old building in the traditional Nanjing style, with white walls, grey roof tiles and flying eaves. Six looked at the shopfront with awe, admiring the large black-and-gold sign under the eaves that read 'The Book Taster's Teahouse', and beneath, in smaller letters, 'In Memory of Lu and Lu'. Walking towards the entrance to the shop, she noticed that the door was decorated with an intricately carved panel of two men playing chess.

But if Six had been taken with the front of the shop, she was even more delighted when she saw the interior. It was just like the pictures of ancient teahouses she had seen in her teachers' books, with about a dozen circular mahogany tables dotted around the room, and benches in the same wood along the side walls. But it also had the air of an old library, with low bookshelves dividing the room into four to give the tables a feeling of intimacy. To the right of the doorway stood a lovely tall table for the preparation of tea that looked like the ones in old paintings where beautiful women held their sleeves out of the way as they warmed cups with hot water and poured tea from delicate porcelain pots. Behind this table hung a blue batik curtain on which the Chinese character for 'Tea' stood out in white. To the left of the entrance there was a a square old-fashioned writing desk, with a full set of calligraphy brushes, slabs of ink (with a stone for grinding it), paper and, beneath it, a big china urn to hold scrolls of paper and larger calligraphy brushes. Along the back wall was a classical zither, a display cabinet of tea sets and, between them, a beautiful wall-hanging painted with the character for 'peace'. The ceiling was hung with calligraphy brushes for wall painting, so large they almost looked as if they could be used to sweep the floor.

Six was struck dumb by the beauty of the room. She felt she had not enough eyes to take it all in.

'Do you like it?' Thick Glasses asked her.

'I love it!' Six murmured. Never in her wildest dreams had she thought she would set foot in such a lovely place.

Thick Glasses began turning on lamps.

'These are replicas of ancient table lamps,' he said. 'The ones on the bookcases are imitation Ming palace lamps in eggshell porcelain. They both provide the right kind of light for reading and appreciating paintings. These days plenty of people know about buying art and putting it on display, but they've failed to grasp that you need soft lighting to appreciate it. Ah well, that's what it's like today . . . People are interested in money, not art. Such a pity . . .'

'Why is there nobody here?' Six asked. Surely a teahouse like this should be the most popular place in Nanjing, she thought to herself.

'We're not opening until next week,' Thick Glasses explained. 'We decorated the place just before Spring Festival and then, over the holiday, we invited some of our bookworm friends to come for tea and snacks so they could give us ideas. I need all the help I can get. I've spent my whole life working in a publishing company editing a youth magazine and doing a bit of English translation on the side, so running a business is new to me. My wife and I have put everything we own into this teahouse, with some help from our son. If it succeeds we'll set up more like it; if it falls through we'll just have to shut up shop and find freelance work where we can. If I can't be a chicken's head and run my own business, I'll just have to settle for being a phoenix's tail and working for someone else . . .'

As Thick Glasses spoke, he stroked the books on the shelves.

'I picked up all these books myself from markets and bookstalls. I've just about read them all, or at least had a quick flick through. Once we open, I'll get more. And I hope a few like-minded people will donate books. Then we'll be pretty well set up. This is the teahouse of my dreams, I just want to . . .'

'Bookworm, you're back! How many hours have you taken to collect her? If you think that you can run a business as slowly as you drink tea, we'll soon have to sell all those books of yours just to break even. Quickly now, why aren't you giving me a hand? I thought it would be easy to pop over to the supermarket to get some snacks, but on the way back the food seemed to get heavier with every step. My fingers are nearly bent right off!'

A middle-aged woman dressed in bright red had burst in through the door, her hands full of plastic bags.

'Ow, gosh—take them. That's right, there's one on each finger. Kang's coming along in a moment with some heavier stuff. Hello, hello, new friend. Sorry, I can't shake your hand, I've got my arms full. My name's Meng as in "Dream". What's yours?'

'Liu'er as in "Six",' Six replied brightly.

'Six? That's quite a coincidence. Last week we had someone in the teahouse called Nine. At first I thought her name was "Wine" so I asked her if she came from a family of wine-lovers. Take me, for instance, my mother used to say my father was a dreamer whose daydreams never came to anything until he produced a daughter. What do you think of that? Pull back that curtain for me, will you please, so that I can put these bags into our storeroom? Thanks! Look at this, they've dug big creases into my hands . . . Anyway, the woman told me her name was Nine, not Wine. I've got a small brain, you see. Still, it's wonderful to have a girl with a lucky number for a name working for us. We'll all reap the benefits. Now, have you and the Bookworm had anything to eat? No? Gracious, it's nearly five. You silly old bookworm, it's one thing for you not to eat, but how could you let her go hungry? You really are the limit. Oh, never mind, forget it, I've just bought some little pastries for the opening. You two can have some to keep you going and then we'll have a proper family meal later. You'll have to take care of yourself Six, when you're working with him. My husband's a decent chap, with a good heart and a solid brain, but his eyesight and memory are useless. If he sees a little black dog by the side of the road, he thinks someone's hat has blown off. He tries to "eliminate the four pests", as our great leaders once told us to, by swatting nails on the wall mistaking them for flies, but then he'll go and think a ladybird is a nail and try to hang a bag of eggs on it . . .'

Six burst out laughing.

'Don't think I'm just poking fun for the hell of it,' continued Meng with a smile. 'Everything I say is true. We've been married twenty-six years, and I've got enough jokes about him to fill a book! If you don't believe me, you'll find out soon enough. And as for his memory . . . Ever since I met him, I've watched him bump around the room looking for his glasses when he's holding them in his hand. If I phone him to ask if he's eaten, he tells me he'll have to go into the kitchen to see if there are any unwashed dishes. I never believe that stuff of his about traffic jams. He just doesn't know where he's going . . . Go on, eat, you must be starving! Here Bookworm, you have these. I'm sorry, but I have to warn Six about your lunacy (or should I say genius) so that you don't scare her to death.'

While she was speaking, Meng had laid out some egg biscuits in front of Six. They were rather like the deep-fried dough chips they ate during Spring Festival in the countryside, but a lot nicer. Six ate too quickly, and then felt very thirsty. She saw Meng reach for a bottle of water so pointed to the sink in the storeroom behind the curtain to say that she was very happy to drink tap water. Meng did not stop her, so Six put her mouth to the tap, drank a big mouthful and felt much better. Then she looked around the storeroom. It was a small, cramped space just big enough to hold two people with shelves reaching from floor to ceiling. The top shelves held lots of different-sized boxes, the middle shelves were used for the tea sets and the bottom shelves had a number of plastic buckets on them for storage, cleaning and emptying tea leaves into. To the left of the tap was a little table which Meng was using to unpack the shopping.

While Six was gazing about her, Meng took out a piece of white kitchen paper, and discreetly wiped the biscuit crumbs off the tap.

'I'm back!'

A strong male voice resounded through the teahouse and, before long, a young man dressed in white corduroy trousers and a black corduroy jacket squeezed into the storeroom carrying two big cardboard boxes.

'That looks good,' he said to Meng. 'Have you saved any for me? You've only been a capitalist for a few days but you're already exploiting your workers: I didn't even have time for lunch!'

The man put down his boxes, wiped his hands on the curtain, and held out his hand to Six: 'Hi, welcome to the Book Taster's Teahouse.'

Six had never shaken hands with a young, unmarried man before but she remembered reading in magazines that men and women were very casual around each other in the big city, so with a great effort she put out her hand. The warmth of the man's strong grip made her feel quite odd; she could feel the blood pulsing through his fingers.

'Have my parents had time to oppress you yet, child worker?' he asked, laughing.

'Kang!' said Meng crossly, untying a beautiful red scarf from around her neck. 'Don't make such thoughtless jokes. Six has only just finished middle school and it's her first time in the city, so it's hard for her to know whether you're serious or not. She might think you're being disrespectful. Six, don't listen to his nonsense. Young people these days think it's fashionable to make fun of their parents. That's because they've never been sent to the countryside to learn what's what. You'll have to tell him about what life is like in

110

your village so he knows what good fortune really is.'

'There you go finding fault again Mother. I know, I know, when you were younger you all had to attend those Recollect Bitterness meetings where people talked about what life had been like before Communism made it much better, but do we have to have them now? If so, please could you invite us to a Recollect Bitterness Meal. We're starving. Put some food in front of us and you can lecture us all you want about how the country's going to the dogs.'

'Kang's got a point, Meng,' said Thick Glasses. 'Let's put all the things away and then go out for a meal. Tea and sweet things before supper are bad for the appetite. Kang, give Ruth a call so she can come and meet Six. Then Six will know everything about our little world.'

Shu Kang pulled out a mobile phone from an inside pocket, dialled and immediately began to talk in English. Six's mouth fell open when she heard this. Even the English teacher she admired the most had never spoken English so quickly. She was even more astounded when Meng began speaking to her son in English. Six had thought Thick Glasses was the most scholarly person in this family, but even the wife knew English. How lucky she was to be working for such intellectual people! An image appeared in her mind of herself talking freely in English with the members of this family, discussing books, history, foreign countries, the life in her village . . .

She stood there, entranced, but was brought down to earth with a bump when the family started exchanging dubious glances about her silence and Meng came up and put an arm round her shoulders.

'Are you missing your home, little Six?' she asked.

'I . . . no . . .' she stammered. She was embarrassed to tell them what she had been thinking about. Suddenly her daydreams seemed shameful. As if she were a dirty toad wanting to eat swan's meat.

*   *   *

That night scenes from the evening kept whirling in front of Six's eyes like a magic lantern as she tried to sleep in her tiny room in the Shu family's apartment. The supper she had eaten in the little dumpling restaurant seemed like the beautiful scenes Hans Christian Andersen's Little Match Girl glimpsed when she struck the matches, but even better: Six had seen much more than the Little Match Girl's roast goose and old grandmother. She kept pinching herself as she lay on her soft bed: was all this real or a dream?

More than anything else, her thoughts kept

returning to Ruth, a fair-haired, light-eyed bignose from England. From the moment Ruth walked into the restaurant, Six's eyes hadn't left her, and she paid no attention to anything else. She had never met a real bignose before, though of course she had read about them in books. The only time she had really seen what they looked like was when she sneaked off secretly to the cinema the time she had visited the local town for an essay competition. The film showing was called *The Bridges of Madison County* and it was about two middle-aged bignoses who were having an affair. Six had left before the end because she had panicked when the man and the woman had started kissing. If anyone in her village had found out she had watched such a thing in the cinema, she would get a bad name. She had seen how her good friend Moli had been destroyed by getting a bad reputation among the villagers, even though she'd done nothing to deserve it. Her parents had locked her up because she'd lost face for them, and fifteen-year-old Moli had killed herself by drinking pesticide. Six's father and mother were already mocked by the villagers for having no sons. If, on top of that, it was discovered that Six had watched a dirty film, the whole family would be finished.

Six remembered how in awe she had been of the actress in *The Bridges of Madison County*. But now that Six had seen Ruth, the actress paled in significance. She spent the evening watching every move that Ruth made and trying to understand her foreign ways. Ruth often behaved strangely. She couldn't use her chopsticks properly and she spoke Chinese in a very funny way. Her pronunciation was so odd that often it was quite difficult to understand what she was saying. She mixed up the four tones of pronunciation so that she made the verb 'to eat' sound like 'seven' and she asked the waiter for a 'clean fat person' when she wanted a clean plate. Six could see that Thick Glasses and his wife were very fond of Ruth: they kept picking up dumplings in their chopsticks and putting them in Ruth's bowl. Shu Kang lost patience with them and kept shouting 'Stop it, that's enough! Mum, Dad, how many times have I told you not to put food in her bowl? Show a little respect for a foreigner and let her decide for herself how much she wants. Your "Chinese love" is too intrusive.'

Meng didn't agree with her son.

'Ruth's an educated person, and she's come to China to experience Chinese culture. If we do everything in a Western way, treating her as a foreigner, she won't learn. Idiocy masquerading as wisdom!'

'*Ruth,*' said Thick Glasses in English, '*would you like to be treated as a Chinese or Westerner?*'

'Chinese, of course!' said Ruth earnestly, putting down her chopsticks and clasping her hands on her chest. Six smiled. Ruth pronounced the word 'Chinese' so that it sounded like 'middle fruit' . . .

While Ruth, Kang and Thick Glasses were discussing goings on at the university, Meng told Six how Ruth had been sent by a Scottish university to study Chinese in Beijing for a year. Kang had also been at university in Beijing and had met Ruth when they took part in a language exchange. Once Ruth had finished her year's study abroad, she had returned to Scotland to continue the last two years of her degree. They did not see each other again until Shu Kang went to Britain to see her, and the two of them made a short tour of Europe. Now Kang was in Nanjing studying for a PhD, and Ruth had come to join him. In order to earn an independent living, Ruth had found a job as an English teacher in a college for primary school teachers, and she and Kang had been living together in rented lodgings on the outskirts of the city for almost a year now.

'And not a word about getting married . . .' Meng added regretfully.

Six felt her face flush red at the idea of Ruth and Kang living together. How could they do such a thing? Surely they would bring shame on the family!

'Aren't you afraid people will make nasty jokes?' she whispered.

'Make nasty jokes about what?' Meng asked, mystified.

'About your son living with a girl before they're married! Won't people gossip about you?' Six could not understand how such educated people could fly in the face of decency without giving it a second thought.

Meng smiled. 'Six, times are changing. When I was young, even holding hands in public was impossible, let alone cohabiting. If unmarried men and women were caught living together they'd be accused of having "an improper lifestyle", or of engaging in "problematic thinking", and forced to write self-criticisms. My parents weren't even allowed to touch each other in front of other people when they were married! But these days, young people kiss in public without a care in the world, and it's become quite common to live together before marriage . . .'

Six felt overwhelmed by confusion. All she had done was spend three hours on a bus and she had entered an entirely different world. Her teachers at school would say, 'One seed not harvested brings a harvest of sorrow, a family without sons brings death to the family line, but to fly in the face of decency brings the end of the world.' If living with a man before you were married was not considered indecent, then what was?

Seeing Six's distress, Meng patted her rough hand.

'It'll take a while, but you'll come to understand why there are such huge differences between the city and the countryside. In many ways, people in the countryside are living in a different century from those in the city, and it will take them many years to catch up.'

Meng did not feel able to tell Six that, in her view, the Chinese countryside was as much as five hundred years behind the city. She remembered how shocked she had been when she had been sent to live in a village during the Cultural Revolution. Although the place hadn't been that far from a town, still, there had been nothing to eat but a string of salted dried turnip at every meal all year round. The five years she spent there had completely destroyed the young Meng's faith that socialist societies were the most successful in the world. When she got back to Nanjing she had taught herself English and had tried to learn as much as she could about foreign cultures. It seemed to her that, although capitalist countries were, as the Chinese said, 'struggling in deep water and burning in the fire', they were, in many ways, far more advanced than socialist countries. She had racked her brains over why it had to be like this, and used all the spare time she had from her job in the sales department of an army-run factory to give herself the education that she had been deprived of by the Cultural Revolution.

'Auntie Meng, are you all right?'

Six noticed that Meng was staring blankly

into space and worried that she had upset her by asking such forward questions about her son. She realised that there were white hairs at Meng's temples and that she was a woman with many cares.

'I'm fine,' Meng reassured her. 'It's just my way. I often go off into a dream when my mind wanders.'

Kang came to his mother's rescue.

'When Mum's mind wanders she's thinking about serious affairs of state or international relations. You'll soon discover, Six, that the things that worry her are far removed from normal people like you and me!'

'There you go again, you silly boy! No sense of proportion!' Meng scolded her son, at which point she noticed that everyone had finished eating, so she asked for the bill.

Six glanced in her direction and was astounded to see Meng take out three ten-yuan notes. Could a few small dumplings really be so expensive? Thirty yuan was as much as her mother earned for a whole season of vegetables. Perhaps the restaurant they were eating in was grander than she had thought . . .

In fact, the restaurant was a modest little place—a branch of a well-known dumpling restaurant in north-east China that sold dumplings stuffed with pickled vegetables, as well as noodles and pork at a reasonable price. But Six didn't know this. She said goodbye to Kang and Ruth as they rode off on their bicycles, and followed Shu Tian and Meng home in a complete daze, trying to imagine the palatial dwelling in which such a rich and cultured family must live. She couldn't have been more surprised when they arrived at an apartment that was about the size of the Li family's kitchen.

Much later, Six would find out that Shu Tian and Meng had never managed to rise high enough in their jobs to qualify for a larger flat. The fact that they had spent most of their youth in the countryside during the Cultural Revolution meant that they were at a great disadvantage in the job market compared to those who had completed university in the ordinary way. Fortunately Shu Tian had managed to get a job at the youth magazine but he had remained a mid-ranking editor through his whole career. As a result, Shu Kang had been three before the family were able to leave the old-style residential building that they had lived in when first married, with its communal kitchen, toilet and wash room, and where families lit little fires for cooking in the corridors. They had been allocated a small seventh-floor flat in one of the new apartment blocks that were springing up around the city. This flat had a tiny, six-metre-square kitchen, three minuscule bedrooms and a bathroom. They had lived there for twenty years, content with their lot but perplexed when some of their colleagues managed to get themselves allocated large flats with several living rooms.

At the end of the 1990s, the government changed its housing policy and instructed each work-unit to do away with its communal housing and allow its employees to buy their flats. Shu Tian joked that the smallness of their flat at least meant that they didn't have to get into too much debt to buy it. He and Meng watched as their more powerful colleagues somehow found the cash to buy their large apartments—or even to snap up two or three low-cost flats—but they didn't complain. Kang had moved away to university, making it possible to sit down in the kitchen to eat, while Shu Tian was able to give to Meng the study he had created by covering over their tiny balcony and use the guestroom instead, knowing that any visitors could be put up in Kang's old bedroom. Even the queuing time in the morning for the two-square-metre toilet felt much shorter. The couple were extremely adept at making the best of things: being right under the roof meant there was no one to disturb their sleep; a tall building with no lift was a great opportunity for exercise. Too hot in summer or cold in winter? In their view, the best way to a good atmosphere was for two people to stay close and love one another. They also believed that books and study were the way to improve the world. So, when the army factory where Meng worked started looking for a private buyer and told Meng to stay at home on a minimal retainer, and it looked as if Shu Tian might face compulsory early retirement from his publishing company, the couple decided to pool their savings, take some of the money that Kang had been earning doing translation work, and start up the Book Taster's Teahouse. Their waitress could sleep in Kang's room if necessary, and they would just have to invite fewer guests to stay.

* * *

Six's disappointment at the size of the Shu's apartment was offset by her astonishment at the way it was decorated. There were books on nearly every wall, while in the kitchen, woks and other utensils hung from the ceiling, and the walls were lined with shelves of spices, oils, rice, vegetables and crockery. Even the toilet had things suspended from the ceiling while the walls were covered with drawings. The whole place looked to Six just like the art museums she had seen in books. She was particularly taken by the little pot containing coloured pencils and scraps of paper hanging in the toilet. The members of this family really knew how to make the most of their time: they even wrote down ideas while relieving themselves!

The room where Six was to sleep was the least crowded room in the flat. Apart from the bed, it contained only a desk, a bookshelf and a dozen or so cardboard boxes, like the one Six used to keep her textbook in at home. She thought of the nights she had spent awake, listening out for rats in case they were gnawing away at her book. She wondered if city people had to put down rat poison to stop their books from getting eaten: illiterate country rats just loved the taste of words. Casting her eye around the little room, Six thought about how crowded the lives of city people were. Everything had to be stacked in huge piles, whereas her family's possessions were laid out around the courtyard, the kitchen or the storeroom. Even the walls of Shu Kang's room were covered in paper: little notes written in English. She went over to the desk, which was narrower than the desk she used at school. There was a photograph of the whole family on the desk, as well as one of just Ruth and Shu Kang, taken while they were swimming. Shu Kang was in a pair of swimming trunks that clung tightly to his buttocks; Ruth was wearing something that barely covered her body. Six could not stop herself from staring at the picture, her face flushed, her heart thumping. Lying down on her bed fully clothed, she tried to sleep. She could not imagine what the future might hold for her in this strange city. She felt as if her world had been turned upside-down.

6

THE THREE SISTERS EXPLORE NANJING

Early one Wednesday morning, Five got up as quietly as she could and crept through the dormitory to the bathroom. For a country girl used to getting up at dawn, she had found it difficult to adjust to the strange routine at the Dragon Water-Culture Centre, where they worked late and slept until mid morning. But, after three weeks, she was beginning to become accustomed to it. This morning, however, she had forced herself to wake early because she was going to meet up with her sisters for the first time since she had arrived in Nanjing and she wanted to have as much time with them as possible.

In the bathroom, Five washed her face and gave her hair a special wash with Mei Mei's shampoo. Mei Mei had two bottles for her hair: the shampoo and one that she said was called 'conditioner'. Five had never worked out how to use this second bottle. Were you supposed to put it on before or after washing your hair, and did you rinse it out afterwards? She would look longingly at the pretty bottle wishing she knew how to read so that she could understand the instructions.

When Five had first arrived, she had asked the head of the dormitory, Mei Mei, whenever she didn't understand something. To her distress, one day Mei Mei had yawned and said, 'Five, can't you save up your questions and ask them all at the same time? Otherwise I won't get any sleep, let alone do any work.'

It was natural to Five that Mei Mei should be annoyed and she tried to stop pestering her. After all, her family always complained about how slow she was, and how she asked too many questions. Even so, Mei Mei continued to help Five whenever she had a spare moment and Five felt truly grateful. In order to repay her kindness, Five asked Engineer Wu to take her to a shop so that she could buy Mei Mei some shampoo. She spent half an hour wandering the aisles of the supermarket until she found a bottle that looked the same as Mei Mei's and took it proudly to the counter. It didn't occur to her to buy one for herself—she had never bought herself anything—and so she carried on using Mei Mei's shampoo whenever she needed to wash her hair.

Back in the dormitory, Five got dressed as quietly as she could. She put on the clothes she had worn to come to the city. They were her favourites: a bright orange top and sea-green nylon trousers. The other girls at the Water Centre kept going on about how these clothes made her 'look like a hick', and the colours 'clashed horribly', but Five didn't care. She saw that other migrant workers tried to fit in with city people by buying clothes in the duller colours they liked—or in red, which in the country was only worn at festival time—but she wasn't going to spend money changing her wardrobe. She wanted to save all her earnings for her mother and, besides, she liked her clothes. People who had never been to the countryside didn't know how beautiful it was to see girls dressed in brightly coloured clothes working in the grey, barren fields in winter, or standing out amidst the flowers in summer. So, when the girls teased her, she didn't try to argue with them. She knew they all thought she was an idiot, so she followed her mother's advice: 'Don't open your mouth and no one can take advantage of you, no matter how clever they are.'

It had taken three weeks for the girls to find a way to see each other all at the same time. Three, whose day off was Monday, had been to see Six a couple of times. Since the Book Taster's Teahouse had only just opened, Six was allowed to choose which day of the week she would like to take off and she would meet up with Three just outside the teahouse and spend the rest of the day walking around the area. However, Five had not realised that employees of the Dragon Water-Culture Centre had any say about their free day, and so had simply nodded when Auntie Wang suggested that hers might be Wednesday. This

125

would give Five two days to restock medicines that had been used over the busy weekend, and then a further two days to prepare for the next weekend. Although Three had tried to visit Five twice on a Monday, the receptionists hadn't let her in because it wasn't permitted to disturb the employees during their shifts. As for Six, she didn't have enough knowledge of Nanjing to visit Five by herself. Fortunately Engineer Wu had looked after Five. Wednesday was his day off too and, since he didn't have a family, he had spent time showing her the city. Five worried about what would happen if there was a problem with the pumps or pools while Engineer Wu wasn't there, but he assured her that he made thorough checks on Monday and Tuesday: if there was a minor problem they could always shut down one of the pools for that day.

Three wouldn't have dreamed of telling her employers that she was having difficulty meeting up with her sisters. In fact she didn't even mention to Wang Tong that Five and Six had come to Nanjing until it came up in the course of a conversation. 'But, Three,' Wang Tong had exclaimed, 'why didn't you say something? Let's change your day off to Wednesday so that you can spend time with your family.' Once again, Three had been surprised by Wang Tong's kindness. She hadn't expected city employers to be so lenient.

Five was bursting to tell her sisters

everything that had happened to her. As soon as she was dressed, she rushed out and stood beside the huge dragon's mouth in the street to wait for them. The green girl saw her standing there and suggested she come and wait in the reception area, but she didn't dare sit on the expensive sofas. The green girl laughed and said she was being foolish: if she didn't sit there, lots of other people would come and wear the sofas out; she would be saving her employers money. But Five was determined to wait outside. She only began to regret her decision when, after two hours, her sisters still hadn't appeared. Half past ten came and went, and even Manager Shui, who was always the last person to arrive in the mornings, had walked through the entrance, stopping briefly to chat to Five. Soon afterwards, Three and Six came running towards her, panting. Although they, too, had got up early, it had taken several bus journeys for Three to collect Six and bring her to the Dragon Water-Culture Centre.

Three was wearing her uniform: a red T-shirt and black trousers with two white stripes down the sides. Six had on a pretty wool dress that had been given to her by Meng. Five was astounded to see how elegant her younger sister had become after just a few weeks in the city. She wasn't the only one to be surpised: Six gasped when she saw her.

'*Aiya*,' she cried. 'How did Five's skin get to

127

be so lovely and pale?'

Three was just as eager to know about Five's new life. 'Who was the man with the big gut you were talking to just now?' she asked.

Five was about to answer when the two sisters began assailing her with so many questions that she could hardly get a word in edgeways.

'This dragon's mouth is huge. How big is the building inside? What do they do in there?'

'What are the other people like?'

'Where do you live? Are you settling in all right? What do you eat?'

'Is your boss nice?'

'Listen,' Five shouted, 'I've been standing here for more than two hours waiting for you. Can't you keep your questions for later? Are we going somewhere or aren't we? Three, back home you said that you'd take us to try those famous Yangzi Delta sticky rice balls when we got to the city. Are you going back on your word?'

'Going back on my word? I like that! Aren't *you* in a hurry . . . OK then, come on. Follow me.'

Three led her sisters onto a crowded bus where they were all immediately separated in the crush. Standing on tiptoes to try and locate her sisters, Three screeched out instructions about where they should get off.

'Six, it's Confucius Temple. Five, did you hear that? Listen carefully to the loudspeaker

128

announcements. When you get to South Tai . . . Ping . . . Road push your way to the door, but don't get off there. Wait till Con . . . fu . . . cius Temple, and be quick getting off otherwise you won't be able to get out. Do you hear?'

'Yes!' Five and Six shouted in reply.

The other passengers on the bus were annoyed by the noise the sisters were making and all began shouting at once:

'Oi, be quiet. You're not in the fields now!'

'Are you training to be a station announcer or what?'

'If you don't even know how to take a bus, what are you doing in the city?'

'Give them a break,' someone else said. 'They aren't the only ones who know how to shout!'

'Hey, don't you give me that righteous indignation. Go and sow your seeds of compassion somewhere else . . .'

Before long, a full-scale argument had broken out in the bus. Three and Six were terrified and held their breath until they reached their stop. Five was more relaxed. She had no idea what anyone was talking about and was simply worried that the noise would prevent her from hearing when her stop was announced. Eventually the bus arrived at the Confucius Temple stop and the sisters spilled out on to the pavement with relief.

After two years in Nanjing, Three wasn't intimidated by the colourful pedestrianised streets near the Confucius Temple, with their shops and restaurants, but Five and Six were amazed by what they saw. Around the ancient temple complex, all sorts of people were milling about, eating food as they walked along and crowding round the stalls of the many street vendors who kept up a constant, noisy patter. Three told her sisters that, during the time of the emperors, anyone who wanted to enter into imperial service would have to come to the Confucius Temple to take an examination; this was why parents still came to the temple to light candles when their children had exams. Great and important families had made their homes around the temple, she said, but she preferred the little lanes where you could still see the old, traditional houses that poor people lived in. 'Those houses aren't much to look at in the cold months,' she said, 'but you wait until later in the spring. The courtyards will be full of flowers.'

By this point, Five was more interested in her stomach than in flowers. 'Where's this food you talked about?' she asked, worried that Six, whose eye had been drawn by the little boats plying back and forth on the river, would lead them away from the lanes of exciting-looking restaurants and take-aways. Engineer Wu had told her that, although many of the restaurants near the river were for the big bosses, who would sit in splendour and listen to the splash of oars in the water while their wine glowed in the lamplight, there were lots of takeaways for ordinary people. There, for a few yuan, you could sample all the specialities of Nanjing: duck-blood soup, bean-flour noodles, crispy 'money cakes' coated in honey and sesame and, in summer, a bowl of refreshing bean jelly seasoned with spices.

Three laughed at her hungry sister. 'Don't worry,' she reassured her. 'It's always easy to find food here.' And she led Five and Six along the lanes, pointing out the various specialities of the different restaurants and teaching them about Nanjing food in the same way that Wang Tong had taught her when she had first arrived. Five's eyes were like saucers when she saw the array of local delicacies: flatcakes fried in duck fat, steamed dumplings filled with vegetables, dried tofu with tiny shrimps, spring-onion seedcakes and as many different types of sticky rice ball as you could think of . . . Three told her how young girls in Nanjing adored eating *wangjidan*, an egg boiled with a half-developed embryo inside, because they thought it kept them healthy and beautiful. They spotted several girls squatting on the pavement beside a *wangjidan*-vendor's stove, plucking the fine floss of feathers off the embryo before dipping their eggs in salt and pepper and wolfing them down.

Three bought some snacks, and took her sisters towards the river in search of a place to sit down. Soon they came to a stone bridge, which she said was called Half-Moon Bridge.

'Why Half-Moon?' Five asked.

'Oh, I know this,' said Six. 'I've read about it. It's called Half-Moon because if you stand on the bridge on the night of the fifteenth day of the eleventh month, when the moon is at its height, you'll see the reflection of the bridge and exactly half the moon no matter which side you stand on. I think the bridge has another name. Something like "The Separation of Culture and Virtue"—two things which of course are supposed to be indivisible like the moon.'

Five looked at her sister in bewilderment. 'Doesn't Nanjing have the same moon as us?'

'It's the same moon all over the world,' said Three in exasperation. 'It's just that the bridge has been made in a clever way to cut the moon in two.'

Five was still confused. 'How long does it take for the moon to grow back together once it's been cut in two?' she asked.

'*Aiya*, you're the limit!' said Six. 'The moon is never actually broken. The bridge makes it look as if it is . . .'

'Don't worry about it, Five,' said Three more kindly. 'When it comes to the fifteenth of the eleventh we'll bring you here and show you. Then you'll see.'

'Come on, eat while you're talking, or else you'll be on at me for not keeping my word,' said Three.

The three girls sat down at a stone table beside the Half-Moon Bridge, and Three produced several skewers of stinky tofu fritters, some Suzhou sticky rice balls, and a bag of crispy dried turnips.

'Hm, this smelly tofu fritter isn't as good as the Tofu Lady's,' said Six, biting a lump of tofu off her skewer. 'OK, Five. Now you've got food in front of you, answer our questions and tell us who the man with the big gut was . . .'

'He's our General Manager. Everyone calls him Manager Shui. He's a really good guy. Three, I want a rice ball, which is nicest?'

Three pushed some rice balls towards Five and then chose a skewer of tofu for herself saying it was best eaten hot. 'In what way is your Manager Shui a good guy?' she asked.

'I don't know . . . He's just good. I mean, he doesn't talk to me in a cold way like other city people, and he's never scolded me, or told me I can't do the job . . .'

The rice ball in Five's hand hovered at her mouth as she tried to describe Manager Shui's good qualities.

'Are people cold to you?' Three asked Five in concern. She was used to city people being rude to her in the restaurant, but she didn't like to think of her vulnerable younger sister being treated in such a way.

'How else would they be?' said Five. 'Everyone in the village treats me that way. Why would city people be different?'

133

'Can't you do something about it?' asked Six, who had also stopped eating.

'Do what? Put up with it, that's what. Doesn't our mum say that the fewer things in life you have to worry about the better? You just have to keep going and things will turn out all right in the end if you're tough about it.'

'Well, what work do you do?' asked Six, biting off a second tofu fritter.

'I'm called an "assistant". It's a bit like what Four does at home: passing Mum and Dad things when they need them and generally lending a hand. So, what's your job like?'

'I asked you about yours first . . . Why's it called a "Water-*Culture* Centre"? What's water got to do with culture?'

Five was flabbergasted that her educated sister didn't know this and she did.

'How come you've never read about it in books?'

'I've not read every book there is!' Six said grumpily. 'Well? Explain to us . . .'

'Engineer Wu says that knowing how to put herbal medicines into pools to make people well is an art, and is part of what's called "Culture".'

'But how does the business make money?' Six asked, finishing off the last morsel of tofu.

'People pay to come and bathe in the water . . .'

'Bathe? What, you mean with no clothes on?'

Both Three and Six gaped at their sister, open-mouthed.

'I know. I was shocked too. The first time I saw a customer wearing nothing but a little pair of pants I nearly died of fright. I hid in the office, and I was too scared to come out for ages.'

'Then, later on you were all right?' Three was filled with anxiety. She had heard about how some country girls were dragged into dirty behaviour when they came to the city. Perhaps, because of her, Five would be lost for ever . . .

'It's not like that,' said Five. 'At first I thought it was, but then the head of my department, who we all call Auntie Wang, showed me a book about it with pictures. There were lots of proper doctors in that book . . .'

Six was amazed. She had never imagined that her stupid sister could cope with such a situation, let alone explain it with clarity. She found herself looking at Five with new eyes. 'So, if there are doctors, why do the people bathe?' she asked.

'If you two interrupt me again I won't say,' said Five crossly. 'The clients soak in different types of medicine for an hour, then they wash away the medicine with fresh water, and then they go to something called a "treatment room" to have a massage. Some of the masseurs work on their bodies, others on their feet. My friend Mei Mei's the best foot masseur and she told me all about it. She says you can make all of a person feel better through their foot. She showed me a picture of how the soles of our left and right feet are connected to our whole body—stomach and everything. She's a miracle worker. She can tell what's wrong with someone just by placing her hands on their feet, and she can cure them too. Engineer Wu says she gets it right twenty times out of twenty.' Five stuffed a rice ball into her mouth.

'Do they give you enough to eat?' asked Six.

'Oh yes, there's food at every meal, you can come back for seconds too. At first I was really packing it away, but after a bit I stopped because I saw that nobody else was asking for more. In fact, some people were even leaving food. I didn't want people to laugh at me for being a greedy pig.'

'*Aiya*, but you must get hungry!' cried Three who had never had a moment's hunger at the Happy Fool and was worried about her sister.

'Of course I get hungry! I got stars in my eyes at first, and my legs were like cotton wool, but after a while I got used to it. My country girl's stomach must be as small as a city girl's by now.'

Three and Six burst out laughing at their foolish sister's belief that she could become like a city girl just by eating less.

'Don't laugh! Why are you always laughing at me? If any of the clients laugh at me, Auntie

Wang or Engineer Wu speaks up for me.'

'Who are the clients?' asked Six.

Five looked at her sister in wonder. Her question seemed very stupid. 'I said just now. The clients are the ones who come to spend money on bathing and massage.'

Three still wasn't convinced that Five's workplace was completely above board and tried to find out more.

'You're sure it's not one of those places where men and women do it together in little rooms?' she asked.

'Well there aren't any little rooms,' said Five, not understanding the question. 'The smallest one is big enough for two beds . . .'

'Two beds!' exclaimed Six. 'Five, you're not doing anything dirty, are you? My boss has talked to me about city people who make dirty money out of country girls.'

'*Aiya*, what are you saying? It's not a dirty job at all. The Green Girl says there are books about this "nurturing of the body and mind" that are three thousand years old. Long ago it was only for the emperor but, recently some clever people have remembered about it.'

'Who's the Green Girl?' asked Three, feeling more reassured.

At the mention of Ms Lin, Five became very animated: 'Three, she's even more beautiful than those girls in your film-star pictures!'

'What do you mean by beautiful?' asked Three, amused.

'How beautiful? I can't explain it. Her waist, her face, the way she walks . . . Oh, if only you could meet her. Then you'd believe me! She's just impossibly pretty! Not like some of the women clients. Oh, those women are face-changers. You should see them! When they come in, their faces are as pretty as a peach-blossom, but get them in the water and there's no colour to them at all . . . Even their snow-white arses are prettier!'

'What about the men?' Three and Six asked simultaneously.

'Well, city men are quite nice looking . . .' Five didn't have time to finish before her sisters butted in.

'How do you know? Have you been spying on them?'; 'How many city men have you seen?'

'What are you saying? I don't spy. But sometimes I do see things. When men and women come to the centre, they pay at the reception desk and get a set of these things called "tokens". Tokens are bits of bamboo that come in different sizes depending on how much money you spend. You have to hand over a token whenever you go to a pool or treatment room. When they've bought their tokens, the men and women go to separate rooms to take their clothes off. The men put on a pair of pants and the women change into these really tight clothes that remind me of that magic headband in the story of the

Monkey King, which squeezes his temples to punish him if he disobeys his master. Once Auntie Wang took me to the women's shower room to check there were enough towels, and there was this woman having a wash. She hadn't drawn the curtain, and I swear she had absolutely no hair on her hidden parts . . .'

Three gasped. 'You mean you saw a White Tiger?' Three asked fearfully.

'I did . . . I did . . .' Five said excitedly. 'Later on I saw that woman bathing next to a really handsome man in the Pool of Tranquillity. They were getting ever so close. I was dead worried the woman was going to suck out all his vital essences and kill him.'

Six thought about what her mother had said about White Tigers. In the past, before any marriage could take place in the village, the matchmaker would perform an inspection of the bride-to-be. She would check that she wasn't broken already, that she had no moles anywhere on her face, and that she wasn't a 'White Tiger'—a woman without body hair. It was believed that such women would destroy a man. Her mother had told them how, during the Cultural Revolution, these inspections had been forbidden and therefore many men had married bad wives without knowing it, and suffered a terrible fate.

'*Aiya*, have you eaten the whole bag of crispy turnips?' shouted Five, interrupting Six's thoughts. 'I knew it! You're asking me all these

139

questions so you can scoff all the nice food while my mouth's busy . . .' Five stuck out her bottom lip.

'Don't panic, I've saved some for you here,' said Three, waving a bulging paper bag in front of Five's face. Six, meanwhile, realising for the first time that Five could teach her something she didn't know, asked what the names of the other pools were at the Dragon Water-Culture Centre. Five listed them proudly.

'Apart from the Pool of Tranquillity, there's the Pool of Mental Cultivation, the Pool of Beauty, the Pool of Yin and Yang and the Pool of Strong Bones. They're all heated differently and I go round with Auntie Wang to check that they are exactly the right temperature. Auntie Wang says that city people don't do hard labour, but they tire their brains out every day, so lots and lots of people get sore heads. That's why they need the Pool of Mental Cultivation. It has waterfalls that wash over their heads and neck muscles. The Pool of Beauty is to cure skin problems and make you more beautiful, but I've never seen anyone in there with scabies like people have in our village, and not many ugly people bathe there either . . .'

Once again, Three and Six could not restrain their laughter at their sister's ignorance of city life.

'*Now* what are you laughing at? . . . The

Pool of Yin and Yang is the one I don't really understand. Auntie Wang says it's to help men and women to have kids, but having kids is a woman's business, so what's the use of men going in? Still, perhaps if Mum could've gone in there, she would've had a son. But then we wouldn't be here . . . Anyway, the Pool of Strong Bones is only for men. It's half hot and half cold and it helps them grow big muscles. As well as the medicine, it's got these waves. I nearly got knocked over by one when I was helping Engineer Wu fix something in there. It scared me half to death. Still, it's the most popular pool with young city men—they really like that pool. Auntie Wang says they're trying to get some meat on their bones. How ridiculous! Why don't they just go and work in the fields? The way I see it, because city men already have enough to eat and everything else they want, they think they need to go looking for something else. All the same, the men in that pool are worth a look. They don't mumble to themselves like the potbellied men in the Pool of Mental Cultivation. Instead they fool around in the water. It gives that pool a special atmosphere. Very male . . .'

Five's last few sentences had Three and Six staring at her in astonishment.

'Look at you two, gawping like idiots!' cried Five. 'Don't worry. If you want come and have a look at some big muscles yourselves, I can ask Engineer Wu. Perhaps you could get a job in the Pool of Strong Bones . . .'

Three jumped up and thumped Five on the back. 'How can you talk like that, Five! You've only been in the city three weeks and already you're trying to lead your sisters astray!'

'*Aiya*, I'm only teasing. There are male assistants to look after the men and their changing rooms are miles away from the women's . . . Maybe your heart isn't made of stone after all, Three. I can see images of men in your eyes! Six, what do you think?'

'I'm wondering how someone like you can get all this straight in your mind,' said Six, feeling guilty immediately for implying that Five was stupid. However, Five did not take it to heart.

'It took me a week of running errands with Auntie Wang before I could find my own way back to the "foot massage room" where I sleep, and in the beginning I thought everything was magic. Some strange things happen, that's for sure. You should see the clients when they walk in. They're all limp and listless, like wheat sprouts after a dry spell. But when they go out the door they've got rosy cheeks and a spring in their step, like plants after a good watering . . . Oh, and another thing, what sort of lamps d'you think they have?' Five asked mysteriously.

'Electric of course,' Three and Six answered together.

'That's what I thought they'd be,' said Five

grandly, 'but now I know that they have these things called "Kongming lanterns". Bet you don't know what they are!' Three and Six shook their heads.

'They're these paper lanterns that rise up to the ceiling when they are lit because of the hot air. There are lots of them floating about in the steam above the pools. They look really beautiful. Auntie Wang says they are sometimes called "sky lamps", and she told me the stories people tell about how they came to be. Some people say that a clever man from the time of the Three Kingdoms invented them to send signals to his armies. Others that they were used in south China to worship the gods. And there's another story about how, during the Qing dynasty, the people of Fujian Province brought them back from foreign countries, and used them to give the all-clear when villagers were hiding from bandits in the mountains. Auntie Wang says that in some places, they still release sky lamps during Lantern Festival.'

Six was extremely impressed by her sister's short lesson and told her so. 'It seems as if you're really learning a lot, Five,' she said, congratulating her sister.

'Well, I'm lucky. Mei Mei is in charge of my dormitory, and she takes really good care of me. She even lets me use her things . . .'

Three was troubled by this. 'What are you doing, using other people's things?' she asked.

143

'We can't let city people think we won't pay our own way . . .'

'Don't worry, I know. I asked Engineer Wu to help me buy her a bottle of shampoo . . .'

'So what do you use to wash your hair?' Six asked.

'I share her shampoo,' said Five bluntly, 'just like I share Four's comb at home.'

'Oh, Five,' said Three, 'using other people's belongings isn't the same as borrowing your family's things! What did Mum tell us before we went away? "Even if there's no rice in the family bowl, it's better to starve than take someone else's gruel"!'

Five looked crestfallen and a tear dripped on to her nose. 'But how can I buy things for myself when I hardly see you and I can't read the labels? I can't exactly go up to all those clever city people and ask them to read things out for me. They'll laugh at me and I don't want them to think that everyone in the countryside is as stupid as me.'

Five's words had a sobering effect on Three and Six. It wasn't her fault that she hadn't been to school. The two years that Three had spent at primary school had been extremely difficult for the family and they'd hardly been able to afford cooking oil. Fortunately, Four couldn't go to school because she was deaf and dumb. When it came to Five's turn, their father was determined not to waste good money trying to educate a girl who was clearly so slow on the uptake. He would have found a reason to keep Six out of school too if the teacher hadn't come and begged him to let her stay. He would rant that Six's eight years of education were the family's downfall. It was as if she had studied them into poverty . . . Still, how could their father have known that, in the city, writing was central to everything?

'Do you earn any tips?' Three asked Five gently.

'Yes, we get tips every day, and at the end of the month we get our official money. Auntie Wang says I'm a new girl, so my wages are the smallest you can get in the company. Even so, I'm earning a lot more than Dad. I never thought I'd lay my hands on fifty yuan so soon. I asked Mei Mei to change my money into a fifty-yuan note. When I have another fifty, I'll get a hundred-yuan note and give it straight to Mum. That'll give Dad a shock.'

The three sisters were silent as their thoughts turned to their mother—a woman who had never lived a moment for herself since the day she married . . .

*   *   *

It was pleasantly warm in the early spring sun and Nanjingers, who had been waiting for this moment all through the long damp winter, were taking the opportunity to get out of their houses and into the fresh air. Pedestrians

145

wandered across the Half-Moon Bridge while old people sat on stools in the sun. The men played chess, chatted and read the papers; the women cleaned and prepared vegetables, drank tea and gossiped gently among themselves. There were a few three-year-olds sitting on their grandmother's knee or in a pushchair, but hardly any other children to be seen.

Meng had told Six that, from the moment they started nursery school at three, city children had very little time to play. Quite apart from their three hours' homework each day, their parents also wanted them to spend time studying calligraphy, music, painting or some other activity in the hope that they might prove to be talented. On Saturdays, the local Children's Cultural Palace was swarming with children taking art, dance or music lessons, and some even spent another three hours taking tuition elsewhere. Sunday was the only time for games, but children who were not doing well at school had to use this day to prepare for next week's lessons and take supplementary classes.

'Excuse me, would you mind getting out of the way so that we can take a photo?' said a man who was walking towards them, camera in hand. Three whispered to Five that he was a 'tourist', visiting Nanjing from another Chinese town, and that soon the city would be full of people using their holidays to visit new places. They might even see some bignoses from foreign countries too.

As the sisters got to their feet, Three scooped up the discarded tofu skewers and paper rice-ball wrappers from the ground and threw them into a nearby bin.

'You can't put rubbish on the floor in the city,' she said to her sisters. 'It's like dropping rubbish in front of someone's home in our village: people will think you are not showing respect. Let's go, I'll show you where I work, it's only a few steps away. We won't go right up to it, though, otherwise my boss will offer us a free meal.'

'Yes, yes, let's have a quick look so we know how to get there, but don't let's bother anyone,' Six agreed.

Five was about to say that she too was longing to see the restaurant where her sister worked, when a woman wearing a uniform just like Three's appeared in front of them carrying a basket of vegetables.

'*Aiya*, Three, are these your sisters? Well, let me introduce myself. I'm Wang Tong, Three's boss. Where are you all off to? It's almost lunchtime. Come back with me for a bite to eat before you go sightseeing.'

Five was astonished. Was Nanjing a magical place where, if you thought about someone, they appeared before you? She watched in admiring silence as her sister tried to reassure Wang Tong that they had already eaten.

'Now, now, Three, you mustn't feel you have to stand on ceremony with me. I know you haven't eaten! What are you worried about? It can't be the cost. I hope you've told your sisters that you're like family to us, and relatives can eat one free meal a week, with a thirty per cent discount for the second and ten per cent for the third. Come on, stop shilly-shallying!'

The sisters followed Wang Tong to the Happy Fool where they found a woman admiring the vegetable display in the window.

'Your sister's handiwork makes us a fair bit of money, I can tell you,' said Wang Tong, ushering the girls into the restaurant. 'Now sit down and make the most of this quiet period before the lunchtime rush begins. If it gets busy then you might have to go and chat elsewhere. Now, I know exactly what Three likes eating so I'll bring you three of her favourite dishes. If you don't like them, then leave them. It's not a problem.'

Before Three had time to thank her, Wang Tong turned and sped into the kitchen. It was clear that there was to be no arguing with her, so Three decided to show her sisters the displays of fresh fruit and vegetables on the walls while they were waiting for the food to come.

'This all looks very nice because it's spring,' said Six, 'but what do you do in winter?'

'Well, the city isn't like the countryside: you

148

can still buy vegetables that are grown under plastic, and things like melons and cauliflowers that are imported from abroad. To stop the melons dripping juice, I wrap them in the cling-film stuff that people use here . . .'

'That sounds horrible,' interrupted Five. 'Why would anyone like to look at out-of-season vegetables which probably aren't that fresh anyway?'

'Things don't have to be fresh to be pretty,' said Three. 'In the winter we use a lot of preserved fruit, as well as dried goods, like prunes and turnips. I make dried vegetables into flowers, or cut them in half so that you can see the pattern inside. City people are so busy, they don't have time to learn how to dry fruit and vegetables. Here, they can get a lesson while they're eating . . .'

'These city people need a teacher for everything,' muttered Five. 'Why can't they just learn from the street or their home, like country people?'

'That isn't a city talent, it's the wisdom of the countryside,' said Wang Tong, who had appeared at their table carrying a tray of food. 'We're lucky to have Three to enlighten us. Now, here are some appetisers to start you off. I haven't given you any of the "wild food" Nanjingers love so much. I'm not sure your country appetites are suited to such tiny portions. This is Zhenjiang preserved meat; this is pickled white cabbage from the north-east (you don't see much of that down your way); this one's a local, radish-peel salad (we don't prepare it in the same way as you do). When you're ready, the kitchen will make a bowl of noodles with spring onions for each of you, and spare ribs in Beijing sauce to go with them—how does that sound? Three knows what we've got here. Three, if your sisters want anything, let the kitchen know. I'll have to leave you to your own devices now because it's going to get busy, but remember: this is your day off. I won't let you lift a finger to help . . . Yes, coming!' called Wang Tong as some customers came through the door. 'Good afternoon, over here please, what'll you have today? We have all the vegetables on the board . . .'

Despite having eaten earlier, the sisters tucked into their lunch with relish. While they were eating, Three tried to explain the meaning of the restaurant's name to Five, who didn't think 'The Happy Fool' was very dignified.

'The name comes from something the owner's mother used to say,' Three said, mimicking Wang Tong's tone of voice as she gave her sister a lesson. 'She believed that there was so much unfairness in the world that you could never be happy unless you closed your eyes to it, and were content with being foolishly blind to things that worried other people.'

Five was not convinced. Her own foolishness was a constant source of unhappiness to her, and she couldn't understand how someone could consider stupidity a good thing. Perhaps Three's boss wanted to keep her employee stupid so she was easier to order about. Five didn't say this to Three, but she silently thanked her good fortune that she herself had ended up with a job in a place so grand and impressive that its name had a dragon in it, not a fool.

By the time the sisters had polished off a big bowl of noodles each and a large platter of spare ribs, there were lots of customers waiting for a seat, so they hurriedly said their goodbyes. Six was eager to show Five where she worked, so they decided to take two buses back to the Book Taster's Teahouse, which was in the north-west of the city.

Five was a little perplexed that her sister seemed so delighted to have a job in a teahouse. She remembered how, when labourers had come to work on the road near her village, a teastall had been set up so that they could rest on the ground drinking huge bowls of tea. How could her sister get so excited about something like that? But as soon as she saw the elegant black-and-gold sign under the eaves of the Book Taster's Teahouse, she understood that this wasn't any old teastall. In fact, when she got inside, it seemed like fairyland. There were beautiful lamps everywhere, as if from an emperor's palace, and three-footed incense burners on the mahogany tables. It was as if the place was full of gods and spirits!

A man with glasses got up from a table where he was sitting with a group of people, and came to greet the three girls. Before Five had a chance to take in what he was saying, he had ushered Six behind a curtain and told her to make tea for her sisters while he attended to his friends.

'That must be Six's boss,' said Three. 'She told me that, although he's not much to look at, he's very talented. He's so clever at calligraphy that he painted the sign outside himself, and Six says he got their family car in exchange for some calligraphy that he did.'

'What does the sign outside say?' asked Five, wondering how the teahouse's name would measure up to her Dragon.

'It says "The Book Taster's Teahouse: In Memory of Lu and Lu",' said Three.

Five was unimpressed. 'That doesn't sound very important.'

'I think Lu and Lu were important wise men,' said Three, 'because this teahouse is full of learning. It must be a good place for Six to continue her education. She told me that sometimes even foreigners come here.'

'Bignoses? What kind? Uncle Two told me he's seen some strange black and white ones in Zhuhai. Some even had red hair! Are the ones

Six has seen like that too?'

'Ask her yourself in a minute. Six, what's this notebook?'

Three had walked over to the desk by the door and was looking at a beautifully bound book on the table.

Six put down her tea tray and came over. 'It's a place where customers can write down ideas and jokes, or contribute a piece of calligraphy. Come on, I'll read you a joke. Here's one I haven't seen before. Someone must have written it today. It's called "God Makes People".

'The first time God made people, he modelled a batch of them out of clay and put them in the kiln to fire. But God was very tired and he nodded off. When he took the clay people out of the kiln they were all burned black. So God modelled more clay people and fired them again. This time he didn't sleep but sat waiting in front of the kiln. After a while he got impatient, so he put out the fire and took out the clay people to see how they were getting on. But it was too early, the clay wasn't properly fired yet, so they were all white. Finally, God decided to make yet more clay people. This time he was careful to watch the sun until the time was exactly right. When he opened the stove and brought out the clay people, he

153

was happy: they were perfect—not black or white, not overcooked or undercooked, but yellow, just like us!'

Six burst out laughing but neither Five nor Three could see what was so funny.

'How come this God has to do his own work?' asked Five. 'And why can't he put right his mistake without having to start again? Mum says the Bodhisattva Guanyin can change whatever she wants; she doesn't get things wrong the way we do. If this God heard our prayers, what good would he be able to do?'

'He wouldn't hear our prayers,' teased Six, 'because this God doesn't understand Chinese.'

'Shhh!' said Five in alarm, reaching out to put her hand over Six's mouth. 'You mustn't ever badmouth the gods, or they'll get revenge on you!'

Meanwhile, Three was leafing through other pages in the notebook. 'Why is this person writing in Pinyin?' she asked.

'That isn't Pinyin, it's English. Listen, I'll translate the joke for you. It says . . . um . . . "A Chinese person who'd just started learning English bumped into an English person on the street, and apologised in English: *I am sorry*. The British person replied *I am sorry too*. The Chinese person, thinking that he ought to be as polite as the British person, said: *I am sorry three.* The English person was puzzled: *What are you sorry for?* The Chinese person, determined not to appear rude, said: *I am sorry five.'*

Six laughed until tears came to her eyes.

Once again, Three and Five did not get it at all, but Five was astounded that her sister could read and understand something foreign.

'Where did you learn foreign language?' she asked in admiration.

'You should call it "English", not "foreign language",' said Six. 'English is one just kind of foreign language, while other countries speak different languages. We had English lessons in school but I didn't learn very much. My boss's family can all speak English fluently, though, and perhaps I'll learn more here because lots of foreigners visit the teahouse.'

Five suddenly remembered what Three had told her. 'Have you really seen bignoses, Six?' she asked in awe. 'What do they look like? Are they scary?'

'It's not very polite to call them "bignoses",' said Six, 'and they're not scary at all! My boss's future daughter-in-law is from England. She has yellow hair and blue eyes, and she's really nice. The only problem is—she can't speak Chinese that well.'

'Blue eyes?' said Five in amazement. 'How old is she, not to be able to talk properly?'

'It's not that she can't talk properly, it's that her pronunciation of Chinese isn't very good.

Think about when strangers come to our village and people try to speak Mandarin to them. Her Chinese sounds like that: full of mistakes. Still, she speaks the best Chinese out of all the foreigners I've met.'

'You mean you've seen other foreigners as well?' asked Five, longing to know more. 'Was it like in the joke just now? Black ones and white ones?'

'It's not as simple as that,' said Six. 'The black people aren't always completely black— more yellowy-black or coppery-black—and the white people can be pinkish white or greyish white. Most of Ruth's friends are foreigners. They talk in a strange way and wear these funny rough-looking cotton clothes, not like proper people's clothes, but they're all very nice. They come from places like Italy, France, New Zealand, America, oh yes, and Iceland. The man from Iceland says that in winter it's dark as night all the time, and in the summer the sun never goes down.'

'So how do they work in winter, or sleep in summer?' asked Five.

'I asked him that. He said: "In summer we use curtains to shut out the light to sleep, in winter we use street lamps for light." I'll introduce you to some foreigners if you want, Five. They're very easy to talk to. It's a shame there aren't any here today, they usually come in two or three times a week . . .'

'What do they come here for?' asked Three,

enthralled by the idea of foreigners with multicoloured eyes.

'Some come to read and chat, some to drink tea, others to write . . .'

'They can write?' asked Five, not quite believing her.

'Some of them can. They're learning to speak and write Chinese and they often come in with Chinese friends to practise their language. Look,' said Six, turning to a page in the notebook, 'this is their writing. It's worse than mine, isn't it? Can you see the errors in this character, Three? The two moon radicals are written as suns . . . Thick Glasses can't have seen this: he always corrects the foreigners' mistakes.'

Three stared at the foreigners' characters with fascination, but Five, who had never learned even the rudiments of reading and writing, quickly lost interest. She turned instead to the bookshelves next to them.

'Six, how come this book's wearing so many clothes? It's even got a belt round its tummy!'

Six was about to explain how the book wasn't wearing clothes but a 'jacket' and a 'bellyband' when Meng walked into the teahouse carrying two heavy bags of food. Her daily visit to the supermarket was a trial for poor Meng, but she had no choice. She couldn't drive (and, anyway, she was frightened their old Xiali would fall to pieces beneath her if she did), and the door-to-door delivery firm she contacted was too expensive: they would only deliver a fixed quantity each day and, since the teahouse had only just opened, she didn't need so much. Still, she consoled herself that her walks to and from the shop would be a good chance for her to work off some of the plumpness she had got from all those years of sitting in a chair reading.

'Six, are these your sisters? It's easy to guess: you all seem to come from the same mould. I'm glad you've made yourselves some tea. Have some of these "Pretty Girls' Fingers" to go with it. They're delicious little biscuits with crushed hawthorn berries inside. Don't stand on ceremony, eat.'

'We've eaten, we had lunch in Three's restaurant,' said Six, anxious about abusing her employer's hospitality.

'Three's restaurant? Good, good! But these are tea snacks, to be eaten at three or four in the afternoon while you're having a long, leisurely chat. I need to get Shu Tian to make a phone call: a company's booked a tea party for tomorrow evening and we need some extra helpers. Excuse me.'

Five stared at Meng's departing figure. 'She wears very elegant clothes for her age, doesn't she? I never would have thought a dress in a dull autumn-leaf-colour like that could look so good.'

'You're right, it does look good,' said Three

sadly. 'She can't be that much younger than our mother but Mum looks all old and shrivelled, and this woman seems even younger than our eldest sister.'

*   *   *

The three sisters sat in the teahouse until 4.30 and then spent the rest of the afternoon window-shopping. Although Three had visited a few big shops with Wang Tong and her husband, and Five had been out with Engineer Wu, it was the first time any of them had wandered the shopping streets without a city person as a guide. They felt exhilarated by the sense of freedom and confident because they knew there were people in the city who would take care of them. Five was particularly delighted by their expedition as it gave her the opportunity to look, finally, at the thin figures standing behind glass. At first she was disappointed to find out they weren't real, but her disappointment gave way to fascination as she saw what beautiful clothes they were wearing.

After two hours of staring into shop windows with their sister, Three and Six began to find it tedious.

'Why do you like these fake people so much?' asked Six.

'I don't know . . .' said Five, her nose pressed against the glass. 'I think it's because they remind me of Mum.'

Three thought this was very peculiar. 'They look nothing like our mum. And, anyway, they're not real.'

'I keep thinking how beautiful Mum would look if she was wearing clothes like this,' said Five passionately.

'But Mum could never wear those kind of clothes,' said Six, pushing her nose against the glass too. 'They're only for thin people.'

'You're wrong,' said Five. 'I've seen city women who are Mum's size wearing similar clothes and they look just the same as these fake thin people . . .'

'But you don't know what Mum's size is,' objected Three.

'What do you mean?' cried Five. 'Aren't her measurements written in your heart?'

The sisters were silent as they made their way back to the Dragon Water-Culture Centre to drop Five off, each thinking about their mother. It was half past eight and, around them, the lights of Nanjing were beginning to glitter in the evening sky.

Three looked at her sisters, remembering how amazed she had been when she had first seen the city lit up at night. In the countryside, night was pitch black and there was nothing to do but sleep. Three had never imagined such light, not even in her dreams. Her vision of Paradise was of a place where fairy maidens held up large oil lamps for their Heavenly

160

Queen. But the glow of these lamps was dull in comparison with the neon-lit streets of Nanjing.

The entrance to the Dragon Water-Culture Centre was lit so spectacularly they could see it from way down the street. Five was thrilled. All day she had been fighting a growing sense of inferiority as she admired Three's art and Six's learning. After all, what did she do but serve near-naked customers in pools of water? She had comforted herself with the thought that she worked in a place with such a grand name that it must be more important than the restaurant and teahouse. Here was confirmation. The gorgeously illuminated dragon was by far the most amazing thing she had ever seen in her life, and shone like a beacon in the night.

7

SIX AND THE TEAHOUSE CUSTOMERS

As the weeks passed, the plane trees along the streets became fat with leaves and the hot Nanjing summer began to set in. Six had begun to get used to life at the Book Taster's Teahouse. She smiled to herself when she thought about how anxious she had been when she first arrived. The first weeks had been the worst. Fortunately, there had been no opportunity for her to embarrass herself at an ostentatious opening party because the Shu family hadn't held one. Instead there had been a small gathering of friends, who had all been very kind to Six and forgiven her mistakes. However, other things hadn't been so easy to cope with. A few days after the informal opening, two visitors to the teahouse had given Six a terrible fright.

It was all because of the way in which the teahouse had announced its opening. Six had been surprised that Thick Glasses and Meng hadn't celebrated their new venture in a more lavish way. At first she thought that city customs were different from the countryside where people would blow trumpets, set off fireworks and put up brightly coloured lucky pictures at any opportunity; she recalled how even old Lu Daye from the poorest family in the village had lit a few rockets when the roof beam went up on the ramshackle mud hut he had built as a home for his son and new daughter-in-law. But when she saw the family-style restaurant next door celebrate its opening with a big meal, and how the congratulatory gifts of tall baskets of flowers stood by the door for nearly two weeks, she realised that the Shu family's low-key party had been a deliberate choice. She asked Thick Glasses about it, but he had simply shrugged: 'Why spend money filling the stomachs of city functionaries when they are already walking wineskins? Our business comes from study and friendship, it's different.' But it seemed that Six wasn't the only person who was surprised by the way in which the teahouse had opened.

In its second week, two elderly ladies came in and demanded to inspect the business licence, saying that they were from the Neighbourhood Committee. It was Six's first day alone in the teahouse. Thick Glasses was with a friend who had offered to help fix his broken-down old car again, and Meng had things to get on with at home. Remembering what Meng had told her to do in such circumstances, Six led the two women to the framed certificates hanging above the writing desk. She then stood back and watched nervously as the two women with their short hair and sombre clothes scrutinised them for a long time.

'Are all three in order?' asked one of the women, who was dressed in clothes of a greyish blue. 'I've forgotten my reading glasses, I can't see properly.'

'There's nothing wrong with the words and official stamps,' said the other, who wore a grey waistcoat, 'but what I don't understand is why they've started trading without holding an opening?'

'That's right. We'd have been invited if there was an opening, but we only found out about this place yesterday.'

'Girl, where's your boss? We've got some questions for him.'

Six stepped forward, trying to control her nerves.

'I'm sorry, he's not here, but you could leave a message if you like,' she replied courteously.

'Not here? Well, has he got a mobile phone? If so, tell him to come back right now. Tell him the Neighbourhood Committee is inspecting him.'

The two women spoke in very serious voices.

Six called Thick Glasses's mobile phone but his response wasn't much help. 'Can't it wait a bit,' he shouted, 'my friend's just got the bonnet off the car . . .'

Six took the phone from her ear momentarily and told the two women what her employer was saying. The one in blue immediately snatched it away from her.

'Now then, Boss Shu, is your car more important than the law? How could you open a business without mentioning it to the Neighbourhood Committee? Get back here so we can sort this out right away, or else we'll leave you a fine when we go! Well, we're waiting. Do you want to talk to the little girl? Here!' The phone was returned to Six's hands.

'Serve them two pots of tea and the best snacks we have,' said Thick Glasses, 'and keep them talking. I'll be done in twenty minutes. I'm sure you can occupy them till then. Once those old people start gassing, they forget all about the time. Try your best!'

Six did as Thick Glasses told her, and set out tea and cakes on the table in front of the antique display cabinet—the best place to sit in the teahouse. Then she carefully selected two small, illustrated books from the shelves and handed them to the old ladies. Meng had been given these books by a friend, and had told Six that they contained art by the leaders of the nation. It wasn't that the calligraphy and drawings were anything special, but the books were to be kept in the teahouse as a kind of protective charm against anyone who came bothering them.

Six was surprised by how effective the books were: as soon as the old ladies saw the names of the artists, they cried out in pleasure.

'*Aiya!* Who'd have thought our leaders

would be so good with a brush? What wonderful calligraphy!'

'Girl, what are you actually selling, tea, books or art?' Grey Waistcoat asked, gesturing to the bookshelves and the scrolls and paintings on the walls.

'Only the tea is for sale,' Six answered. 'The customers can read these books while they are drinking their tea. My boss says that the more people read, the less social unrest there'll be. And look, we have a book over here that contains writing from our foreign customers!'

Six brought over the notebook from the writing desk and laid it out in front of the visitors.

'*Aiya!* Comrades from friendly nations also visit you?!' asked the woman in blue in amazement.

Grey Waistcoat seemed more at ease with the idea. 'These foreigners read Chinese books then?' she asked.

'Yes,' said Six enthusiastically, 'they've come from all over the world to study Chinese culture. They all speak very good Chinese but, if you're willing, you might care to give them some advice about their pronunciation.'

'Really?' said the woman in blue, who was clearly very interested. 'I've seen a few foreigners at the Sun Yatsen Mausoleum, but they were all jabbering away to each other in their own language. I've never heard any foreigners speaking Chinese.'

'Well, I've seen quite a few in Shanghai, where my son and daughter-in-law live,' said Grey Waistcoat. 'The shops there even have signs in foreign letters. In fact, you could almost say that foreign words are taking over: even the Chinese signs don't sound Chinese! *Nai-kee*—what does that mean? There are so many shops with strange signs and window displays. You've got no idea what's in them. Designer labels—that's what my son says they sell. He and his wife won't wear anything else. I mean to say, wearing clothes is all about being comfortable and looking presentable, wouldn't you say? What use is a brand name? Who's going to put their hand into your collar to look at the label?'

'Aren't these brand names to show social status?' asked the woman in blue. 'That's what my son says.'

'Come off it!' scoffed Grey Waistcoat. 'Do you think you can become a celebrity just by wearing expensive clothes? That's like saying we old things can become young again by wearing clothes for girls.'

'Perhaps brand names do reveal social status,' said Six, thinking that someone should stand up for the woman in blue. 'After all, poor people can't afford them, and people who aren't aware of fashion don't buy them. Isn't fashion now a kind of culture?'

'Culture? Nonsense! I can't be doing with people who use Modernisation and Culture as

167

excuses for bad behaviour,' Grey Waistcoat said, her face stern.

Six cowered, but this time the woman in blue leapt to *her* defence.

'But things aren't the way they used to be. Back then we all wore blue to show we were good Communists, but, if we're honest about it, we didn't have enough to eat. These days, everyone wears different clothes and, if you have the money, you can eat delicacies from all over China without leaving Nanjing. Take that cake you're eating. In the old days you could only eat Rolling Donkey cakes in Beijing, but now you find them everywhere. It's like the TV. Just by having one in your living room, you can say you've seen the world.' And with this, she stuffed a Rolling Donkey into her mouth, whole.

'Don't get me started on television! Just look at the films they show these days . . . They don't seem to inspect or cut them at all. You even see people in the bedroom, naked as the day they were born. And look at the result: today's children have no idea how men and women should behave. Go to Shanghai in summer and you'll see what I mean. Women run about the streets wearing less than men, their bare feet shoved into a pair of slippers without any socks! I think they're picking up bad ways from the West. They don't eat our good spring greens, they go for fast food cooked in oil that hasn't been changed for ten days; they don't drink our nice tea, they go for that fizzy muck Westerners call beer so that men grow such bellies they spill out over the tops of their trousers. Talk about fashion! When my daughter came to see me for Spring Festival she was wearing jeans cut so low her bottom was almost showing. She said this style was fashionable all over the world! I gave her a proper talking to. I mean, a nice girl like that, doing herself up half like a prostitute, half like a lunatic . . .'

Six could see that Grey Waistcoat was getting more and more angry so she tried to calm her down.

'Madam, you're right. This is exactly why my bosses opened this teahouse: so that more people can drink our Chinese tea, look at our Chinese paintings and calligraphy, and discuss our Chinese books. You see, if foreigners start to be influenced by us, the people who try to copy foreigners will appreciate our Chinese culture too. Don't you agree, Madam?'

The two women looked at each other, then nodded. 'Of course,' said the woman in blue, stuffing a sesame rice-ball into her mouth. 'We agree with you entirely.'

After that, the two old women spent some minutes walking around the teahouse munching on their cakes and looking at the displays of books, paintings and calligraphy. Eventually they came back to their table.

'It's good that you've opened this teahouse,'

said Grey Waistcoat, savouring a mouthful of tea and admiring the teapots in the cabinet. 'We in the Neighbourhood Committee will give it our full support. We just need the formalities to be complete. After all, your boss seems to be a learned man.'

'Madam, you are too kind!'

At some point Thick Glasses had slipped back in. Now he came over with a pot of fresh tea in his hands, and exchanged the teacups for a good set from the display cabinet.

'So *you're* Boss Shu?' exclaimed Grey Waistcoat, looking suddenly cross again. 'Every time that old Xiali of yours goes past my front door the whole family starts coughing from the smoke. Now tell us, why didn't you have an opening before starting to do business?'

'Well, it's like this,' said Thick Glasses, catching Six's eye. 'These days there's far too much serious extravagance and waste about the place. Although everyone is always talking about fighting corruption, they don't give officials an opportunity to be honest and upright. I thought it was about time that cultured people took a stand and did something to show people what real Chinese traditions are all about. That's why I started a teahouse where people could learn more about Chinese culture. I also wanted to show that, when our local officials gave us their support, it was because we did good things, not because we held a party. That's why we sent a printed announcement to all the local government offices when we opened. Perhaps there's been a mistake at the post office, and they haven't been delivered yet? I'll send you another to make up for it.'

'Was it in a big red envelope with foreign writing on it?' the woman in blue asked, realisation dawning on her face.

'Yes, yes,' said Thick Glasses enthusiastically. 'We decided to send English cards to show that our teahouse was a place of learning. In order to demonstrate our support for Chinese industry over foreign imports, we made the cards ourselves by hand.'

'The paper looked very cheap and the printing was uneven, so I threw it away!' said the woman in blue. Grey Waistcoat looked faintly embarrassed that she hadn't been able to read the English words on the announcement.

'Well that doesn't matter,' said Thick Glasses with a big smile. 'We don't expect your Neighbourhood Committee to act as an archive! It's enough that we know you received our announcement, so that you are aware of our respect and obedience. The promotion of Chinese culture is a matter for everyone, high and low alike. As you can see, our leaders take it very seriously!' Thick Glasses leafed through the book of calligraphy on the table with a meaningfully casual air.

At this the two old ladies nodded furiously.

'Very true, very true! We must all unite in cultural pursuits. From now on, if you need anything, don't hesitate to ask. The Neighbourhood Committee has a finger in every pie round here, we're right behind you. Goodbye.'

The two ladies strode towards the door.

'Mind how you go now! A good day to you!' said Thick Glasses as he ushered them out. Then, as soon as they were out of earshot, he turned to Six to congratulate her.

'Six, I never knew you were so wise! You had those two old ladies set up to swallow the bait all by themselves . . .'

Six's legs were so wobbly that she too sat down. She was astonished by the performance that Thick Glasses had just put on. Surely this wasn't the same man who couldn't express himself clearly and got all his affairs in a muddle! Not only had he coaxed the old ladies into good humour, they had left full of heroic pride.

After that, the teahouse was never again bothered by the Neighbourhood Committee, but there were still a few unwanted visitors. Six could not abide the people from the Business Administration or the Tax Bureau, who came in without so much as a greeting, never said 'thank you' when they left, and expected to eat and drink for free. Moreover, they always came just before lunch, with the unspoken expectation that Thick Glasses would invite them to go to a local restaurant to eat. If no invitation was forthcoming, they would whip out leather folders from under their arms, and subject Thick Glasses and Meng to an interrogation.

Once Kang dropped in when this was going on.

'Dad, Mum, what's up?' he called out. 'Have you broken the law?'

Meng looked embarrassed to be talked to like this in front of two officials from the Bureau of Commerce, and scolded her son. 'What kind of talk is that? We've got permits, we pay our taxes on time, how can you ask your own mother and father such a question?'

'In that case, has Dad been caught for speeding?' Kang asked, looking at Thick Glasses.

'Hardly! My car can't even get up to the normal speed, let alone break the speed limit.'

Meng and Thick Glasses watched helplessly as their son walked over to the officials.

'Comrades, my parents are clearly embarrassed to tell the truth in front of their son. Since you are such fair and impartial messengers of the law, please tell me what they've done wrong, so that I can draw lessons from this matter, or help them to mend their ways.'

'They haven't done anything . . .' stammered the men in confusion.

'That's very odd,' said Kang, turning to his parents but continuing to look completely deadpan. 'If you've done nothing wrong, why do you both have such hangdog expressions? We're all citizens under the red flag: you're legitimate taxpayers, they are upright officials, nobody is anybody else's prisoner. Why then are you behaving like the terrified masses quaking before their feudal masters? You will damage the reputation of our officials by behaving in this way. Wouldn't you agree, Comrades?'

'This is grown-up business, you stay out of it!' snapped Meng.

'Mother, that is very wrong of you. Everyone has responsibility to uphold the law and support a fair society. I'm a PhD student in Sociology, studying ways to improve the system of social management. You know that standing idly by can lead to great harm. Besides, treating a PhD student like a child is stripping me of citizenship rights which have been mine since the age of eighteen. Am I right? What do you say, Comrades?'

'Young people certainly know what's what these days,' said one of the officials.

'Indeed,' said the other. 'PhD students really are a mine of knowledge and information. Well, we won't disturb you any further, it's been a pleasure . . .'

As soon as the two officials were out of the door, Kang started grinning, but Meng was

174

cross.

'What's got into you this morning, young man?' she said, sinking into a chair. 'Don't you get enough of a kick out of your normal mickey-taking? Well, you've done it now! You've put on a good show of being upright and unafraid, but you've no idea how much your father and I are going to suffer! We've managed to get away with not having a splashy opening, we've weathered the annoyance of the local officials for not paying sufficient tribute to them and now, when the new head of the regional Bureau of Commerce comes to inspect our teahouse, you overreach yourself and read them a lecture! Looks like this shop isn't long for this world, PhD son of mine!'

'Not necessarily,' said Thick Glasses, giving his spectacles a polish. 'Who's to say the new man running the Bureau of Commerce isn't completely straight, unlike the rest of our corrupt officials? And even if he's not, we'll weather it. The ancients used to say that "the wise man shows no fear in the face of the unexpected, and no anger in the face of wrongful accusations". If the Bureau of Commerce closes us down, then we'll just sell off the books and paintings to recoup our investment, flog the calligraphy and furniture to pay the rent and give the tea sets as New Year presents.'

Kang sat down beside his mother and began rubbing her shoulders.

'That's right, Mum! Have you forgotten the words you made me recite every day from the moment I started primary school? *Be upright in your dealings with others, and pure and honest in your actions.* You're doing well if you can be upright in your dealings and run a pure and honest shop in these times! If they do shut us down, I'll get all those foreigners to write an open letter condemning them. That'll show 'em. They're scared of foreigners. Still, I really don't believe it'll come to that. No one can close down a shop these days just because he's heard things he didn't want to hear. China's not like it was ten years ago!'

'Kang, you're still young,' said Shu Tian. 'You haven't seen enough of life to know how quickly things can change. In China, how many heads have rolled over a careless word? OK, we've lived through twenty years of the Open Policy, but has the definition of the Party been reformed? Have they introduced freedom of the press? China isn't like the West. Western societies have had Religion to tell them what's right and wrong.'

'I don't see it, Dad,' Kang objected. 'Lots of Westerners haven't believed in God for a very long time . . .'

'There may be people who don't believe in God, but they have grown up with festivals such as Christmas and Easter, living in a cultural tradition that has remained the same despite all the changes. What's the law in

176

China? In ancient times, the emperor was the law. Then, when feudalism ended in 1912, China couldn't find a master. The warlords scrambled for power, each seeking to be a king in his own domain. And then came Mao, who stopped all their fighting. Do you remember singing *The East is Red*? In our time, everybody worshipped Mao Zedong as a god. You're supposed to be studying society— hasn't it occurred to you that Mao's power came, not from a cult of personality, but a desperate hunger for belief? An uneducated population, eking out a living from the soil, needed a god to bring order to the universe. They needed a god whose words everyone would obey, so they could be steady and secure in their poor lives. Despotism was the only way this could happen: everyone was either an enemy or a comrade. Now the Chinese want democracy, but how many people really understand what democracy is? Is there true democracy in the West, with its criminal gangs, wars of religion and governments who take certain actions in opposition to the will of the people? Did the students at Tian'anmen really know what they were calling for? There are some Chinese who don't see any difference between the student uprising at Tian'anmen and the Cultural Revolution: both were driven by young people, both wished to sweep away the old order in the name of "Democracy". But democracy isn't something that comes just by waving a flag . . .'

* * *

Little by little, Six's understanding of the conversations she heard around her grew. Thick Glasses and his family could sit for hours discussing modern Chinese society. Sometimes they even forgot to eat proper meals and it was almost closing time before they realised they had nibbled their way through more than half of the next day's stock of food. Six found it very difficult to follow political discussions and instinctively shied away from them. She preferred it when the conversation moved on to history or culture. Whenever Thick Glasses or Meng had a spare moment, she would ask them to tell her stories about China's past. This was how she learned the story behind the words on the teahouse sign: 'In Memory of Lu and Lu'.

'In the Tang dynasty,' said Thick Glasses, 'there were two great tea-tasting masters: one called Lu Yu and one called Lu Tong. Lu Yu had loved tea since the moment he was born. He loved it as much as his own life. For years he travelled through China, carrying with him nothing but a bamboo basket containing his tea set. Over mountain passes and along great rivers he went, tasting many famous teas, until one day he came to the gates of a mansion from which issued a wonderful aroma of tea.

' "What do you want?" the doorkeeper asked coldly.

' "Tea," said Lu Yu with a smile.

'The doorkeeper thought he had misheard. "Food?" he asked.

'Lu Yu corrected him with great courtsey. "I request that you grant me the gift of tea."

'The doorkeeper felt there was something very odd about this man with his bamboo basket. He'd never heard of a beggar asking for tea. He took a look at his face, and saw that his delicate features were not those of a poor man, so he gave him a bowl of tea. As soon as Lu Yu raised the fragrant bowl to his lips, he knew that he had never tried this particular tea before. "Good tea," he thought to himself. And then he thought: if the gatekeeper's tea is of such high quality, the owner's tea must be better still. And so, given an inch he took a mile: he addressed the gatekeeper once more.

' "I'm sorry to bother you again, but I would like to beg an audience with the master of the house."

'The gatekeeper could see that this man was out of the common run, so he went in to find his master. Lu Tong was reading in his study. He too was someone who had loved tea all his life.

' "If it please you, Master, something unusual has happened. A man who came begging for tea is asking to see you."

179

'When Lu Tong heard this he was both irritated and amused. "Whoever heard of a tea-beggar," he thought to himself. "Perhaps I have misheard."

' "What did he want?" he asked.

' "Tea," the gatekeeper repeated seriously. "He's asking for tea."

'Lu Tong thought for a moment. Then he said, "Let him come in."

'When the gatekeeper brought in Lu Yu, Lu Tong saw immediately that he was no ordinary man. He had a scholarly appearance and a courteous manner. Taking some leaves of the famous "Jade Belt Tea", he steeped them in a pot and then poured a bowl for his visitor.

'Lu Yu inhaled the fragrance of the tea as it filled the room. "Good tea," he said, nodding his head. But then he added "Such a pity!"

' "A pity?" asked Lu Tong. "What's a pity?"

' "The poor quality of your tea set is a pity," replied Lu Yu.

'Lu Tong immediately asked humbly that his visitor enlighten him, and so Lu Yu lifted up his bamboo basket and pulled away the white cloth to reveal a purple pottery tea tray on which sat a purple pottery teapot and four bowls.

' "The fragrance from your teapot fills the room," he said. "But the fragrance from mine fills the house."

'Filled with curiosity, Lu Tong took Lu Yu's teapot and used it to brew some tea. To his

180

joy, as soon as the water seeped into the leaves, the room and the courtyard were filled with the most beautiful scent.

'From then on,' concluded Thick Glasses, 'Lu Tong and Lu Yu became sworn brothers, and their knowledge of tea became famous. That is why their names grace the doorways of many teahouses, and why Meng and I decided to follow this tradition.'

Six loved listening to Thick Glasses and Meng's explanations, but there were some things she didn't like to ask about. She was troubled, for instance, by the fact that Thick Glasses and Meng would occasionally put a sign on the door that said 'Closed for Inspection' in order to allow a group of middle-aged men to meet undisturbed. These men didn't read, or write in the visitors' notebook. Instead they simply drank tea and talked. Sometimes Meng would ask a friend to come and play the zither for them. Six knew that these people were not like normal customers, but she couldn't understand why her employers never let other people into the teahouse when they were there. Eventually Meng gave her the answer.

'Those poor people,' said Meng one evening, as they were tidying up after a group of men had left. 'They have to live in such a hole-in-the-corner way.'

'Why?' Six asked shyly. 'Are they bad people?'

Meng looked at Six, clearly wondering whether she should confide in her.

'They are all good people,' she said after a while. 'It's just that they are different in their bodies.'

'They don't look different to me . . .' said Six in confusion.

'I'm going to tell you,' said Meng, 'but please don't tell anyone. These men are homosexuals . . .'

'But isn't that against the law?' said Six, wide-eyed. She could feel a chill running down her spine, and the tray in her hands was shaking.

'That was before. These days homosexuals cuddle openly on the street.' Meng took the tray from Six's hands.

'Then . . . why are these ones afraid of being seen?' asked Six, made courageous by the fact that Meng had raised the subject herself.

Thick Glasses was clearing a table nearby. 'Because they are married men,' he said. 'Think about it . . . Can you imagine how unhappy their wives and children would be if they found out?'

'Then what did they get married for? Weren't they cheating those women?' Six could not understand how Thick Glasses, who had always been so kind-hearted, seemed so unconcerned about the poor wives. Perhaps men always took the man's part . . .

'When they were young, homosexuality was

against the law,' Meng chimed in, pouring some tea for Six and Thick Glasses. 'People say that single women bring trouble and gossip to their door—it's not much better for single men. There was no other way for them to remain respectable but to get married and treat their lovers as friends. It makes me very sad to think how these men have been leading lives of deception for so long. Almost all of them are silent and withdrawn. It's not good for your health to live in this way . . .' Meng's voice was subdued.

'But now that there's no law against it, why don't they follow their feelings?' Six felt very sophisticated saying such a thing.

'Their women might turn a blind eye, but what about the children? What child nowadays could endure having such a father?' Meng topped up her husband's tea.

Six thought about this. 'You're right,' she said. 'If I found out my dad was homosexual I think I'd die of disgust . . . But then, if Dad was . . . like that, how sad it would be for him to have to live a life he didn't want.'

From then on, Six made a special effort to treat the male visitors with consideration, but she still felt awkward around them. Her favourite customers were the foreigners whom Ruth brought to the teahouse. This was not just because Six was curious about them: their hunger to learn about Chinese language and culture gave her a great feeling of pride at

183

being Chinese, and a sense that, even though her stock of learning was meagre, to these foreigners, it seemed like a bottomless well.

She was constantly surprised by the things she found out. She had never realised there could be such differences between people. Once, for example, she overheard a Japanese teacher from Ruth's college talking to Ruth in Chinese about the Japanese custom of present giving. When the Japanese gave gifts, she said, most bought things that were of no use at all to the owner, because the recipient could pass them on to someone else, and that person could pass them on to a third party. In Japan, you didn't open a gift in front of the giver, but the next time you saw them you had to mention the gift and express your thanks.

'That's very different from England,' said Ruth. 'When we get presents, we open them straightaway so that we can thank the giver. But you Japanese are like the Chinese: you have to wait until the guest has left to see what the gift is.'

Ruth asked Six why Chinese people did not open presents in front of people. Six had never even thought about it, but remembered how her mother had said that 'only people possessed by ghosts and demons open a gift in a hurry and lose face!'

One day, Ruth came to the teahouse with a Canadian couple. The man was an old university friend of Ruth's and they were in

China on their honeymoon. Wishing to congratulate the newly-weds, Six brought some snacks to them while their tea was brewing— peanuts and honeyed Chinese dates (to represent many children of both sexes).

'*I wishing you early have son!*' she said in her best English.

The foreigners didn't appear to understand Six's poor pronunciation, but they certainly understood Meng when she came forward and said, '*How many children would you like to have? Do you like a big family with many kids?*' They were both overcome with embarrassment at Meng's words, and even Ruth blushed. Once Ruth and the couple had left, Meng asked Thick Glasses why her words had caused such a reaction.

'Don't you know you should never ask newly-weds that question in the West?' he said smiling. 'They consider it a private matter . . .'

Six's tongue hung out with astonishment when she heard this. Who would not want others to wish them a son?

Six often found herself perplexed like this. Even the smallest little thing, such as seeing a magpie in the street, could cause misunderstanding. The magpie was Six's favourite bird so when she saw one hopping about on the pavement outside the teashop, she eagerly pointed it out to Ruth and her friends. To her amazement, they averted their eyes and called out, 'Don't look!' and 'Is there only one?' Ruth explained that, in many European countries, a lone magpie was said to bring bad luck. Six then told her about how, in her village, everyone believed that a single magpie brought good things. Her mother would say that, when a magpie called from a branch, an important guest was on his way. When her big sister was married off, the bride-gifts from the husband included a pair of beautiful pillowcases embroidered with magpies, symbol of love and constancy. And, when Six left the village, her best friends had given her a pair of insoles for her shoes, embroidered with a magpie and a wild goose, a symbol of their good wishes for good luck and freedom.

The foreigners who were only just beginning to learn Chinese would meet up in the teahouse to practise with each other. They gave each other language tasks, such as talking about their favourite things. When people replied 'Going for a walk', Six was bemused. What did this mean, and why did Westerners like the idea of walking? At home she had walked miles to school and back, even when she was exhausted. And city people were always stressed as they walked—or half-ran—to work, to the cinema or to a restaurant. She had never seen anyone walking for pleasure.

The more Six learned about foreigners the more she came to believe that the Chinese were the wisest and most industrious of all nations. After all, they never took words from other languages, but always drew a new character if they needed to create a word. Six had realised this when listening to a conversation between English students during which they used the word 'taboo'. She asked Shu Kang its definition and he told her that it was actually a borrowing of the Polynesian word *tabu*. Six was astounded to hear that the English could be so lazy.

The ignorance of the Westerners who came to the teahouse also amazed her. She had learned all about Western history at school. She knew of Britain's dark colonial past and its exploitation of slaves, America's bloody civil war, Holland, Spain and Portugal's battle for hegemony of the seas; she had studied French *bas-relief*, the ruins of ancient Rome, and Greek myths. She had therefore expected that foreigners would know all about Qin bricks and Han tiles, the poetry of the Tang and Song dynasties, the Four Great Inventions and the novels of the Ming and Qing . . . But one day, a friend of Ruth's had actually asked Six to list the Four Great Inventions, as if he had no idea that they were 'paper, movable type, gunpowder and the compass'! And not one of these foreigners seemed to know about the *Book of Odes* or *The Dream of the Red Mansions*. 'Impossible, impossible!' Six would cry. 'Every middle-school student here knows your Shakespeare, Dickens and Victor Hugo.

How can you not know our Cao Xueqin and Tang Xianzu? We're not a small country, we have so many people and such a long history! Why don't you know this?'

At the same time, however, Ruth's friends claimed to know a lot of things about China that Six didn't, and were constantly asking such difficult questions that even the Chinese university students who came to the teahouse to practise their English had difficulty answering them. The foreigners said Chairman Mao had starved very many people to death, but Six remembered the teachers in the village saying that without Chairman Mao, their grandfathers and grandmothers would all have died of hunger . . . Then there were stories of how Chinese people had built railways for the north Americans, of how European herbs had been brought over from China, how the suicide rate in China was the third highest in the world, how more than twenty countries around the world had adopted several hundred thousand Chinese female orphans between them, how Chinese overseas students in the West were the richest students, but didn't know how to ask questions in class . . .

Six didn't know where the foreigners had heard all this information about China. Was this the 'Propaganda' Kang talked about when he described how the Western media would say things about China that weren't true? Why was it that the China these foreigners described sometimes seemed unrecognisable to her?

She decided to ask Thick Glasses and his wife about it. They exchanged a glance, then Thick Glasses said, 'Six, why are our two ears on two sides of our heads? So we can hear sounds that come from different places. The things your villagers used to say about the city don't necessarily resemble the things you see for yourself here, do they? And is your Second Uncle's version of city life the same as Three's? China is very big. The north and south, the east and west, the countryside and the cities are all different. People say all sorts of things about them according to the knowledge they have managed to pick up. Some are true, some are false, but there's nobody in this world who can be the final arbiter. It is important to think and see for yourself. You can't believe everything you're told, but nor can you suspect everything either, do you see?'

Meng looked at her kindly. 'It's good that you're making friends with the foreigners, but you shouldn't talk too much about things you don't understand, especially not politics. Some of the people you meet in this teahouse won't be as good as others. These people won't mug you or steal from you, but they might bring a false accusation against you for using "reactionary language". Nobody with a brain in their head would believe that a little girl like you could be a reactionary, but a lot of people in China don't have the education to know that you have to think things through before leaping to conclusions. They have little understanding of how to be a decent person. Those people might see your words as an opportunity for promotion, or to earn some extra money; they won't consider the rights and wrongs of the matter. You've come to the city to see the world. It's very important to look around you before deciding what you think. You're still young. You need to see more of life, and read more books. Reading will allow your intelligence to grow wings and take flight. Look at me—at my age there are still heaps of questions to which I haven't found an answer!'

'Really? There are still things you don't understand?' Six could not believe it.

'Yes, we all have them. The more you read, the more you want to know, and so the more questions you have.'

It was after this conversation that Six began to understand why Thick Glasses and Meng would take certain books home with them in the evenings. The library, so lovingly put together by Thick Glasses for his customers, was growing. As the teahouse became better known and attracted more business, lots of people were contributing books to the shelves. It was Six's job to enter these new books into a log. She would painstakingly divide them into categories, with a serial number for each. Who knows, she thought to herself, maybe some day the teahouse would have enough books to open a quiet room solely for reading, like the big bookstores she had seen in the centre of town. But there were some books that Meng and Thick Glasses didn't want entered in the log, and which they immediately hid in the storeroom behind the blue curtain before taking them home at closing time.

At first Six thought that the couple were simply greedy for more books to add to their personal collection. After all, Meng had told her that she still had a lot of questions to answer. But as time went by, she heard customers say things like, 'This book is still banned, but the ban on that one has been lifted', and only then did it really dawn on her why not every book could be put out for people to read.

She was surprised to find that it was often the upstanding Guan Buyu who brought in these secret books. Although she had never returned to his book-lined office, he often came to the teahouse to meet up with some friends, and was always friendly and pleasant to Six. He even confided to her that his teahouse meetings were actually a 'reading group' that had existed clandestinely for years, and was now able to use the teahouse as a base. One day she plucked up courage to ask him about 'banned books'. How was it possible to know which book was off-limits? Thick Glasses had told her to check with him before she entered books that touched on religion, freedom of speech, law, or relations between men and women, but there seemed to be so many opportunities to make a mistake. Guan Buyu told Six that she was not alone in being confused: the policies of the Nanjing officials were many and ever-changing, making it virtually impossible to be a hundred per cent sure what the ruling was on a controversial book. It was therefore best only to lend books to people you knew and trusted. With ordinary customers, even regulars, you should be extremely wary. Better to say that there were 'no new books' than to put others in danger. It had never occurred to Six that reading books could be dangerous, but she took Guan Buyu's warning to heart. She couldn't bear the idea of landing a book lover in trouble.

She noticed that Thick Glasses and his family also took care with some of the jokes that were written in the visitors' notebook. If she asked Kang to explain a joke to her that she didn't understand, he would pretend not to hear her; a short while later Meng or Thick Glasses might discreetly rip out the page from the notebook.

One day she rescued one of these discarded pages and read the following:

In the 1980s, at the time of the Open

Policy, the three Chinese leaders Deng Xiaoping, Jiang Zemin and Li Peng were out driving a car called China when they came to a three-way junction. According to the road sign, straight ahead was Socialist China, to the left was Russia, which was in the process of disintegration, and to the right were the capitalist nations of America and Great Britain. Both Jiang and Li looked towards Deng for guidance. Without so much as a pause for thought, he said, 'Signal left, but turn to the right'.

Six had absolutely no idea what these words meant, so she tried reading another joke a little further down the page:

One day a little boy was given some homework by his teacher. He was to write a sentence using the words Nation, Party, Society and People. The child didn't understand what these words meant or how they were related to each other, so he asked his father over supper. The father tried to explain in words the boy would understand.

'Imagine these words apply to our family. Granny is the Nation: without Granny none of us would be here. Daddy is the Party: his word is law. Mummy is Society: she takes care of everything in the home, but if she gets angry there's no peace for anyone in the house. And as for you, you're the People: you should obey the Party, help Society and win glory for the Nation.'

The boy was still not entirely sure that he understood, so he put off doing this exercise until he had finished all his other homework. By that time it was very late. He did his best, but he still couldn't make a sentence, and he was worried his teacher would hold him up to ridicule the next day. He decided to consult his family again.

Pushing open the door of his grandmother's room, he saw that she was already asleep. Pushing open the door of his parents' room, he found them in the middle of making love. His father yelled at him to get the hell out. Not understanding why, the little boy returned in tears to his room to complete his homework.

The next day, the boy's father received a call from the teacher wanting to know if the homework was all the boy's own work.

'Why? Has he said something "counter-revolutionary"?' asked the father, anxiously.

'No, no . . .' said the teacher. 'It's just that it's so good.'

That evening, when the father opened his son's exercise book, he saw five big red stars and the words:

'When the Nation sleeps and the Party plays with Society, the People weep.'

Six couldn't follow this joke either, but she was troubled by it. From then on, she avoided certain pages in the visitors' notebook, in the same way that she avoided books that spoke too openly of what men and women got up to in bed. Once, after closing time, she had glanced at a few pages like this, and had gone so weak at the knees that she couldn't do her work. It was right to ban such books, she thought. After all, if people in the village read them, there'd be nothing growing in the fields!

Little by little, Six got to know the regulars at the Book Taster's Teahouse and they got to know her. Although she dreamed of having conversations with the more bookish customers, she realised that, no matter how much she learned, they would always see her as a waitress. The politeness with which they treated her came from a strong sense of hierarchy, and was driven by compassion and pity more than anything else. In the end, the people she liked best, and who put her most at ease, were those who came for the tea and jokes, rather than the books. After the teahouse had closed for the day, she would pore over the visitors' notebook to read the messages these people had left, noting the way that the personality of each customer lived on in their handwriting. There was the affectedly scrawled style of the educated businessmen who came in a hurry and left in a hurry; the rigid pattern-book characters of men in their forties, who had a lingering fear that any irregularity in length or line thickness might incur criticism; and the fine, delicate script of the women. She would close the book thinking about how women wrote very little in the notebook, but how the few words and phrases they left were like tantalising hints, leaving the reader craving for more. She longed for the day when she could see into the hearts of city women so that she could learn to be like them.

8

DIAGRAMS AND DIALECTS

Five's vision of the great dragon at night had stayed with her during the weeks that followed the day off with her sisters. The moment she had seen its glittering scales shining through the dark, her feelings about her job had changed. It seemed to her that she was living and working in a truly magical place, and she was sure that it must contain some secret that would help her, a mere chopstick, become something better.

She continued to see her sisters on her free day, but she didn't always enjoy their outings. Sometimes Three couldn't join them, and said that Five and Six were now familiar enough with the city to cope without her. However, without Three as their guide, the two younger sisters argued about what to do. Five wanted to spend the day looking at the thin people in shop windows, while Six insisted on meeting up with students from the university. When they were with Six's friends, Five felt desperately uncomfortable. The bignoses jabbered away in their 'foreign language' and she could do nothing but sit silently and watch. Things weren't much better when the conversation was in Chinese. None of Six's friends, not even the Chinese ones, could believe that she didn't know how to read, and when she tried to talk to the university students about farming, they didn't understand a word. This was partly to do with the Anhui dialect that Five spoke, and partly because Six wasn't very interested in 'translating' what Five had to say. How Five wished she had the courage and the knowledge to go off on her own, but she was tied to Six by her ignorance. Things were better when Three came out with them. They would visit big shopping centres or shopping malls with food courts. There Six could meet her friends, and Three could go for a walk with Five nearby, so that all of them could enjoy their time in their own way.

Five thought a lot about how she could find the secret hidden in the Dragon Water-Culture Centre. She dreamed of returning to the village for Spring Festival having proved that a stupid girl can be clever in the city. She thought about how relieved Uncle Two would be when he came back from Zhuhai for the festival and saw that she had heeded all his warnings. But Three and Six both said that, if you wanted to live your life in comfort, you had to earn serious money—and if you wanted to earn serious money, you had to go to school. Was this really the only way? Engineer Wu repaired the machines just by looking at pictures, and Auntie Wang never so much as glanced at a sheet of paper. Mei Mei was the only one who got up early in the morning to read books, and yet she was just a humble worker rather than a manager. Six had read a *lot* more books than Three, but she was still no good at arranging vegetables. The more Five thought about it, the more she was convinced that there must be a path to a decent life that didn't involve reading and writing. And so she made herself a little plan: to follow Engineer Wu and Auntie Wang's example, and use her eyes and ears to learn everything she could about how the Dragon Water-Culture Centre functioned. If she watched and listened carefully, she didn't need to ask questions. After all, her mother often told her that whenever a woman opened her mouth, it caused misfortune. It didn't do to go advertising your skills to the world. What was important was not what you said, but what you did.

It was Engineer Wu who first noticed the change in Five's behaviour. He realised that she had begun to accompany him whenever he worked overtime, without claiming for the extra hours. He asked Auntie Wang if she had asked Five to do this, but she was just as surprised as he was. They decided that Five must want to learn technical skills, which was good news for the Dragon Water-Culture Centre: the more an assistant knew, the better her ability to cope in an emergency. Besides, this way Engineer Wu had a helper.

For Five, it was as if she was learning to see and hear for the first time. She watched how Engineer Wu would prod part of a machine with a screwdriver, then stick his ear to another section and listen. Sometimes he simply put a hand on the machine and stood there lost in thought until the problem became evident to him. He estimated everything by sound and feel, only using measuring devices as a last resort when he had to open up machines for repair. Sometimes he had to work late into the night to resolve a problem. People said his hours were as long as Manager Shui's, but Five didn't mind staying with him. She loved following him as he moved among the pipes and the pumps. Captivated by her new insights, Five began to listen to machines too. She even got up early so that she could accompany Engineer Wu on the rounds he made before the Dragon Water-Culture Centre opened. The pools were cleaned and sterilised the night before, but they needed to be checked again in the morning, along with the showers, thermostats and fire safety equipment.

Five was particulary fascinated by Engineer Wu's big book of drawings, which he called a 'flow chart' of the Dragon Water-Culture Centre's plumbing. It was full of little arrows, squares and circles, and Five longed to understand it. If she could learn the laws of the pump room in the same way that she had learned the laws of nature—sowing in summer and reaping in autumn, or using nets for shrimp and hooks for fish—she could be a big help to Engineer Wu and Auntie Wang. She begged Engineer Wu to let her borrow the diagrams, but he said they were more important to him than money, and he would be lost without them.

When she had made the morning rounds with Engineer Wu, Five would run off to Auntie Wang to begin the job she was paid for. The preparation of medicines for the pools was a strictly monitored process. Each preparation room would boil or steam their special pre-soaked herbs for a given time, and then add them to the pools in fixed quantities. At this point, Auntie Wang would look at the colour of the water, test the temperature with a thermometer and sniff the smell by the side of the pool to check that everything was up to standard. Five learned all this so quickly that Auntie Wang was quite taken aback. She was particularly impressed by the fact that Five could gauge the temperature of the water simply by feel, and didn't need to use the thermometer. When Auntie Wang told her she had 'natural genius', Five couldn't see what was so special. Wasn't looking at water just like looking at the sky to tell what the weather would be? If there were fish-scale patterns in the sky, then there would be no need to turn over the slices of sweet potato that had been put out to dry; if there were little hooks of cloud at the sky's edge, it meant a rainstorm was on its way. In stuffy weather, bugs would bite; cloudy days with grey water were best for fishing . . . all this you could know by looking. As for her sense of smell, what was so special about that? It was easy to know about things through smell. When her dad had checked the strength of pesticides by using the little pieces of white paper that Six had told him about, she had always known the answer before the white paper came out of the can, just by sniffing. She never said so, of course. In fact she had often wondered why her father, who had worked the land all his life, could be so slow on the uptake. Her mother said that it came from smoking fruit-tree leaves in his pipe, which had left him without much of a sense of smell.

Soon Five had made herself invaluable to Auntie Wang, and it wasn't long before the managers of each pool began to notice her skill and add their own praise to Auntie Wang's. However, they were much more dubious when Auntie Wang decided she was confident enough in Five to allow her to check a pool on her own. It wasn't until Auntie Wang had checked Five's results twenty times and found them exactly the same as her own that the pool managers started to trust her. Indeed, there were many people in the Dragon Water-Culture Centre who thought that this silent little ugly duckling might be in the process of becoming a swan.

Five was aware that people's attitudes were changing, but she didn't fluff up her feathers. Her mother had always said that, just as a guard dog should keep its tail between its legs and not bite without reason, so an honest person should keep her head down and not show off. Instead of chatting with the other girls, Five would spend her free time studying Engineer Wu's pictures and comparing them with the real machines. She also took every opportunity she could to look at Mei Mei's foot-massage diagrams. At first she was utterly bemused by these pictures of the sole of the foot that showed its links to the different parts of the body. Then she realised that the human anatomy wasn't that different from the pig's—and she was very familiar with the insides of a pig because her family always slaughtered one shortly before Spring Festival.

Whenever her father killed a pig, he called his daughters to watch so that he could give them a lecture:

'Now, listen carefully. We may not have any sons in this family to slit the throat, flay the skin or open up the stomach, but I want you to watch these male tasks so you know how it's done; and I want you to learn how to do woman's work well so that you are not laughed at in your husband's home.

'Six, I don't want you kicking up a fuss about blood just because you've had a few years of schooling. Everyone needs meat, whether they are educated or not, and you can't have meat without blood. Your Uncle Two says there are people in the city who don't eat meat in order to protect animals. Protect animals? That's a joke! Are animals more important than people?

'Now, watch how I do it. Remember, you must stab to the heart with one blow. Don't make the animal suffer by stabbing more than you have to!'

Everyone in the village said that Five's father was a good hand at killing pigs: he always hit the mark with the first stroke of the knife. As soon as the knife fell, the pig, hanging trussed up by its four feet from a tree, struggled, shook and screamed, and gouts of blood gushed out. At this point, the sisters could never stop themselves shaking; their throats tightened and they found it difficult to breathe. When he saw that the pig had given up the ghost, their father would blow through a length of iron pipe he had found somewhere and inflate the carcass of the dead pig until it was tight as a drum. Then he would remove the hair and skin, and cut off the tail and head. What frightened Five the most was watching the belly cut open. One slash of the knife and all the organs tumbled out into a big basin, and a blast of bloody stench hit them in the face. Sometimes her father would even reach into the empty belly of the pig and poke about, to clear out whatever remained inside. Their father then chopped the pig into big pieces so that the best back loin, the belly pork, the front and back legs and the trotters could be sent to the market for sale, and thus provide new clothes for the entire family. (Almost all of the pig was sent to market, even the suet on the stomach; the family was left with the smaller pieces of fat from around the intestines, the scrag end for preserving, the tripe and chitterlings, which they ate to celebrate Spring Festival.) While their father chopped, their mother taught her daughters how to clean the innards, bone and joint the meat, and lay it down for salting. As she wielded her knife she would show them which bits were the heart, lungs and liver, telling them the functions of the innards, which were roughly the same for people. And so the sisters learned how, when washing the heart, you had to cut down to the thick blood vessels in order to get rid of the valves on top, and squeeze out the blood inside; how when washing the liver, you first had to remove the gall bladder; how when cleaning the intestines and stomach, you had to wash them carefully with salt before dousing them again in vinegar to get rid of the smell. The best fun was turning the larger and smaller intestines inside out, although it was very smelly work. The girls would squirt each other with water from the intestines and fall about laughing. Five loved how the pink lungs became snow-white and slippery when they were washed. You had to keep squeezing them out over and over again but she felt a great sense of 'achievement'—a word that Six had brought home from school and insisted on using all the time.

When Five looked at Mei Mei's foot-sole diagram, she thought about all the things her mother knew. Even though, like Five, she had never been to school, she had a great understanding of the human body. Her mother's skills were an inspiration and, before long, Five had spent so many hours poring over the picture, she felt courageous enough to think she understood it. One evening, when Mei Mei was lying on her bed complaining about how exhausted she was, Five offered her a massage.

'Do you want a rub?' she said. 'I've rubbed Mum's feet at home and she said it felt really good. Want me to try?'

'Really? All right then, give it a go.' Mei Mei stretched out a foot from her quilt. 'Start with the right foot, it's got more stamina, it doesn't matter if you press a bit hard.'

Five beamed and took Mei Mei's foot.

'Your feet are so soft and narrow!' she exclaimed admiringly. 'Now I can see what Uncle Two means when he says that city people's toes are all packed tightly together because their feet never have to grab the ground when walking; when we country folk walk along the dykes with carrying poles, our toes are all splayed from gripping the mud.' Five started to rub Mei Mei's foot, but after a few seconds the normally softly spoken Mei Mei gave a yell of laughter so loud that the girl in Bed Six stuck her head out from underneath her quilt: 'Hey, keep it down a bit, I'm trying to get an early night.'

'Sorry, sorry!' Mei Mei and Five apologised hurriedly, sticking out their tongues in the way Chinese girls do when they apologise.

'Are you laughing at me?' Five asked quietly.

'Massaging a foot isn't like scratching an itch,' said Mei Mei. 'Come on, you lie down on my bed and I'll show you.'

Mei Mei jumped up and arranged her pillows so that Five could lie down. Then she pulled up a stool and took Five's foot in her hands.

'Goodness,' she said, 'you really do have a wide pair of feet. You must be very good at field work. Now listen carefully. There are lots of different techniques when giving a foot massage: you can knead, pinch, pat, prod, push or use all sorts of other kinds of pressure. When you touch the foot using these techniques, particularly at the meridians and places where the blood vessels and nerves are concentrated, you can feel what's wrong in the body . . .'

Mei Mei pointed to a place between Five's

toes. 'Look at this, for example. The skin here is very thick. That means your brain is tired.'

'My dad says I haven't got a brain,' said Six.

'Nonsense!' said Mei Mei. 'Everyone's got a brain. But of course, not everyone uses it. However, I think you've been using your brain a lot recently. See this swelling under the big toe? I bet it feels tender, right? What have you been up to these last few days to make your foot behave like it belongs to a big intellectual?'

When Mei Mei got no reply, she looked up to find that Five had fallen fast asleep. Quietly she went to fetch a big clean towel and curled up on the dormitory's spare bed. It didn't cross her mind to get under Five's quilt because she knew that the smell of stale sweat would be unbearable. She had once tried to persuade Five to wash her bedding more often, but Five had said that she couldn't remember which month her mother said she wasn't supposed to wash her quilt, and she was afraid of offending the Nine Star Goddess, giver of sons. She had promised to check with her sisters which were the lucky days for cleaning, but she kept forgetting.

*   *   *

The next morning Five woke up surrounded by a beautiful fragrance. At first she thought that she was still dreaming—she had spent the night dancing and singing in grassy meadows—but gradually she realised that she had gone to sleep in Mei Mei's bed. She looked across at the spare bed and saw Mei Mei wrapped in a towel, fast asleep. It was only eight o'clock so she closed her eyes and tried to recapture her beautiful dream.

The ten beds in the girls' dormitory were arranged in two rows on either side of the room. Mei Mei, who was the dormitory head, slept closest to the door, in Bed One; Five was opposite her, in Bed Ten. The girl who had slept in Bed Nine had left and not been replaced. All sorts of girls worked at the Dragon Water-Culture Centre, but most of them came, if not from the city, then from a town. It was difficult for Five to talk to them. They looked down on her because she came from a village, and their conversation was full of words that Five didn't understand—words like 'trendy', 'sushi', *'ku'* (cool) or *'yi-mei'er'* (email). It took Five ages to work out that 'hunk' meant a 'handsome boy', and 'babes' were pretty girls. But it wasn't only the words they used that made them difficult to understand. They all spoke different dialects! There was a girl from Ningbo, a city very close to Shanghai, who Five couldn't understand at all. She had arrived quite recently and always looked very smart, but she had a high-pitched voice that was almost unbearable to listen to, and used different words for 'I', 'you' and 'her'.

Then there was the girl from Hubei Province who used the same word for 'shoes' and 'children'. Even the girl who came from Anhui, Five's province, presented problems: the northern Anhui dialect she spoke was so different from Five's that when, at the start of each day, she said, 'Who wants to die? If none of you are dying, I'll go and die!' she filled Five with fear, until she realised that the girl was actually saying, 'Who wants to wash? If none of you are washing, I'll go and wash!'

Five even had difficulty remembering these girls' names. In order to do so, she secretly created a foot diagram in her head. The five beds on one side of the room were the left foot, the five on the other side, the right. Mei Mei was, of course, the first toe of the right foot. Then came the girl from Sichuan, who was forever fretting about whether her chilli sauce was going to run out. The third toe on the right was the one from the north of Anhui while the fourth was the Hubei girl with pebble glasses. The fifth toe of the right foot and the first of the left foot were both from north-east China. Every day they complained about the heat in loud voices that sounded like they were quarrelling. Whenever they were in the room, Mei Mei would hide herself away somewhere else to read; but Five found these two girls the easiest to understand.

The second toe on the left foot was from Xinxiang in Henan Province. Her elder sister and her younger brother were foot masseurs too. Mei Mei said that foot masseurs from Henan were like sports shoes from Wenzhou—they had taken over all big cities in China, and had a very good reputation. The third toe of the left foot was the new girl from Ningbo, the fourth toe wasn't anyone and the fifth was Five herself.

Of course there were dozens of other girls at the Water-Culture Centre who didn't sleep in the dormitory and whose names and job titles Five had difficulty with. She was at a complete loss to remember who did what shift until Auntie Wang devised a system for her: the soles of the feet were women and the tops of the feet were men; the left foot was the early shift and the right foot was the late shift. Auntie Wang would say things like 'The left sole needs more towels' or 'Take these disposable slippers to the top of the right foot'.

Auntie Wang and Mei Mei always looked out for Five because they were becoming increasingly fond of her. Despite her growing skill, there was still so much she didn't know, and so much potential trouble for her to get into. One night Mei Mei's heart skipped a beat when she had to rescue Five from a situation that would have been embarrassing for her, and possibly disastrous for others.

It was Mei Mei's job to stay awake until all the girls in the dormitory were safely in their beds. She was used to the fact that Five often returned to the room much later than the others because she was spending time with Engineer Wu. However, when at half past two, Five still wasn't back, she started to worry. Mei Mei went to the reception desk to check through the signatures in the clocking-on book. Manager Shui was very particular about employees signing in and out, rather than using punch cards, and so Five marked her name with a figure '5'. There was no '5' indicated as having left the building, though, and the security guard on the door said that, as far as he was aware, everyone had finished work.

Mei Mei's immediate thought was to try the pump room because she knew how fascinated Five was by it. The employees had nicknamed this area of the Water-Culture Centre the 'Tiger Stove', after it was called this by a civil engineer from Shanghai, who had come to bathe at the invitation of Manager Shui. The man had joked that Shui's business was just like the 'Tiger Stoves' in the old quarters of Shanghai that sold hot water to the locals so that they could wash and drink tea. He said there were many explanations why these hot-water shops were called 'Tiger Stoves'. Some people thought it was because the wood-burning stoves used to heat the water looked like tigers, with burning eyes and the flue for a tail. Others thought it was because Western-style houses in Shanghai had lots of chimneys, and the English word for 'roof' sounded like the Shanghai word for 'tiger'.

At night, the Water-Culture Centre's 'Tiger Stove' was only dimly lit, and Mei Mei was afraid. It felt as if a ghost might pop up from behind a row of pipes at any moment. With her heart racing, she was just about to turn back when she heard panting, and the voice of Engineer Wu whisper, '*Aiya*, quick, hurry, I can't hold out much longer.'

'Hold on a bit. Soon, soon . . .' replied Auntie Wang, wheezing and gasping.

'How close are you?'

Engineer Wu sounded as if he was about to take his last breath.

'Almost there . . .' panted Auntie Wang.

There was some grunting followed by an ecstatic 'Yesss!' from Auntie Wang and an 'Ahhh. . . .' from Engineer Wu that sounded like a low, drawn-out growl.

A thought popped into Mei Mei's head. People talked about how well Engineer Wu and Auntie Wang got on. Could it be that they were . . . But before the thought could develop in Mei Mei's mind, she quelled it. Hurriedly turning back to leave the Tiger Stove, she bumped into someone in the dark. They both squealed with fright.

'Who's that?' everyone said at the same time.

Mei Mei was so terrified that she didn't know what to do, but she realised that the person she had bumped into was Five, and she too was shaking like a leaf.

'Who's there?' whispered Auntie Wang, coming towards them.

Five was just about to reply, when Mei Mei clapped a hand over her mouth, and ran for the exit, pulling Five with her. The two girls hid in a storeroom until they saw Engineer Wu and Auntie Wang go out of the building through the iron side door. They they rushed back to the dormitory, avoiding the security guard as he did his rounds. Fortunately, all the other girls were sound asleep after their hard day's work. 'Remember, we didn't hear or see a thing,' whispered Mei Mei to Five who had jumped into bed and was still quaking beneath her quilt. 'This whole thing was a dream . . . Otherwise neither of us will be able to keep our jobs. Remember—it was just a dream . . .'

That night Five dreamed she was standing in a snowy field, holding up a big pig, waiting for her father's knife to strike. She woke up to find the girl in the next bed looking at her curiously.

'Where were you last night?' she asked. 'When I got up to go to the toilet, your sofa was empty.'

Five froze as the events of the previous night came rushing back.

'She got into my bed for a chat,' said Mei Mei hastily. 'We talked and talked and she fell asleep on me. It was a real squash. I tried to

214

sleep but in the end I had to send her back to her own bed. I didn't sleep well all night, when it was nearly light I'd had enough, I sent her away to her own sofa. Isn't that right, Five? From the way you were tossing and turning, it seemed as if my bed made you have an interesting dream . . .'

'Yes, I did!' said Five. 'I dreamed you told me it was just a dream . . .'

The whole dormitory erupted into laughter and Mei Mei took the opportunity to pull Five into the bathroom:

'Remember what I said. Forget all about it.'

Five nodded earnestly. She knew that Mei Mei had her best interests at heart.

It wasn't too difficult to pretend nothing had happened. The next day was Auntie Wang's day off and, even though Five's heart jumped like a startled rabbit every time she bumped into Engineer Wu, he treated her exactly as he always did. Five was beginning to wonder if the whole thing really had been a dream when Auntie Wang casually dropped into the conversation, 'I know you like little Mei Mei, Five, I like her too . . . But you mustn't keep her awake at nights. She's the mainstay of the Foot Massage Section. Next time you want someone to talk to I'll take you home for a chat myself!'

For several days after this, Five was terrified that Auntie Wang knew everything. But Heaven came to her rescue by sending two

215

new assistants for Engineer Wu who distracted Auntie Wang's attention. The two men were both called Zhao, though they were not related. One was an electrician, the other a plumber. Big Zhao the electrician was extremely tall. He was a tough man with a rough voice to match, and was called the Internal Combustion Engineer behind his back because he was always losing his temper. Zhao the plumber was tall and thin and rapidly acquired the nickname of Beansprout Zhao. His favourite occupations were chatting up girls and reading jokes on his mobile phone. He had Auntie Wang in stitches at least three times a day.

Five never understood exactly why Auntie Wang was laughing but she knew that Beansprout Zhao's jokes were dirty. She had heard one of them once when he came over to their table at suppertime.

'Auntie Wang, I got a text message today,' he said, grinning. 'D'you want to hear it?'

'You and your jokes,' Auntie Wang said teasingly. 'Have the girls chased you away from their table again? Go on then, if it's funny, Mr Mobile Phone.'

'OK . . . So there's this elephant and camel, and they're quarrelling. The elephant gets very angry and says, "What's so special about you then? Just a pair of women's tits on your back!" Well, the camel isn't going to take this lying down, so he says, "I'm better than you

216

anyway, with that man's thing on your face!" A passing snake laughs at this. "What are you laughing at, Snake," says the elephant furiously. "Where's *your* face then? Growing on your dick!"'

'Waaaa . . . you're killing me, you wretch!' said Auntie Wang, pounding the table with laughter. 'Get along with you, or I won't be able to eat any supper!'

Five was horrified. If her mother knew she'd heard such a story, she'd be in big trouble. Five was always very cautious with the men at the Water-Culture Centre, remembering her mother's advice that there were no men who didn't have a roving eye. Her mother said that all men ate from their family's wok while looking into other families' bowls. Even her father had got mixed up with the woman who watched the teastall for the road menders. For a few days it was as if his soul had left his body. Five thought it must have been the woman's fault because her father was always saying that women who provoked men were the troublemakers. That was why she took such care over her behaviour, staying close to Auntie Wang and Engineer Wu. She didn't want to be considered stupid *and* have a bad name. What could she do now that she had discovered that her protectors did that awful thing the villagers called 'stealing chickens and dogs'?

Time had passed quickly at the Dragon Water-Culture Centre and summer was approaching. Five couldn't believe how long she had been there. In the countryside the days spent bent over the earth, without being able to see even the raised edge of the field, felt endless. The only time the backbreaking work eased off was at the ends of the lunar and solar calendar, and there were hardly any days of rest for the villagers. Five thought about how she would long for the Mid-Autumn Festival and the Dragon Boat Festival when, for the only times in the year, they would eat steamed buns made from white flour rather than the usual sweet-potato flour. City people, on the other hand, seemed to have a festival every two or three days, and the Dragon Water-Culture Centre was constantly changing decorations and gimmicks in order to attract clients. No wonder the days went so fast in the city: there was always something to look forward to.

At first Five had wondered how, with all these festivals, city people could get any work done. But then she realised that city people didn't take festivals seriously. Mei Mei, for example, knew nothing about how children must wear special clothes for the Duanwu Festival in order to protect them against the Five Poisonous Creatures. Five had heard from her mother that on the Duanwu Festival, snakes, scorpions, centipedes, geckoes and spiders all came out to poison people. Adult skin was old and thick, so grown-ups were safe, but the Five Poisonous Creatures could do real harm to tender children. Was it surprising, then, that city people were so unhealthy? The fact that they didn't take their festivals seriously was also demonstrated by the fact that the employees of the Dragon Water-Culture Centre rarely stopped working on a festival day. How could you call it a proper festival when you didn't take the day off? The exception seemed to be International Labour Day, on 1 May, when, to Five's confusion, everyone prepared to down tools and disappear.

There was no such thing as 'Labour Day' in the countryside and Five was confused. Engineer Wu explained there was no point in the Centre staying open because most of the people who came to bathe were business people, who would be at home, or wealthy people, a lot of whom used the holiday for a short trip out of the city. Nanjingers were making the most of government's recent relaxation of laws on travel. Before, you had needed a permit to leave town on business, or to see friends and relatives. For visits longer than a day or so, you had to register at the local police station where you were staying. Now things were different and people could use their extra money to enjoy themselves.

The idea of spending money to enjoy yourself was completely alien to Five. After all, her father had dismissed even a short visit to a nearby village to see a film as foolish behaviour. But even if she had wanted to use the holiday to spend her money, she couldn't. Three and Six were too busy with the holiday-rush at the restaurant and teahouse to meet up with her, and without them, she couldn't find her way around the city. She therefore decided to spend Labour Day sitting in the dormitory looking at diagrams.

Mei Mei was the only other girl to stay in the dormitory. Five was delighted to see this. Since their night-time meeting in the pump room, she hadn't had an opportunity to be by herself with Mei Mei and there were so many things she wanted to talk to her about.

'Aren't you going out?' she asked excitedly.

'No. Going out means spending money, so there's no point. How about you?'

'I've got nowhere to go,' said Five, too embarrassed to admit that she would get lost in the city on her own in case Mei Mei thought her stupid.

'Do you want me to take you somewhere?' Mei Mei asked solicitously.

'No, it's all right. I don't want to spend money either. I want to save it for my mother and my family. What are you saving for?'

'University,' said Mei Mei quietly, even though there was no one in the room to hear.

'University!' exclaimed Five, feeling as if she had suddenly discovered a big secret. 'Why do you want to go to college? You've got so much learning already.'

Mei Mei looked hesitant, as if she didn't want to say any more, so Five offered to give her a foot-rub if she told Five all about it. Since the last time she had tried to rub Mei Mei's feet she had been practising hard.

'OK,' said Mei Mei stretching out a foot to Five. 'I want to go to university to study medicine. For generations there have been doctors in my family, but the tradition has been broken by me.'

'Because you're a girl?' asked Five.

'No, Five, not because I'm a girl. My mother and my grandmother were doctors.'

Five was amazed. 'How could that be?' she asked.

'It was because my great-grandmother didn't bear any sons. My great-grandfather comforted himself with the idea that he would hand on his medical knowledge to his son-in-law. But when my grandmother married, my grandfather proved talentless as a doctor while my grandmother gained a reputation for making successful remedies. Soon all his patients were coming to her instead. The same thing happened with the next generation. My grandmother passed on her knowledge to both her daughter and her son, but the son, my uncle, was a hopeless doctor. He tried to become a vet, but when laws were passed forbidding the ownership of pets in cities, he was allocated to a hospital. Hardly anyone who came to my uncle for treatment for a serious illness got better; as for smaller illnesses, he prescribed treatments that, like Western medicine, treated only the superficial symptoms and not the root cause.'

'Wait a minute, I don't understand your story,' interrupted Five. 'I know about vets—there's a vet who often comes from the local town to my village. But what do you mean by "superficial symptoms" and "root cause"?'

Five's eyes were full of a desire to learn.

'Some medicines treat only the surface of a problem,' Mei Mei explained, 'whereas Chinese medicine cures people from the inside. For example if you have a skin disease, that's because there's a problem with your blood. When you've cleaned out the poisons in your blood, the skin will get better by itself. Don't worry about not understanding, Five. It would be difficult for anyone who hasn't studied medicine . . .'

'Is your dad a doctor too?' asked Five, going back to pinching Mei Mei's toes.

'Yes. But that's the only thing I know about him. I'm a bastard. My mother brought me up by herself.'

Five looked up in surprise, and her hands froze.

'That's right, I'm a bastard,' continued Mei

Mei. 'I'm not afraid of telling you because I know you won't pour scorn on me, or tell the others. My parents didn't get married because my father deceived my mother. He was her teacher at a medical school in Shandong Province. He seduced her by saying he'd help her with her study, but when she became pregnant he told her he was married, with a son. My mother was expelled from the university for extra-marital pregnancy and sexual misbehaviour.'

'That's not fair!' Five said furiously.

'Thank you, Five. I know it isn't fair, but things like this have been going on for thousands of years, and usually it is women who turn other women in. My mother said that, in the early eighties, you had to show your marriage certificate or papers from your husband's work unit to get an abortion, otherwise nobody would help you because you were committing the crime of sexual misbehaviour. The only other option was to hide in the countryside and have your baby there. But my mother knew nobody in the country. Eventually, a cleaner at the university took pity on her, and took her to her home, a little village at the foot of Mountain Song where the Shaolin Temple is, and she gave birth to me there. After that, she had nowhere to go until, in 1984, the chance came to work in a herbal medicine shop in Hefei. At first she couldn't take consultation fees because she had no medical qualifications, but gradually word spread of her skill. A local official came for a consultation and Mum cured his bad back. He pulled some strings to get her a permit to practise medicine . . .'

'Was it very hard for you when you were a child?' asked Five, trying to imagine what it would be like to grow up with the stigma of being a bastard.

'My mother never told me the truth,' said Mei Mei. 'I always thought my father had died young of an illness. Then in my second year of senior school, a boy from Shandong transferred to my class. His parents had worked in the medical school where my mother studied, and he told everyone that she was a loose woman, and that I was a bastard. I ran home in tears and asked my mother if it was true. She cried until two or three in the morning without speaking, then she came to sit by my bed to tell me about where I came from . . .

'I was so shocked, it was as if I'd been struck by lightning from a clear sky. I was only seventeen and the idea of being branded a bastard was unbearable. I didn't believe my mother had been a victim: I thought there must have been something wrong with her morals . . . And so I took my ID card, and what little money we had in the house, and got on a train. I didn't even look to see where it was going, I just stayed on board till it stopped.

When it did, I found out I was in Nanjing. I hadn't realised I would need a letter of introduction to stay in a guesthouse so I spent the night at a bathhouse. It cost me ten of the fifteen yuan I had. When I look back now I can't imagine what I was planning to do. I was walking down Zhongshan Road when I saw the big dragon's mouth, and heard Banyue talking to someone about looking for new workers. So I went up and asked if they needed anyone. When they heard I knew a bit about medicine and that I came from a family of doctors, they sent me to foot-massage classes.'

'But what about your mother?' asked Five.

'I tried not to think about her,' replied Mei Mei. 'It was only when I had finished my three months of training that I could bring myself to contact her. I telephoned the medicine shop, but they told me she had been in hospital for several months. I asked for the number of the hospital, and got through to my mother. Both of us were crying too hard to speak. Since then we've talked to each other on the telephone once a week, and my mother came to Nanjing for Spring Festival this year. If I get into medical school, she plans to leave the shop in Hefei and come to live with me here. I could never go back to Hefei. It holds too many bad memories for me . . .'

'You must want to get into medical school very much,' said Five, trying to rub Mei Mei's feet in the way that would feel nicest for her.

'So much! I *have* to become a doctor so that I can repay my mother for all that she has suffered on my behalf . . .'

For the rest of the Labour Day holiday, Five and Mei Mei were silent, each immersed in her own thoughts and memories. Five thought about how cruel fate could be to women, and how much her own mother had suffered. Mei Mei's story, and the things she had overheard that night at the Tiger Stove, had made Five realise that life was less black and white than she had believed it to be. The Dragon Water-Culture Centre was full of stories that she never would have heard back in her village. If she listened carefully there was so much she could learn.

9

THREE FALLS IN LOVE

The Chinese say that if Chance brings two people together but they have no Time, love will not flourish. Nor will love grow if two people have the time to spend with each other but no feeling in their hearts. The only true love is when Chance and Time are in harmony.

For Three, there was no such thing as love. As far as she understood it, when a certain moment came in a man's life, he would go out and 'bring back' a woman, or, alternatively, a woman would be 'brought' to him in exchange for a sister, or another female relative, who would be 'taken away' to marry into his new wife's family. Chance or Time didn't come into it; it was simply a question of being 'taken'.

Three was absolutely determined that this would not happen to her. After all, hadn't her father 'taken' her mother—and look what had become of her. It was as if he had gone out and brought back a tool to have children, make clothes, cook, do the housework, raise the pigs, feed the dogs, and endure injustice and hardship. If wanting a man meant living that kind of life, Three would gladly do without one.

She was aware that it wasn't easy to avoid

such a fate. From an early age, Three had used her eyes and her ears, listening to village gossip and observing the goings on around her. Clearly, in certain seasons, people were on heat, just like animals. But why did women have to pay with the rest of their lives simply for wanting a man on a spring morning? It seemed to Three that people were far more stupid than beasts: a sow could give birth to ten piglets and then suckle them all, while people only managed one baby at a time, or two at most; newborn animals could open their eyes and stand up a few days after birth, but newborn people lay around for over a year before they could take their first step. The chickens in the yard were as free as air; they didn't allow themselves to be pushed around by the cocks . . . It was said that people distinguished themselves from animals by their skills, but as far as Three was concerned, no amount of skill could save you from pain and suffering. Her mother was the most capable woman in the village, yet her life had no sweetness: she was rated lower than a beast just because she had been unable to bear a son. Fortunately Li Zhongguo was basically a decent man, unlike some husbands, who beat and cursed their wives for not giving birth to a 'roof-beam'. He hadn't smothered or drowned a girl child and left her mother's heart bleeding. But who was to know what any future husband of Three's might be like? He

228

might be worse than her father . . . The older Three got, the more her dread grew. She could see no alternative: for a woman, a man was the root of all troubles and a source of bitterness.

But Three could not remain a stone-hearted girl for ever. Just as spring must come before flowers open, young girls need the right circumstances for love to grow in their hearts. When Three's heart began to put forth buds and green shoots, there was nothing she could do, no matter how hard she tried to resist.

*　　　*　　　*

Three's love arrived in the midst of an argument. One day, just as the lunchtime rush was starting at the Happy Fool, three men came into the restaurant and ordered a bowl of bean-flour noodles, a dish of fried greens and three glasses of beer. Wang Tong had popped out to the market, so Three was alone with the cook. She dealt with the order as fast as she could and, within five minutes, was back at the table with the food. But as soon as she had turned away to deal with other customers, one of the men hurled his beer glass to the floor and stood up.

'Is the idea to treat everyone like fools in this restaurant just because it's got a foolish name?' he shouted. 'I've just found a worm in my fried greens! People go on about how fresh your vegetables are. Too right! You don't even bother to wash them—just chuck 'em straight into the wok, mud, worms and all. Look at this, everyone! This worm may be the same colour as the veg, but it wouldn't be here if they'd washed the leaves properly. Can you see? It's still moving . . .'

At this, one of the man's companions stood up and started carrying the offending plate around, displaying it to the other customers. Within seconds the restaurant was in turmoil, with everyone using their chopsticks to explore their food in search of insect life. Three was terrified. In all her two and half years at the Happy Fool, she had never encountered such a situation.

'Brothers . . .' she said, rushing up to the men. But they interrupted her as soon as she opened her mouth.

'Who are you calling "Brother"?'

'Uncles . . .' Three tried again.

'How old do you think we are?'

Poor Three was overcome with confusion. What *was* the appropriate form of address? Grabbing at straws she tried *'xiansheng'*, forgetting that, while in the countryside this word means 'sir', in the city it means 'husband'.

The men roared with laughter.

'You think we're going to marry a woman who puts worms in her food? Not likely. But maybe you're after something else, eh? Perhaps as well as reviving Nanjing's venerable tradition of fresh vegetable cooking, you're bringing back the ancient traditions of Face Powder Lane too . . . Well, what about it? Are you and your friends interested in sexual as well as culinary history?'

Again, the men burst out laughing, all the while continuing to parade the plate around the room.

Three was mortified. Diners were beating a hasty retreat while those customers who had been queuing at the door were rapidly making off down the street. At the same time, a large crowd of onlookers had gathered outside, and people were peering in through the window. Three gave a desperate look at the kitchen but the cook was nowhere to be seen. She was ready to throw herself at the feet of these men to stop them making a fuss.

'Sirs, please forgive me this once,' she cried. 'I'll give you your money back!'

'You think that will be sufficient recompense? Get your boss out here! You can always tell a guilty boss when he hides himself away as soon as there's trouble. Little girl, have you ever heard the word "compensation"? When the Americans find a bug in their food they get thousands of dollars in compensation. I don't suppose you know how many yuan there are to the dollar, do you? Well, there are eight. So that makes tens of thousands of yuan. You reckon you can give us that?'

The crowd at the window was growing so large that people were actually starting to make their way into the shop to watch the scene. A few were taking the opportunity to pocket the tableware. Three could feel herself shaking all over. Her heart was ready to leap out of her mouth; her hands and feet were numb. Gradually the men in front of her, with their big, angry mouths—like the howling mouths of ghosts—began to swim in and out of view. Three thought of her mother's stories of people whose souls were stolen away by ghosts. Perhaps this was happening to her . . . She was just on the point of fainting when a man pushed his way to the front shouting, 'Leave it! That's enough!'

Three came to her senses. Standing in front of her was a tall, burly young man in a white uniform with words 'Yangzi Delta Hotel' printed on it.

'Muckraking, are you, with your little pieces of muck?' continued the man. 'Whoever's seen a bug that's been through the wok and come out alive? Or one with the mud still on it for that matter?'

The young man carefully removed the wriggling worm from the plate of greens and held it up for everyone to see.

'I'm a cook, but this is the first time I've come across a worm that's been through hot oil and can still move. Now think about it, lads. The owners of this restaurant aren't here right now, but I'll bet that, as soon as they get back, they'll go straight to their mates in the police. That's right: their mates. These days you don't get to open a shop by sheer hard work: you need a bit of help from your friends. When the cops arrive, you guys'll be trapped here, and when they go through your pockets, they'll find the mud left behind from carrying that worm with you. Now, I'm sure it's our fate to be friends, and a good friend doesn't like to witness another in distress . . . If I were you I'd hop it while you've still got the chance . . .'

At that moment, Wang Tong's voice could be heard calling through the crowd.

'Let me through, what's happened? Why are you all standing around gawping? Move over, let me in! What do you mean what am I shoving for? This is my restaurant! What are *you* shoving for? I'll call the police! What d'you mean bugs in the vegetables? Even if there was a ghost in the vegetables you still couldn't keep me out of my own restaurant! Out of the way, there! Three, Three!'

As soon as Three heard Wang Tong's voice, she dissolved into tears.

Wang Tong got out her mobile phone in a show of calling the police while the young man began shooing away the crowd of spectators. Three was so overwhelmed by anxiety that she was hyperventilating and couldn't speak. By the time Wang Tong had ascertained from the young man what had happened, the three troublemakers had slipped away.

'Why did you let them go?' she asked, distressed. 'We should have handed them over to the police!'

'Madam,' said the man as he rearranged the tables that had been shoved to the edges of the room by the crowd, 'this is a terrible business and the police should be informed about it. But I'm not sure whether they'd have done anything if they'd come here. You know what the police are like: they can't cope with big things and won't deal with small things. I'm sure you've got good connections in the right places, but why draw them into a small matter like this? Odds are, someone hired those thugs to cause trouble. Things are changing fast round here and there are people who are jealous of the success and good luck of others. I'm from the countryside. Before I came to Nanjing, I used to think that city people were different from country people, but now I've worked here for a few years I've discovered they're all just the same. If someone is having problems, they all crowd round pretending to be sympathetic, but actually, deep down, they're quite pleased because it makes them feel better about themselves. That's why good news rarely makes it to your door, but bad news flies like the wind. If you ask me, today's business is a good sign: it is a measure of your restaurant's success that people are jealous of it. You might even attract customers now, because the clever ones will realise that the food you serve is free of pesticides. Have you heard? These days, rich people are telling their servants to buy vegetables *with* wormholes . . . Anyway, I think this girl here was really on the ball. Anyone else would have hidden in the kitchen while they smashed the place up. If she hadn't handled things so well, they could have destroyed your restaurant. She's very brave.'

Three looked at the man in surprise. She had never imagined someone would call her brave when she had been almost too upset to cry or breathe. Overcome by shame, she thanked him for his help, but begged him not to trouble himself any more.

'That's right, we can manage, thank you,' said the cook who had suddenly reappeared. 'I was in the toilet when those men started shouting, but I'm here now.'

Wang Tong and Three kept quiet. They were both certain that the cook, who had always been rather a coward and hated trouble, had hidden himself away during the fracas. But they did not say anything: for a Chinese man, losing face is worse than a beating.

It was only then that it occurred to Wang Tong to ask the young man's name.

'Forgive me, sir,' she said. 'I've been so angry that I forgot to ask what our benefactor is called!'

'No need to apologise. The name's Ma, but everyone calls me Big Ma. I come from Anhui.'

Three's eyes lit up. 'Whereabouts in Anhui? I'm from Anhui too!'

'Well, they say that fellow countrymen greet each other with tears in their eyes,' laughed Big Ma, 'but I think it means a different kind of tears!'

He had a big, infectious laugh and, to her embarrassment, Three found herself laughing too.

Wang Tong bustled around them arranging chairs. 'Let's all sit down and have a drink together,' she said. 'Since you're from Anhui too, Big Ma, that makes you practically family! I'll put up the Closed sign and Wang, our cook, can bring you a few dishes. We'll open again this afternoon, but for the moment we all need to get over the shock, otherwise our good luck won't return. Doesn't everyone say that "the God of Wealth doesn't find those who aren't easy in their minds"? Let's all raise a glass to our new friend Big Ma and our clever Three!'

Big Ma gave the hotel where he worked a quick ring and arranged to come back later. He confessed that he wasn't actually a chef, but a hotel driver, and had been out collecting the dry cleaning. Then they all settled down for an enjoyable lunch.

It was past two o'clock when they finished, but the suppertime rush wouldn't start until five. Wang Tong suggested that Three take Big Ma to his van, then go for a little walk before starting work again. Three was only too happy to go with her rescuer and followed him into the street.

It was the first time since Three was a little girl that she had accompanied a man through bustling crowds. She was very proud to have met Big Ma, but, at the same time, she was worried that, if someone she knew saw them, she would lose her reputation. After all, for a girl to walk by the side of a man could only mean one thing. She wondered what would happen if she met a customer from the restaurant and they asked her who he was and how they had met. How would she answer the question?

It was as if Big Ma knew what she was thinking.

'You know, I was planning to buy myself a birthday lunch today, at the Kentucky Fried Chicken next door to your shop,' he said.

'Is today your birthday?'

'Yes, it's my birthday. And now you're the first friend in this city to know, apart from the personnel manager at the hotel who took my details for his records.'

'Do I count as your friend?'

'Of course you're a friend. Anyone from Anhui is a friend of mine.'

'What gave you the idea of coming to our restaurant instead of going to Kentucky Fried

Chicken?'

'Well, it wasn't exactly my idea. I was walking past when I saw a big crowd and heard someone shout, "Seems like there's some fooling around going on in the Happy Fool." The name of the restaurant sounded familiar so I pushed to the front out of curiosity to see what was going on. At first I thought I ought to keep my head down because country boys shouldn't rub city people up the wrong way. I was just about to leave when an old guy next to me mentioned that the girl inside was from Anhui. Well, I couldn't not get involved then. So I tried a bit of bluff. I can't say I know much about cooking—apart from making myself the odd bowl of noodles and chopping up meat to eat in flatbread—but I could see that worm had been planted the minute I clapped eyes on it. It was obvious where they'd smeared the mud across the leaves themselves.'

'*I* didn't see anything . . .' said Three, shamefacedly.

Big Ma laughed. 'I thought it was strange that you hadn't noticed. Looks like you were scared out of your wits, getting picked on like that.'

'How did you come to the city to work?' Three wished she could learn everything about this man at once.

'Well, I used to love driving the tractor at home so I persuaded relatives to help me find a job delivering goods in the local town. It was great driving through the streets and looking around: one day there'd be a wedding, the next day a new general store would open. They were always putting up new buildings or widening the roads . . . You wouldn't believe how much that town changed in the two and a half years I was there. Later on I found a friend to help me take the test for my driving licence . . .'

'Driving licence?' Three didn't know what he was talking about.

'A driving licence is a little book that proves you've passed your driving test. You need it before you're allowed to drive on the roads otherwise you can get sent to prison.'

'But why did you need a friend to help you get it?' Three asked.

'We casual labourers don't get anywhere without a few friends in the right places. Those driving test officials have deep pockets: if you don't have connections, you might as well throw your money into a bottomless pit. Of course, I'm not saying your friends can help you with the actual driving. When you do that test there are traffic police watching and it all has to be above board. But there's also a written test and, if you've got a friend, they can help you understand what the questions mean, and the examiner will turn a blind eye if you just copy out the answers.

'Anyway, when I'd got my grown-up driving

licence, I thought I should start earning some grown-up money. I knew you could earn big salaries down in the south, but you had to get someone to put in a good word for you. So I decided to start closer to home. I'd heard Nanjing was a rich city—emperors had lived there—so I went to check it out. My luck was in. The job centre near the big willow found me a position loading and unloading delivery vans for a chain store. But it was hard work. Every box weighed fifty kilos, and I had to lift more than five hundred boxes a day. Later on some of my mates heard I had a driving licence and helped me get myself into the small ads in the newspaper as a driver . . .'

'Why did you have to be in the newspaper to find a job?' Three asked. She was embarrassed about all the questions she was asking, but Big Ma seemed to be a very patient person.

'People pay attention to what's in the papers. It's a bit more reliable than the job centre. Anyone who advertises there is bona fide, if you know what I mean.'

Three wasn't sure that she did, but she was curious now about newspapers.

'Where do you get this paper?' she asked.

'You have to buy one, of course. The best one is the *Evening News*. It costs one yuan a throw.'

'One yuan!' Three exlaimed. 'You could buy half a meal with that!'

'Too expensive for you, eh? It's not

240

expensive if you find a good job. Take this five-star hotel where I work. The wages are more than twice what I got at the chain store, it's not tiring, and I get to drive; we have fixed working hours, and there are statutory public holidays.'

'Statutory public holidays?' Three was in awe of how much Big Ma knew.

'Statutory public holidays are rest days set down by the government. If you add in the days off that the hotel gives, that makes over sixty free days a year. We can take those days off at harvest time to go home and help bring in the wheat. Of course, we can go home for Spring Festival too if we want. But we can't always take the same periods off each year. It wouldn't do for all the staff at the hotel to be on holiday at the same time, so we have to rotate . . . And you? Do you go home for Spring Festival? How long have you been working in Nanjing?'

Big Ma listened carefully as Three explained that her uncle had helped her find a job in the city, but that he himself worked in Zhuhai. The next time she would see him would be when they both returned home for Spring Festival. Three was so busy talking about her new life at the Happy Fool that they made a complete circuit of the Confucius Temple without her noticing. It was only when Big Ma said that he ought to get back to the hotel that she realised the time.

'Do you often come to the Confucius Temple for deliveries?' she asked hopefully.

'Sure,' said Big Ma with a smile, 'I'm over here a lot. There's a well-known dry cleaner's in Red Guard Lane. Our hotel sends loads of stuff there. When you have the same day off as me, I'll take you out. You can tell me all about the art of arranging vegetables. Can you arrange flowers too? City people really like flower arrangements!' Big Ma began fishing out his keys as he walked towards a white minivan. As he started the engine he shouted to Three through the window: 'I'll take you for a spin out to the Sun Yatsen Mausoleum sometime. Bye!'

Three raised her hand in farewell as the van sped into the distance. It was a long time before she let it fall. Then she rushed back to the Happy Fool to ask Wang Tong where she could find books about flower arranging. If Big Ma thought she should know what flower arranging was, then she should. Any craft Big Ma was interested in, she would learn.

*   *   *

Big Ma and Three saw each other several times over the next few weeks. Their conversations were slightly awkward because Three was so shy, but if they stuck to the subject of flower arranging, everything went well. Big Ma would do his best to reply to

242

Three's torrent of questions: 'Who takes care of all the house plants and flower arrangements in your hotel? Can you make flower arrangements in winter? What are hothouse flowers like? Why do foreigners like dried flowers . . . Don't they realise that flowers are at their best with the dew still on them? If city people love flowers so much why do they separate them from their roots? Can a flower stuck in a vase be as pretty as a flower growing in a field? If you put different smelling flowers together, won't the scents all get muddled up? Why do you say flowers are like women?'

The two of them visited parks and botanical gardens to look at the flowers, and went to bookshops in search of flower-arranging manuals. But there was one place that Three longed to see, but to which Big Ma never took her: his hotel. She thought of asking him, but felt too embarrassed. After all, her mother said that unripe fruit was good to look at but not to eat: you had to wait until it was ripe for it to be truly delicious. Three thought she ought to wait for the day when Big Ma offered to take her to see his hotel.

Even when she was not with him, Big Ma occupied a lot of space in Three's head. One day Wang Tong asked her what she was daydreaming about. She was worried that Three had become quieter since her encounter with the worm-wielding thugs. 'Are you still bothered by that business the other day?' she asked.

'No, it's nothing like that . . .' muttered Three, trying to dry up the glasses in front of her as nonchalantly as possible. 'Only . . . What is love?'

Wang Tong's lips curved into a smile, but she spoke as if this was the kind of thing they always talked about. 'Love is being happy when you see a person and sad when you don't. Why? Have you fallen in love with someone and not told me?'

'No, no . . .' said Three blushing. 'Don't worry. When I have, you'll be the first to know, all right?'

In fact, Three longed to tell someone she had fallen in love. She thought of confessing to her sisters, but she was worried that they would start asking her questions she couldn't answer. Even now, she didn't know who Big Ma's family were, or what they did, nor did she fully understand Big Ma's character or why he behaved in certain ways. If her two nosy little sisters started interrogating her, what would she say? The only thing she knew for certain was that this feeling had nothing to do with rutting animals, as she had once thought. Big Ma had not so much as touched the tips of her fingers, but Three already felt that she belonged to him. She had given him her heart. She was sure her mother and father had never experienced anything like this. If her father

244

had, he wouldn't treat her mother like a lump of rock. And how could her mother have felt these things when she was simply 'taken' from her parents? Three wanted so much to run home and whisper her secret in her mother's ear: your stone daughter has burst into flower!

But it seemed that Three was living an illusion . . .

One day, she had arranged to meet Six after lunch outside the bargain warehouse to the east of the Confucius Temple. The plan was to do some shopping there before going on to the Dragon Water-Culture Centre to pick up Five, who wouldn't be free until later. The girls had heard from city people that this was the best time of year to pick up bargains; the same goods would go for several times the price in the month before Spring Festival. They wanted to find some presents to take home when the holiday came. The two sisters were just greeting each other in front of the warehouse when Three spotted Big Ma going in through another entrance. Her heart skipped a beat. There was a girl at his side! For a moment Three couldn't move for shock. Then she started thinking. Perhaps it hadn't been Big Ma after all. Grabbing Six's hand she persuaded her to go straight into the warehouse so that they didn't miss any bargains. She couldn't rest until she had found out whether it really was Big Ma that she had seen.

The warehouse was three storeys high and crammed full of stalls selling pretty, eye-catching things in every imaginable shape and colour. Shoppers had to squeeze through the narrow gaps between stalls, and the sound of haggling was deafening. Men bellowed, women screeched and little children wailed and shrieked. It was as if all of Nanjing's small traders had squashed themselves into the building. Six was thrilled, and immediately headed for the bargain clothing stalls where the prices were slashed through with big red crosses. She was so caught up with trying to decide what to buy for her mother and father, and what her married sister and Four might like, that it was some time before she realised that Three was no longer at her side.

The poor girl was pushing her way through the crowds, her heart crying out to Big Ma. She desperately wanted to find him, but at the same time she was afraid to. Eventually she caught sight of his tall, burly figure standing by a rail of trousers. Sure enough, there was a girl beside him, laughing and chatting away. One of Big Ma's hands was even resting on her shoulder! In that instant Three felt her blood turn to ice, and a chill creep from her head to her heels. The bright colours of the building faded to grey; the noise and bustle vanished, leaving only an awful stillness. She thought she could feel herself dissolving.

When Six caught up with her sister she

barely recognised her. Three, who five minutes before had been vibrant and happy, had suddenly lost all colour. There was not a trace of life on her face, no gleam of humanity in her eyes. She didn't even answer her sister's questions.

Six hastily helped Three outside, sat her down on the warehouse steps, and bought a bottle of iced water to bathe her palms and forehead. After a while, Three heaved a sigh and tears began to trickle down her cheeks. Six asked her what was the matter, but Three would not answer, saying only that she wanted to go home straightaway. Then she walked off without so much as a backward glance. Puzzled and confused, Six went to meet Five, who still couldn't go out by herself, wondering all the while what could have happened to her big sister.

Three went back to her little room and cried bitterly. Why had Big Ma not told her he had a girlfriend? Why couldn't he see what was in her heart? It had never occurred to her that Big Ma would take her out for any other reason than romantic interest. In her village, no man would be seen with a girl unless this was the case.

Suddenly the world of the city, which Three had thought she was beginning to understand, became a harsh and alien place with incomprehensible rules of its own.

Three tossed and turned all night, and the

next day she made such a mess of the restaurant's display, breaking the stems of vegetables and squashing the melon, that the cook had to nip out for extra supplies while Wang Tong was looking the other way. It was the time of year when the market was filled with wonderful peaches. Usually Three adored inventing new ways to hang these fruits on the wall, but today she just couldn't think what to do. She spent the day listlessly watching the customers come and go. That night, and for many more, she soaked her pillow in tears.

10

ENGLISH LESSONS

For the next two months dark clouds covered Three's sky. She became silent and withdrawn, and had no enthusiasm for her work. If Big Ma came to the restaurant to ask her to go out, she hid in the kitchen and asked the cook to pass on a message that she was busy. On her days off, she stayed in her room and didn't see her sisters.

Wang Tong was worried. When Three had come back early from her day off, she had assumed the sisters had had a row that would blow over. But Three's mood didn't improve for several days so she phoned the Book Taster's Teahouse to speak to Six about it. After hearing from Six that she had no idea what was the matter with her sister, Wang Tong began to think again. Slowly she came to the conclusion that it must have something to do with Big Ma. She asked her husband how he thought she should help Three. 'Imagine coming to a city like Nanjing when you had never seen a television or a car,' she said to him. 'Her heart is like a blank sheet of paper, ready to absorb whatever lands there.'

Guan Buyan discussed the matter with his father and brother.

'Remember the expression "marry the dog and follow the dog, marry the cock and follow the cock",' said Old Guan. 'Once a girl marries, she forgets her past and gives everything to her husband. If you really want to help this little girl, introduce her to a husband. Time will do the rest.'

His brother Guan Buyu agreed. 'People are always saying that a first love is for ever, but that's nonsense. Find her another young man and she'll be much better.'

And so Buyan, Buyu and several other well-meaning people from under the big willow tried repeatedly to introduce Three to different young men. But it was no use: nobody could be as good as Big Ma and Three didn't want to meet any of them.

Wang Tong was at her wits' end. She couldn't bear to see Three wasting away in front of her, but nor could she think how to help. She was certain she had to find a way to get Three to talk to someone about her pain, but she couldn't persuade her to go out with her sisters. In the end it was a festival that provided her with the opportunity she needed. Three had always felt a responsibility to help her younger sisters understand life in the city, Wang Tong knew this, so she made use of the coming Double Ninth Festival to half coax, half order Three to meet up with Five and Six. 'How will they know how to celebrate the festival if you don't tell them?' she said encouragingly. 'Why don't you all go to the Qifangge Snack Bar and have a good chat.'

Five and Six had not seen their sister for almost two months, and were shocked by how much she had changed. Three, who had always been so rosy-cheeked and sturdy, had become almost unrecognisable. Her face was grey and lifeless, her shoulders were hunched, and she had lost so much weight that her bones were clearly visible through her flesh.

'Whatever's the matter with you?' asked Five. 'Six said we shouldn't disturb you. She had an idea that you were courting because the cook at your restaurant told her secretly. But how can courting wear a body out like this?'

When Three saw her sisters' concern and pity, she burst into tears, even though she thought she had wept herself dry. Over a meal of duck-blood soup, tofu stewed with meat, and rice-balls with osmanthus flowers, she told them the whole story. Tears dripped into her food as she talked about how she had thought Big Ma was her boyfriend. Five and Six cried too. They were all so overwrought that they took three hours to finish three tiny bowls of snacks, much to the displeasure of the waiters who were annoyed that three migrant worker girls could hog a profitable table after spending only a few yuan. As for the tears, the waiters weren't particularly surprised: the Double Ninth Festival was when Nanjingers honoured the older generations, and around

251

that time, there was always the odd person weeping into their soup over their dead parents.

Five and Six were at a loss as to how to console their sister. It seemed to them that there was little they could say to make her feel better. So, instead, they tried to make jokes to take her mind off things. The fact that there were so many festivals in the city but no one seemed to know exactly how to celebrate them, made them laugh.

'All the books about ancient folk customs were burned after 1949,' said Six, wisely, 'and now there are very few old people who remember them. That's why it's so confusing. Do you remember how Bao Daye in our village used to say that the Double Ninth Festival was about old city people climbing high hills and looking into the distance, hoping for long life, but Uncle Two said everyone in Zhuhai ate rice cakes with red letters on to bring good luck? And here in Nanjing they keep changing their minds. One minute they are buying chrysanthemums, the next they're saying that you need branches of dogwood to "drive off evil"!'

For the next half an hour, Five and Six entertained their sister with extravagant and humorous guesses about what each of the city festivals was supposed to mean, until eventually her gaunt face broke into a faint smile. But when they parted, they could see that the smile was already fading.

*   *   *

Back at work, Five and Six both reflected on their elder sister's experience. Their reactions were very different. Five was furiously indignant on Three's behalf. To her, the whole thing was cut and dried: Big Ma was a bad man of the sort her mother had always talked about. The kind of man who wanted a foot in two boats or to wangle food out of two families. Five was surprised that Three had put so much trust in him. Surely her older sister had been in the city for long enough to have looked for a man before; so many people liked her, praising her nimble hands and saying she was as quick on the uptake as any city girl. Besides, Nanjing was such a big place, with so many men. Why was she determined to hang herself from this one tree? Their father said that, if a dog had gone hungry for three days, it would abandon its master and go to others for food. It seemed impossible to Five that Three had never thought about a man before Big Ma, or that she could be so foolish as to continue to pine for him now that he had proved himself so faithless.

The way Six saw it, Three was not nearly as 'citified' as Five thought she was. For all her success at the Happy Fool, Three still had no real knowledge of urban life. If she had, she

253

wouldn't have mistaken Big Ma's friendliness for love. It was clear he had simply been trying to help her get a better paid job. Six remembered conversations with Three where she had talked in confusion about the 'Three Cs' of the city: cars, computers and credit cards. While Three vaguely understood about cars (although she couldn't think why anyone would buy something that cost so much in taxes, fines and parking fees), she had never got to grips with the idea of computers and credit cards. Six saw that, however long Three stayed in the city, she would never shake off the peasant mentality that had been drummed into her since birth. Even though she didn't want to repeat the anguish of her parents' generation, she couldn't escape the fact that, for an uneducted countrywoman, the goal of life was a husband: a prop to support her, the sun in her sky. The only way a peasant woman could prove her worth was by bearing children and doing housework. So it was that, as soon as Three believed that Big Ma was her own, her virgin heart was lost.

Of course, Six didn't discuss her opinion with Five. If anything, Five was an even more hopeless case. Six still giggled when she thought of the incredible knots Five had tied herself in when trying to explain how businessmen used the conference rooms at the Dragon Water-Culture Centre. 'They've got these magic rooms,' Five had said. 'They're full of televisions, "kara"-something machines that can make people sing, and electric brains . . . Auntie Wang says we're going to open two meeting rooms that can change talk.'

'Change talk?' Six had asked, intrigued.

'You know, change foreigners' talk into the words we speak . . . I think it's called "trans"-something . . .'

'Translate,' Six had supplied helpfully.

It wasn't that Six herself had known what 'multimedia' rooms were when Five had first tried to explain them. But her education had given her the ability to find out about things she didn't know. Her school had been her secret life. She was the only girl in her village to go to middle school, and she had rapidly realised that the boys who attended the school never spoke at home about the books they were reading. She could understand why: their families, who did not even know one end of a book from another, would have no idea what these books were talking about. To village people, even the local town, with its one short street and dozen little shops, was almost a foreign country. At first Six had been puzzled as to why her two uncles, who were members of the Production Brigade and went regularly to the town, did not think to tell everyone about their experiences outside the village. Then, one day, she had asked her Uncle Three this question, and received the following response:

'Silly girl, if people don't have anyone to compare themselves to, they don't know they're being wronged. It's comparisons that make people unhappy: those who don't know good fortune, don't know poverty. We're so poor here that even the town officials don't want to visit us. Why would they? What's in it for them? A mouthful of salty water and a lump of steamed sweet-potato bread . . . If I went around talking about other people's rich lives to everyone, do you think I would be popular? The less people have to worry about, the better. They may be poor, but they're at peace. They don't make trouble, and that's the most important thing. Listen to old men talking about fighting the Japs, or the Revolution; or their sons remembering the Great Leap Forward and the Cultural Revolution: as soon as anyone starts stirring things up, the peasants suffer. Take all these economic changes—what's the betting that they make things worse? Who'll farm the land if everyone's off doing business? And do we really think we can beat foreigners at their own game? As soon as the Boxer Rebellion started—as I've heard it, because the Chinese were wanting to lead a better life—the foreigners cut off more than a dozen heads in this village! No . . . As long as the days pass peacefully and we've got food and clothes, it's best just to keep out of trouble. Keep what you learn to yourself, I tell you. Leave if you're

256

able, and find yourself a husband outside. If you can't leave, then live your live in poverty but at peace. Happiness is accepting your fate . . .'

As soon as she had heard these words from Uncle Three, Six decided that, one day, she would leave the village to see the city, like Uncle Two and many of her male classmates. But now that she was in the city, and she had met people like Ruth, she realised that the city was just a springboard to the rest of the world. Five and Three would never understand things in the way she did. Five was too ignorant to realise that the people in the Dragon Water-Culture Centre weren't all 'kind and good', they were just pitying her. And Three had tragically failed to realise that Big Ma was just being kind because she came from Anhui: she had been like a thirsty plant who took a drop of water for rain.

There was a saying in the countryside: 'When a man goes to the city, the first thing he learns is how to spend money on women; when a woman goes to the city, the first thing she learns is how to look men in the eye.' But, having seen for herself how peasants behaved in the city, Six wasn't sure they really learned anything: their city skills were like flowers cut for decoration—destined to wither without their roots. *She*, however, was determined to get a proper education—to cross the river, even if it meant taking things one stepping-stone at a time. As her mother always said in times of great difficulty and distress: 'There is no road under heaven that cannot be walked; even stones carry the footprints of insects!'

Six had heard one of Shu Kang's university friends talk about the 'Three Modern Items' essential for life in the twenty-first century: computing, driving and English. It seemed to Six that, of these three skills, English was the most important. After all, Shu Kang had said that English was 'the mouse of the computer, and the steering wheel of the car'. Six felt that, if she could master English, she would be well on the way to building her bridge across the river. But, as things stood at the moment, her English was less a stepping-stone and more a pebble. She had to face it: the pronunciation difficulties she had when she spoke Mandarin, rather than village dialect, were as nothing compared to her problems with English sounds. They made her feel as if there were weights tied to her tongue, and her garbled efforts were often greeted with giggles: '*No, no,*' Ruth would say kindly. ' "*Shit*" *is for swearing, not wearing. A "shirt" is for wearing.*' Nevertheless, Six was absolutely determined. She would never allow the fate of her mother and her elder sisters to become her own. She would perfect her English.

It did not cross Six's mind that she should use the money she was putting aside for her mother to pay for English lessons. Nor would she accept charity from her employers, even though Thick Glasses and Meng had offered to help. She kept firmly in mind her mother's words: you can't depend on others to build your reputation; you must earn it for yourself with your own heart and brain. So Six studied English in her own way. First she memorised new words, then she put the words together in the only way she knew how (following Chinese sentence structure), then she fearlessly engaged Ruth and her foreign friends in conversation. At first the foreigners would fall about laughing at her odd word order. She would say things like, 'We everyday in teahouse with friends drink tea'. Gradually, however, the foreigners realised that 'Six's English' could help them with their Chinese. Although they would correct her sentence structure, they took note of the word order she had used and applied it when they formed Chinese sentences. They also realised that Six's tendency to translate bits of Chinese slang and everyday phrases directly into English could help them understand colloquial Chinese. When Six said things like, *'People mountain, people sea'*, *'Morning three night four'*, *'Wang eight eggs'*, *'Wield a big knife in front of General Guangong'* or (everyone's favourite) Mao's phrase, *'Good good study, day day up'*, they would quiz her about what exactly the phrase meant in Chinese until they managed to create a dictionary:

People mountain, people sea—Great crowds of people

Morning three night four—Blow hot and cold

Wang eight eggs—Bastard

Wield a big knife in front of General Guangong—Show off

Good good study, day day up—Study hard so as to make progress every day

Eventually, Six too began to see the funny side of this 'east-west mixture'. When someone said something like *'I'll give you some colour to see see'* (I'll show you!), she would burst into giggles.

Shu Kang and Ruth's foreign friends all liked Six very much. They found her very different from the Chinese students they met at the university. The offspring of one-child families, these students had been the kings of their little families since they were born and had been so hothoused that they had lost the instinct for being interested in things. Perhaps their parents, who had toiled and suffered to satisfy their only sons or daughters, had never even thought to cultivate that interest in the first place. A life where everything these young people wanted was theirs for the taking had warped their innate desire for struggle and new experiences. To Ruth and her friends, Six's eagerness to learn about the world was refreshing.

For her part, Six observed the Chinese students with great interest. In her dull, quiet village, she could never have imagined that there were so many sources of pleasure and amusement available to young people. These students showed her how youth could be a carefree time—free of worry and concerns— but they also gave her the impression that university students could go anywhere in the world: there was nothing they could not do and no words they could not say. Therefore, every time a group of young people had been to the teahouse, Six would go over to the visitors' notebook and, if there were no other customers, read aloud the things they had written.

One day, she watched a group of students fall about laughing over something in the book. When they had gone, she was so eager to see what it was that she asked Meng's permission to go and read it, even though there were still two customers in the teahouse. Meng had become familiar with Six's obsession with the notebook and was happy to indulge it. She nodded kindly and Six began to read:

In recent days our university has been swept by a fad for ultra-short skirts, each shorter than the last. Leader X considers this to be in extremely poor taste, and has therefore put up a notice banning short skirts on the university board. Ever since the announcement went up, it has caused a great furore and students have begun pinning responses to the board. The first came from a girl in the Chinese department who wrote a delightful poem:

Knives are out all over the school
Just because of the short-skirt rule
Who's showing wisdom in this case?
The noticeboard will reveal their face.

The second to make their mark on the notice board were the school medics:

The common cold is caused by a virus, not by the COLD.

Those sharp-eyed guardians of books in the library wrote:

Let ultra-short skirts be fashionable!
With so little space to hide books, we can give our eyes a rest.

After careful consideration, the canteen daubed their contribution:

There's no difference between short skirts and spare ribs: both shrink when in contact with water.

During the lunch break all the other departments in the university wrote their own views:

FINE ART DEPT: *Venus de Milo proves that a tasteful lack in certain areas can be even more beautiful.*
ENVIRONMENTAL STUDIES DEPT: *Surely you aren't trying to tell us global warming is a myth?*
MATHS DEPT: *If we allow the existence of a rectangle 1m in length, then there is no logical reason for a square 0.3 metres in length not to exist.*
HISTORY DEPT: *Helen of Troy's beauty did not change because Churchill and Hitler had different tastes.*
PHYSICS DEPT: *Cloth may be an insulator against bad taste, but air is an excellent insulator too.*
LAW DEPT: *The law exists to protect us against the evil thoughts brought out in the accuser by short skirts, not the short skirts of the defendants.*
BIOLOGY DEPT: *The basic difference between humans and apes is not the length of skirts, but the different thoughts induced by long and short skirts.*
POLITICS DEPT: *The move from long skirts to short skirts and on to ultra-mini skirts, is an embodiment of a democratised*

collective.

PUBLIC RELATIONS DEPT: *Lowering the vision of the other party in negations is the very thing we've been striving so hard to achieve all these years.*

Finally, the Association of Low-Income Students added:

Give us bigger bursaries!
We're so poor our clothes don't cover our bodies.

When Six finished reading, everyone in the teahouse burst out laughing. She had no idea why. The effort of reading had prevented her from following the meaning of the words. But even if she had, it was unlikely that she would have understood the innuendo-laden humour.

Most jokes were still a mystery to Six, but she was gradually beginning to understand the concept of humour. A Danish student had shown her how pain can be changed into happiness through laughter. She had met this student when he brought a carton of ice-cream into the teahouse and asked if she wanted to try some. Six had been delighted at the idea of sampling this famous American food that she had heard so much about, but the first mouthful sent her into shock: it was so cold that the nerves above her eyes throbbed in agony. The Dane had taken Six's face in both

264

hands, saying, 'What are wrong, Little Six? Is your face hurting?' No man's hands had ever touched Six's face before and she felt instantly dizzy, as if her body were melting away. She became fascinated by this man with kind hands and a kind nature, and so tried to help him with his Chinese as much as possible. It was when they were doing an exercise on the subject of 'mothers' that he showed her how surprising humour can be.

'My mother is very thin,' Six said slowly, so he could understand, 'but she holds up the whole house. My mother has never been to school, but she has taught us all how to live. My mother does not love beauty for herself, but she has raised six beautiful daughters. My mother is not talkative, but every word she says helps you understand life. My mother is very hard-working, but she has never made anything nice for herself to eat or wear. My mother is very brave, but she often cries because she doesn't have a son . . .'

'Six, you have spoken about your mother so beautifully,' said the Danish man (he spoke such bad Chinese that he pronounced 'mother' as 'horse'). 'Do you want to hear about mine?

'My mother is very fat, she has a belt for a watchstrap. My mother is very fat, her waistline is like a race track. My mother is very fat, when she goes for a paddle at the seaside it has an effect on the tides. My mother is very fat, when she goes to the beauty parlour it takes them twelve hours to give her a facial. My mother is very fat . . .'

Before he had finished, Six's tears had turned to laughter.

Six encountered a great deal of humour of this kind, as well as ideas that were very different from those of Chinese people. Once, an English girl left a piece of homework with her so that she could correct the Chinese. She liked it so much that she copied it out and stuck it over her bed:

Money can buy a bed, but it can't buy good sleep.
Money can buy a house, but it can't buy a home.
Money can buy food, but it can't buy flavour,
Money can buy a gym, but it can't buy health,
Money can be used for trade, but it can't buy friends,
Money can buy qualifications, but it can't buy ambition.

Six often asked Meng about the things she was learning. One day she asked her about jokes. 'Why do people want to invent so many of them?' she wanted to know.

'Because they like to laugh,' was Meng's first, casual response, but when she saw that Six wasn't satisfied with this answer, she elaborated. 'Chinese people don't have much happiness to talk about. Their lives have been full of tears, troubles and bitterness, and their memories provide few opportunities to smile. Without salt, food has no flavour; without laughter, people are boring. If we don't claw a few laughs out of our lives—even if those laughs are bitter chuckles, cold smirks, foolish giggles or idiot grins—then the great Chinese tradition of wit and wisdom will lie down and die. Laughter is like chopsticks. Without chopsticks the traditional Chinese way of life would be gone. The same goes for our sense of humour. Your father may say that his family line will end because he only has a handful of "chopsticks", but chopsticks are essential to life.' Meng gave a sigh. 'Actually, I don't think Chinese women have learned to laugh enough. It's a firmly held belief in our culture that a good woman does not laugh or cry—but, until we do so, we can't be truly good women.'

Six thought a lot about what Meng had said. She was full of admiration for the cleverness of her reasoning. But, if Meng was right, why was it that her parents and her teachers had always said, 'Laughter is a sickness: when a man laughs he's playing the fool; when a woman laughs she's playing the strumpet'? Was it because village people were poor and city people rich? Or because they had different definitions of laughter? It seemed to Six that it was the latter. And perhaps those different

267

definitions even made city people look completely different from village people, so that when you walked down the street in Nanjing, you could tell at a glance who had come from the broad avenues of the city and who from the muddy tracks of the country.

She wondered, too, about what Meng meant by a 'truly good woman'. Her mother never laughed. Did this mean she wasn't 'truly good'? People in the city seemed to have so many ideas about women that it was hard to know what to believe. She had read something in the visitors' notebook that had preoccupied her for days.

The Differences Between Male and Female Workers in the Eyes of the Boss

- *When the boss sees a male subordinate with a family photo on the desk, the boss thinks, 'Hmm . . . He must be a good, responsible man who takes care of his family.' When the boss sees a female subordinate with a family photo on her desk, the boss thinks, 'Hmm . . . work isn't the most important thing in her life, no point in expecting her to put her heart into the company.'*

- *When the boss sees a male subordinate with an untidy desk, the boss thinks, 'He's so industrious! Look, he doesn't even have time to tidy his desk.' When the boss sees a female subordinate with an untidy desk, the boss thinks, 'Look at that! She's clearly got no organisational ability!'*

- *When the boss sees a male subordinate talking to his colleagues, the boss thinks, 'He must be discussing recent business developments. That's the spirit!' When the boss sees a female subordinate talking to her colleagues, the boss thinks, 'Humph, she's gossiping and finding fault again. Oh well, it's in women's nature to have long tongues.'*

- *When the boss sees that a male subordinate is about to get promoted by his manager, the boss thinks, 'This man must have great potential.' When the boss sees that a female subordinate is about to get promoted by her manager, the boss thinks, 'This woman must be having a thing with the director.'*

- *When the boss sees a male subordinate arrive late, the boss thinks, 'Was he burning the midnight oil again last night?' When the boss sees a female subordinate arrive late, the boss thinks, 'Did her husband want it again last night? Or have they just . . .'*

269

- *When the boss sees a male subordinate hand out wedding invitations, the boss thinks, 'He'll be more responsible now. Let's give him a big red envelope of lucky money as a bonus to encourage him.' When the boss sees a female subordinate hand out wedding invitations the boss thinks, 'Let's not make her red envelope too big. Soon she'll get herself pregnant, take two months' maternity leave, and end up quitting her job to look after the kid.'*

- *When the boss sees a male subordinate leave for a better job, the boss thinks, 'Here's a man who understands how to make the most of a good opportunity. Too bad the company can't keep him.' When the boss sees a female subordinate leave for a better job, the boss thinks, 'That's women for you—untrustworthy!'*

Guess whether the boss is a man or a woman? Give me your answers please.

There were several answers written at the bottom of the page and Six saw that one of them was in Meng's handwriting. 'Boss could be either!' Meng had written. 'We say "poor women", but the boss's opinions are often given to him by his wife . . .' Six wasn't sure she

270

agreed. She wanted to add, 'It's all men's fault! They did this to women', but she thought of a phrase a customer had just taught her—'Lack of forbearance in small matters spoils great plans'—so she kept her thoughts to herself.

The next time Six met up with Five, she told her what Meng had said about only being a truly good woman if you knew how to laugh and cry. Five immediately took issue with this.

'No one in our village says Three's a good woman, do they? But she never laughs or cries. In fact, they criticise her for being made of stone *because* she doesn't laugh or cry. No, it's women who have sons who are the truly good women!'

'What about our mother then?' asked Six. 'She can't have sons, but she's not a bad woman, is she?'

'*We* may not think so, but everyone in the village does. Perhaps "good" or "bad" depends on where you are,' said Five, sagely. 'I know that everyone in the village thinks I'm stupid. Think what our mother says about me: "Three may not have woken up to her female nature, but Five hasn't woken up to anything at all"! But at the Dragon Water-Culture Centre they say I've got a miracle talent. Even the section heads, who've never admitted that country people are good for anything, say I'm a clever girl with my Four Orifices wide open . . .'

'Seven Orifices,' Six corrected her. 'It should be seven: two ears, two eyes, two nostrils and a mouth.'

'No, four,' insisted Five. 'Two nostrils, and one ear and eye. The Dragon Water-Culture Centre people say I can only get the other ear and eye and my mouth once I've been to school and learned to read . . .'

Six burst out laughing. 'They're very interesting, your Water people . . .'

'What's so funny?' said Five, crossly. 'How many people can even use four Orifices properly? If the streets were full of such people, why didn't they find anyone to check the water and the medicine before me? Even Auntie Wang has to use a thermometer! Six, d'you think you've got more Orifices open than me? Come to the medicine pools and try your luck, you'll know that your Orifices can't beat mine . . .'

Six smiled. But when she got back to the teahouse that evening, her happiness was tinged with sadness. She knew that, every day, she was learning things that would take her further and further away from her sisters. And what about her mother—her best teacher of all? Could she leave her behind? Much as she rejoiced at her entry into the world she had dreamed of, at the same time she felt a sense of loss at her fading attachment to her home . . .

In the years to come, who would understand what Six had left behind? She was like a flower from the countryside that had caught the eye of a visiting artist. The painter, photographer or poet could transform that flower with their brush, camera or words; they could bring it to the city to be hung on the walls of high-class art galleries, or preserved and cherished in albums and books. People might admire that flower, but how many of them would truly appreciate the significance of its colours and the source of its fragrance?

11

UNCLE TWO VISITS THE GATES OF HELL

One afternoon in January, Five was at the Pool of Tranquillity checking the water when Lin rushed in with a message. Five had stopped thinking of her as the Green Girl when she realised that Lin didn't always wear the same coloured clothes. After nearly a year, she was finally learning everyone's names.

'Five,' called Lin, out of breath. 'Manager Shui wants to see you! You must come at once.'

Five barely looked up from what she was doing. Since the autumn she had been the official Tester at the Dragon Water-Culture Centre and she took her duties seriously. Apart from Engineer Wu and Auntie Wang, there was no one else who could do her job, and the other staff had to wait for her say-so before using the pools. Now she was like her father, she thought: at home, nothing could happen without a 'yes' from him. Not even her clever sisters had jobs where other people had to obey them. She imagined what it would be like when she returned to the village and everyone realised that her mother hadn't given birth to a foolish child after all. They would have to respect her mother after that.

'Five!' urged Lin. 'Hurry up, it's urgent. Leave the testing to Auntie Wang and the others.' She grabbed Five's uniform and pulled her up. 'Come on, quick-fire.'

'Fire!' shouted Five in alarm. 'Is Manager Shui's office on fire?'

'No, no, not a real fire . . . "Quick-fire" means . . . Oh, never mind. Come on!'

Lin took Five's arm and frogmarched her off to Manager Shui's office, without even giving her a chance to wash her hands.

When they arrived, Five was amazed to find Three talking to Manager Shui, who was sitting at the big desk in the outer office. It was weeks since she had seen her sister and she was struck by how pale she was.

'Three, how did you get here? And why did you go straight to our Manager Shui without telling me you were coming?'

'I can't explain properly, let them tell you,' said Three, looking anxiously at Manager Shui whose huge stomach wobbled as he swivelled round on his chair.

'Now Five,' he said slowly. 'You mustn't panic when you hear what I have to say. Just listen carefully and everything will become clear . . . Now, you have an uncle who works in the south, right?'

'That's right,' said Five in surprise. 'Uncle Two.'

'Well, it seems your Uncle Two came to

275

Nanjing yesterday on his way home to Anhui. Finding that it was late and not wishing to bother anyone, the good-hearted old man unfolded his quilt in the doorway of Mr Guan Buyu's office and settled down for the night. He had just gone to sleep when he was arrested by the police.'

Five felt herself go weak with shock. 'The police have got Uncle Two?'

Manager Shui leant forward and signalled to her that she should sit down. 'As I said, don't panic until I have explained everything. He was probably arrested on charges of loitering or being an unemployed vagrant . . .'

'But that's not a serious offence, is it?' interrupted Three, to the admiration of Five who didn't know what 'charges' meant, let alone 'offence'.

'No, it's not a serious offence,' said Manager Shui calmly, 'but it gets a lot of people into trouble. Since ancient times, we Chinese have never been allowed to move about the country freely. Even when visiting friends and relations we need permits and letters of introduction. If you wish to spend a long time in a place, you must register with the local officials—that's the Production Brigade or local government in the countryside, and the work unit or police station in the city. Since the Open Policy in the eighties, country people have been permitted to come to the city to work, but the paperwork has remained the same. The police usually turn a blind eye to these formalities, but when they find themselves at a loose end, or they're short of cash, they start picking up people for things like not having a letter of introduction, working illegally, or failure to abide by the hygiene regulations, etc . . . They'll find a problem even if nothing's the matter . . .'

Five was confused. Although she understood only half of what Manager Shui was saying, it seemed to her that he was implying the police were bad, and she couldn't understand how an upstanding citizen like him could criticise the police in this way.

'Dad says the police are there to catch bad people . . .' she protested.

'And indeed they are, Five,' said Manager Shui. 'But despite their uniforms and big peaked caps, they're human too, and there are good people and bad people among them. It's like the powerful officials in the countryside: there are good ones and bad ones, right?'

'Then are the policemen who got my Uncle Two bad?' Five asked.

'I wouldn't go so far as to say that,' said Manager Shui, 'but I suspect they've made a mistake in arresting your uncle . . .'

Three looked at Manager Shui in despair. 'We're done for!' she moaned. 'My boss is always saying that you have to have connections if you want to sort out problems like this. Connections mean you can go through the back door. They make big problems small, and small problems disappear. But, if you don't have connections, then no problem becomes a problem, small problems turn into big ones, and a big problem can be the end of you. What are my sisters and I to do without connections?'

'Don't be alarmed,' said Manager Shui. 'Perhaps it was better for your uncle to spend a night in a police cell than outside in the bitter cold.'

This thought cheered Five. 'That's right,' she said. 'Uncle Two could have frozen to death otherwise!' But Three was not so easily consoled. 'He'll hardly be comfortable at the police station either!' she cried. 'Bao Daye from our village used to say that, if you spend a day in the cells, you lose a layer of flesh . . .'

'Now don't worry,' said Manager Shui, getting to his feet. 'I'm going to sort things out . . . What kind of friend do you think I am, Five, not to tell me that you had sisters working in the city? I only found out when young Three appeared in my office. Apparently, your Uncle Two told the police he knew Mr Guan Buyu. Well, when Mr Guan found out what had happened, he sent a message to Three telling her to come and find me. He knows I've got good contacts with the police. You're my best worker, Five, I'm not going to let your uncle languish in prison, am I? I've made a phone call already. They've told me to come to the police station around midday to pick him up. Since it's already almost half-past eleven, I suggest that you two come along with me to sort this out. I have to be at a government Cultural Businesses Meeting this afternoon.' As Manager Shui was speaking he shut down his computer—by now Five knew that the glass window with fishes swimming behind it was a clever electric brain that could solve all sorts of problems.

'But I've not got my money yet,' exclaimed Five, leaping out of her seat to race back to the dormitory for her savings.

'Five,' said Manager Shui, gesturing to her to stay put, 'all your money put together wouldn't come close to footing the police's bill! Now listen. You serve important people every day when they come to bathe here at the Dragon Water-Culture Centre, and they'll help us out when we need them. That means a lot to me. Let me help you this time. You just carry on working well and we'll be quits.'

'But how many years will it take me to pay you back?' Five asked anxiously.

Manager Shui burst out laughing at her earnest honesty. 'Oh, little girl . . . Just work until you don't want to work any more . . .'

Ten minutes later, Three and Five were sitting in the back of Manager Shui's black Mercedes on their way to the police cells. Five spent most of the journey with her eyes squeezed shut. She had only ever been on a bus before, and the car made her feel dangerously close to the road. Three, on the other hand, had been in Big Ma's delivery van a couple of times, and was therefore more calm. It was she who spotted her uncle as the Mercedes drove into the forecourt of the police station. He was standing just inside the building, flanked by two men who were gesturing in gratitude to the policemen inside. As the Mercedes edged nearer, caught up in a queue of cars waiting to park, Uncle Two was led out through the door, and Three saw that the two men were Guan Buyu and the boss of the teahouse, Shu Tian. Six was also with them. Without seeing the black Mercedes, they all squeezed into Shu Tian's old red Xiali and were about to set off when Manager Shui drew up beside them, wound down his window and asked, 'All settled, then?'

'You took your time, good sir!' said Shu Tian, opening his car door. 'But, as it happens, we had a big stroke of luck today, and there was no need to wait for your chariot to arrive. My broken-down Xiali sufficed.'

'Great stuff!' said Manager Shui. 'You must tell me all about it. How about coming to my place? We can have a talk and give the three sisters and their uncle a chance to get over the shock.'

'That sounds good,' shouted Guan Buyu over the revving of the Xiali's engine, 'provided I get to a meeting in a hour.'

'I've got a meeting with the City Government,' said Manager Shui, 'but I can manage a brief break . . .'

Three and Five were hardly listening. Instead they were smiling in relief at Six and Uncle Two who were sitting in the back seat of the other car.

Shu Tian agreed with Manager Shui that he would follow him back to his house. On the journey there, Guan Buyu chatted away to Six in an attempt to put Uncle Two at his ease.

'I feel guilty,' he said to her. 'I ought to have given you and your sisters a telephone number so that you could reach me if you needed me. And I should have made sure that the Tofu Lady told Uncle Two how to contact me. I'm so sorry you and your uncle had to go through such a terrifying experience. But it would be just the same for us Nanjingers if we came to the countryside. When we leave the city we're completely lost! It only takes a cow or a sheep to walk up to us and we're frightened out of our wits. What good are all our city skills if we can't even take a crap in your privies without running screaming from the pig, our trousers round our ankles? We end up cutting short our days out in the country because we're desperate for the toilet. It's the same when we go abroad, as I have done a few times. We're so scared by the different language and customs that we find ourselves jumping out of our skin if the guy next to us so much as farts.

281

No, when all's said and done, at home we're master of everything, but as soon as we arrive at a place we don't know, we turn into cowering wretches . . .'

Guan Buyu's crude words shocked Six, who couldn't equate them with the polite, cultured man she knew. However, their meaning rang all too true to Uncle Two, who rubbed his unshaven cheeks as he listened. He had been crying so hard that his face was covered in snot and tears. Yes, indeed, he had been a cowering wretch . . .

It had all come about because of something the Tofu Lady had said. All the workers were leaving Zhuhai for Spring Festival, and he and her husband had travelled back together on the train. Gousheng had offered to put him up for the night so that he could meet up with his nieces before going on to Anhui and, in the morning, Uncle Two had stopped by the Tofu Lady's shop to eat some stinky-tofu fritters. While she was serving him, they had discussed his nieces, and the Tofu Lady had mentioned that it was a while since she had seen Three. Her absence had been a matter of some debate amongst the regulars at the big willow. Some people said that she was ill, others that she'd run off with a man, but no one knew for sure. Even Mr Guan Buyu, who was always so well up on the latest news, was wondering what had become of her. They had lost track of the other two sisters as well, because they only ever came to the willow tree when Three did.

Uncle Two was so anxious when he heard this that he decided he should try to find the girls immediately. Although the Tofu Lady tried to dissuade him, assuring him that the girls were probably on their way to find him, and warning him that Nanjing was bigger than he thought, he was adamant. But when he reached the main road with its streams of heavy traffic, Uncle Two was afraid. He only knew the roads between the train station, the Tofu Lady's shop and the bus station. Now he was confronted with millions of people and hundreds and thousands of streets. Where was a peasant like him supposed to find his relatives? He got out the willow whistle Three had made him, and blew it as hard as he could, but it was now too dried out and cracked to make a noise. Uncle Two's heart was filled with foreboding, and he tried desperately to think what to do. Suddenly he remembered Mr Guan. He knew where the girls were! The big willow wasn't far from the Tofu Lady's place, so it shouldn't be too hard to find.

To his relief, Uncle Two found the tree without difficulty but again his luck failed him. Mr Guan's office was closed for the day. A passer-by said that people who had urgent business often waited for Mr Guan because he was known to come to the office in the evening to read. Uncle Two decided to bed down in the doorway. He opened one of his bags of luggage, got out the second-hand overcoat he had bought for his wife and wrapped himself in it. Then, covering his knees with the tattered padded jacket that had kept the cold night-wind off on the building site, he propped himself up in the lee of a few wooden boxes using his other bag as a pillow. As he lay there, the exhaustion of forty-eight hours on the train overcame him, and he began to snore.

He awoke with a start to a stern voice and a dazzlingly white light.

'What are you doing? ID! Letter of introduction! Get up, get up, I'm talking to you, hurry up!'

Still half asleep, Uncle Two had no idea what was going on, but he saw the peaked cap and police uniform and his instinctive reaction was to search for his papers, hidden deep in his clothes. Yet, try as he might, he couldn't extract the bulging envelope from its hiding place and the more he panicked, the more his hands shook and the harder it became to get the thing out. The policeman was becoming increasingly impatient. 'Get a move on!' he shouted. 'Stop messing around and show me your papers!'

'I . . . that is, I have documents,' stammered Uncle Two. 'I've got them all: ID card, work permit, letter of introduction . . . Bloody hell, I can't get them out . . .'

'No bad language! This is a civilised city, not like your crude, dirty countryside. Huh, are these all your documents? Is that you? You don't look like the big tough guy in the photograph with your old man's beard! And where's that woman's coat from?'

'Woman's coat?' Uncle Two was completely scared out of his wits, 'What woman's coat?'

'I'm asking the questions! So that thing draped over your shoulders isn't a woman's coat? It's been such a short time since you stole it, you haven't had a chance to look at it properly, eh?'

'This . . . this . . . I mean to say . . . it's coming back to me now. I bought it for my wife.'

'Now it comes back to you? If you'd bought it yourself, would you need to think about it? Get your things together and come with me. You country people should be planting your fields, but no: you're too busy thinking of coming to the city to make a fat profit. And when you're here, you still reckon you're not earning enough, so you pocket a bit here and a bit there to take home for Spring Festival. Aren't I right? Hey, get that woman's coat out of your bag! How dare you pack it away when you still haven't proved it's yours. Fingers still itching to nick something else, are they?'

Without waiting for an answer the policeman pulled out a strange black machine and shouted, '03, 03, this is 26, over . . . I've caught someone red-handed here. Get a move on, I'm cold, over . . . Two bags of luggage, over . . . What do you mean wait for the next van? How many have you brought in? Over . . . Well, I don't care if you have to squeeze him in. Just get here soon, it's bloody freezing today, over!'

The policeman put his machine back inside his jacket and turned to Uncle Two.

'Why are you shivering? If you're cold, put on that woman's coat of yours. We can deal with that issue when we get to the station. We policemen don't have hearts of stone, you know. It's not as if I've handcuffed you. Handcuffs on a bitterly cold day like this would freeze you to the marrow.'

'I'm . . . I'm not cold, I'm . . .' Uncle Two could scarcely get the words out.

'Not cold? Then why are you shaking? Don't tell me you're scared! If you're brave enough to commit a crime, you should have the guts to take the consequences. Don't go about thieving if you're going to get scared afterwards. If there's one thing I can't stand it's a wimp.'

'I haven't stolen anything!' shouted Uncle Two, finally finding the courage to speak up for himself.

The policeman was momentarily taken aback. 'Then what are you shaking for? An honest man doesn't jump at shadows. If you haven't stolen anything there's nothing to worry about. Just explain it all when we get to the station . . .'

'But why should I go to the police station if I haven't stolen anything?' asked Uncle Two, his brain suddenly lucid.

'Well . . .' This time it was the policeman's turn to be confused. He thought for a moment and then said, 'Prove you haven't stolen anything!'

'Prove it? But how can I do that? I just haven't, that's all,' said Uncle Two, stumped by the policeman's logic.

By this time, the policeman was overcome by impatience. 'Look, whether you've stolen anything or not, you're coming with me! Let's worry about the reasons why later, eh? Do you want to go home for Spring Festival or don't you? Trying to argue the toss with a policeman indeed!'

Uncle Two bent his head to bow and then, thinking better of it, stood up straight, a look of utter bewilderment on his face. The policeman heaved a sigh.

'Bear up,' he said, in a kinder voice. 'And remember: don't try to chop logic at the police station. So long as your crime isn't serious, the punishment will be light, but if you go looking for trouble, things could get worse. Believe me, you'd do well to listen to my advice. You country people have no idea how things work in the city. Here's the thing: every work unit has an end-of-year quota and the police are no exception. If I hadn't caught you, some other policeman would have pulled you in. You were throwing yourself at the barrel of a gun sleeping in full view of everyone like that! All you have to do is explain that you didn't understand the city rules. So, come on, it's not that bad . . .'

The policeman talked on but Uncle Two's overheated brain was so tired and confused that he drifted off into a reverie in which he was assailed by the voices of his fellow labourers roaring in his ears:

'Haven't you heard? The cops might put up signs saying "Confession leads to leniency, resistance will be met with severity", but they really mean "Confession leads to severity, resistance will be met with even more severity". Keep your head, give 'em a present and you'll be home for Spring Festival . . . Otherwise, guilty or not, you'll end up inside being duffed up by the old lags as a "welcome present". If you're lucky you'll get off with a few scars; unlucky and they'll break your arms and legs. Prison has to be bad otherwise it wouldn't deter criminals from breaking the law again.

'And don't try to protest. Whatever you say, you'll be wrong-footed. Wrongly accused? It was your own ignorance that brought it upon you, and how will you learn the rules and regulations without a dose of punishment? Cops too brutal? You're lucky to be living in the "modern democracy". At the time of the emperors, your whole family would have been

288

executed alongside you, and probably a few friends as well . . .

'You might think the Open Policy was intended to make things better for you, but think again. When laws are changed, it's the officials who benefit, not the peasants. Forget what you've heard about foreign countries, and how people there can influence the law. Don't be so childish! Can someone who works in the fields sit in a big fancy Hall of State making laws? It's all people with power and influence playing games to deceive the common people . . .'

Uncle Two thought about his gangmaster on the building site, who owed him three years' wages. Some of his fellow workers had tried to sue the man, but the court had sent them packing because they didn't have contracts. Then a few of the workers whispered that the court had been paid a bribe and said they should go out on strike, but their bosses had warned them off. They were working on a key State project, they said, and any strike action would be considered anti-Party and anti-State. Who would risk that kind of charge?

Ever since Uncle Two had gone out into the world, he had prided himself on his caution. He'd watched fellow workers get into difficulties and listened to their complaints, thinking all the time that they were foolish not to learn how to do things the city people's way

. . . But here he was, arrested for waiting at a door. Who would have thought *that* could be a crime?

A piercing howl of police sirens roused Uncle Two from his reverie, and a fifteen-seater minibus screeched to a halt in front of him. 'Get in the back of the van!' said the policeman as he opened the door.

Inside, the minibus had been divided into two sections: the front two rows of seats were for the five policemen, while those they had arrested were crammed into the back behind an iron grille. Uncle Two clambered in and squatted down by the door with his back to the others. He could hardly move, the bus was so full. He couldn't see exactly how many people were behind him, but he could smell them: the sweaty armpits of people who hadn't washed for many days, the fishy reek of feet, that dusty, smoky smell found only in the hair of migrant workers, and the terrible odour of bad breath that came in great gusts every time anyone opened their mouth. Uncle Two had never been able to understand how it was that country people could brush their teeth every day and still have such bad breath, but it was the case—and never more so than now. Crouched in the back of that van, just one of a stinking mass of bodies, Uncle Two felt overwhelmed with despair. He had no idea where his three nieces were, and his wife and family had no idea where he was. How could this have happened? Although he tried to suppress them, great sobs began rising up in his chest.

'Quiet there! No noise!' one of the police bellowed from the front. This gave Uncle Two such a start that he choked, and started hiccupping.

'Fuck it, I told you to shut up. Which one of you bastards is being courageous enough to ignore me?'

'I'm . . . hic . . . sorry . . . hic . . . I . . . can't . . . hic . . . stop,' wept Uncle Two.

'Leave him,' came the voice of the policeman who had arrested him. 'If heaven doesn't rain on us, the people fart at us. Just let him get on with it.'

Before long the van stopped and the back door was opened by a policeman who shouted, 'Out, hurry up, everybody stand by the wall over there, bring your stuff, stand properly, don't shuffle about, get in a proper line! Move it!'

Uncle Two practically fell out of the bus into the small courtyard as the people behind him began to push to get out. This meant that he was the first in the queue for questioning. He was led into a small interview room, which just had space for a small table and two chairs. As Uncle Two was sitting down, the policeman who had arrested him came in to talk to the man behind the table.

'I've put them all into the other interview

rooms, Officer Huang, because it's so cold out. When you need someone else for questioning, go via the back door, rather than getting chilled to the bone. I'm off out again. Who's to know if we're not saving a life or two today: you could die being out in this weather. Are these bloody ignorant peasants trying to kill themselves?'

'If you put the ones we've questioned with those we haven't, how am I supposed to tell who's who?' asked the policeman called Huang crossly.

'Just look in your notebook to see who you've talked to. There are eleven more to go after this one.' The policeman opened the door to leave.

'And when you bring in even more, where are we supposed to put them, eh? The second half of the night's going to be even colder. We can't just make people stand in the yard!'

'Fit 'em in somehow,' said the policeman, who evidently wanted the conversation to finish. Officer Huang shivered in the chilly draught from the open door.

'That's all very well, but how am I supposed to question them all?'

'Put in some overtime . . .' And with that, the policeman walked away.

Uncle Two watched nervously as Officer Huang leafed impatiently through his notebook: 'Come on then. Name? Age? Where are you from?'

'Li Zhongjia, forty-two, Chuzhou Prefecture, Anhui Province.'

'How do I write that? Li as in the fruit tree? Zhong as in loyalty? Jia as in family?'

'That's it,' stammered Uncle Two. 'My elder brother is Zhongguo—Loyal to the Nation. My father said that after loyalty to the nation comes loyalty to the family.'

Officer Huang seemed to find this way of naming sons amusing because he gave a little chuckle.

'Do you have papers?'

'Yes, these are my identity papers, this is my work permit, this is the letter of introduction from my local government . . .' Uncle Two pulled out the big envelope from his breast pocket, and once again unfolded the papers with their big red official seals.

'And have you got a temporary residence permit for Nanjing?' asked Officer Huang sorting casually through the papers, and making a couple of ticks in his notebook.

'For Nanjing?' asked Uncle in confusion.

'The permit that allows you to reside or stay in Nanjing.'

'But I wasn't planning on staying here. I'm just passing through on my way home. I get the bus here. I was waiting to see someone.'

'So when did you arrive in Nanjing and who were you waiting to see?'

'I got off the train yesterday and went home with someone who'd been travelling with me

293

. . .' Uncle Two did his best to remember every detail, for fear that the policeman would accuse him of not admitting to something.

But Huang interrupted him. 'I've no time to listen to your petty details. Who were you waiting for and can they vouch for you?'

'Well . . . his name is Mr Guan . . .'

'Telephone number?'

'I . . . I don't know . . .'

'You don't know? Then how can we find him to bear witness for you? Is there anyone else who can confirm your story? If there isn't, you can forget about going home for Spring Festival!'

Uncle Two was filled with horror at the idea that he might never escape this place. 'Perhaps . . .' he stammered. '. . . Everyone under the willow tree knows Mr Guan. He helps lots of country people find work . . .'

'Are you talking about the job centre near the big willow tree?' Huang asked.

'Yes, that's the place!'

'Is that where you were arrested?'

'Yes, yes,' said Uncle Two eagerly.

'So tell me about this woman's coat you had on you . . . Where did you get it?'

'I bought it second hand, for my wife.'

'Receipt?'

'Do I need a receipt when I buy clothes?'

'Of course! If you don't have a receipt, how can you prove you haven't stolen the goods?'

'Honestly, I've never taken other people's

things! May Heaven strike me down if I tell a lie!' begged Uncle Two, pointing to the top of his head in desperation.

Uncle Two's agitation seemed to make Officer Huang very frustrated.

'All right, I've finished with you. Go and wait for sentencing.'

'Sentencing?' exclaimed Uncle Two, his knees going weak. 'Sentencing for a crime?'

'What do you think we brought you in for, if not to sentence you?' said Officer Huang, escorting Uncle Two into the other interview room. Though it was crammed full of people, there was not a sound to be heard. Huang pointed to another prisoner, asked his name, and took him away for questioning.

Uncle Two sat down in the tiny space the man had just vacated and tried to find somewhere to put his bags. The man next to him gave a shove.

'Bloody hell, who d'you think you are coming into prison with all your luggage?'

'Sorry, sorry.' Uncle Two didn't know what to do.

'You can put one of those bags on my knees,' a voice said from beside him.

'Thank you, Brother!' said Uncle Two, trying unsuccessfully to turn round to look at the good-hearted person.

'It's natural for companions in adversity to help each other out,' the voice said wanly.

'Are you all right?' asked Uncle Two quietly.

'You sound rough . . .'

'It's nothing . . . A row with the missus. I went out to drown my sorrows, had a few too many, and mistook a police car for a taxi on the way home. As if that wasn't enough, I laid into the cop inside thinking he was the taxi driver . . .'

The man was just about to continue his story when the door flew open and a stern voice called out, 'Quiet! No talking allowed! The next one to speak will stand in the yard!'

That night, Uncle Two went over his life as if he were standing in front of the gates of Hell. Even if he escaped this nightmare, he would never be able to hold his head high again. It had taken him years to achieve the respect of his fellow villagers. Although during the first decade of his life he had given his parents great joy merely by being a boy, after that no one would respect him unless he proved himself a man. It had not been easy. People considered him a 'weak seed' because he had no sons. He had carried his unhappiness around with him, unable to find a solution to his problems, like a teapot without a spout. Eventually, he had carved out a living by leaving his home and labouring with the sweat of his brow, but this incident in prison was going to send him right back down to the bottom of the heap. Even if by some miracle he got home, wouldn't the people in the village revile him? Nobody would believe he'd been falsely accused. In the eyes of the villagers, the police had a god-given authority. He remembered how the older generation had revered Chairman Mao. To them, he knew everything there was to know: Chairman Mao could build a house, turn a seam, hang a dog, or dry sweet potatoes in the most economical way. Well, the police were like Chairman Mao to the current generation: never wrong. There was no getting round it, he was done for. As his wife said, the tongues of the people in the village could chew a person to death!

As fish-belly white leached into the sky, and a shaft of weak sunshine came into the room where Uncle Two was incarcerated, he heard a groan beside him.

'This is the season for executions . . .'

Uncle Two's blood froze. 'What are you saying, Brother?'

'I'm saying,' said the low voice, 'that a lot of us here are going to be a New Year gift for Yama, king of the dead.'

Uncle Two shivered. He remembered stories about the ghosts of wrongly accused men who had died unjust deaths. When, next year, the Ghost Festival came on the fifteenth day of the seventh month, would he too be one of those wronged ghosts? He would never see his wife and daughters again! Or his friends from the village! Or his brothers . . . Suddenly Uncle Two realised just what the muddy lanes and fields of his tiny village meant to him: the tender green shoots of spring, the scents of summer, the gold of autumn and the lazy pleasures of winter . . . He recalled how even villagers who had made trouble for him, occasionally showed him kindness—like his sister-in-law who, though she cursed him endlessly, had also once given him two bulls' penises to 'strengthen his *yang* energy'. Nobody was really that bad . . . 'If I get out of this alive,' thought Uncle Two to himself, 'I'll never get angry again. No matter how much people shout at me, I won't mind. Anger and laughter are part of being alive! Is anything more important than living? Let me live . . .'

Uncle Two prayed to all the gods he could think of, from the Christian Jesus and Virgin Mary to the Bodhisattvas, Guanyin and the Tibetan Master of Zangmi. He even prayed to Chairman Mao, Jiang Zemin and that new leader, Hu Jintao, saying their names over and over again. But when the iron door finally opened, and a figure in a peaked cap stood tall before him in the bright light, the gods that had sustained Uncle Two's courage disappeared without a trace, leaving behind nothing but his heart, which was pounding so hard he thought it would jump out of his mouth.

The policeman read out a list of names and told those to whom they belonged to go and stand by the door. When he read out the name 'Li Zhongjia', no one answered.

'Li Zhongjia? Aren't you Li Zhongjia?' the policeman asked, coming up to Uncle Two.

Uncle Two saw the gates of Hell before him. 'I . . . I don't want to die!' he whispered, his face deathly white and his teeth chattering.

'Go and stand outside,' said the policeman in a neutral tone. 'In a short while we'll let you go home.'

When he heard the words 'go home', Uncle Two thought of films he had seen where the bad guys said, 'I'll see you home' and then murdered their victim. He flung himself at the policeman's feet. 'Kind sir, I implore you . . . I haven't stolen anything . . .'

'Hey, what are you doing?' said the policeman stepping back. 'Stand up. We're sending you back home, what more do you want? Your family's come to fetch you. Get along with you, outside!'

It wasn't until Uncle Two saw Six waiting for him that he realised he had left the gates of Hell far behind him.

*   *   *

Guan Buyu, Shu Tian and Six listened to Uncle Two's sobs and tried to imagine what he was thinking. It seemed strange that he should cry when he'd been released. Surely he should be happy? Shu Tian and Guan Buyu had only ever heard sinister stories about the police, so they were relieved that he bore no visible traces of ill-treatment; Six thought him a bit weak for weeping over a short night in prison. None of them had any inkling of what this honest country man had endured, or the sleepless nights he would continue to suffer for months to come.

The red Xiali followed the black Mercedes through the gates of a high-class European-style housing development near the Sun Yatsen Mausoleum, and up the driveway of a big villa. The two cars parked and Manager Shui led them all to his front door.

'Well, Brother,' he said, turning to Guan Buyu as he got out his key, 'where were you yesterday when this poor peasant was getting such a scare? People say that the police are better these days, and don't get their kicks the way they used to—from arresting anyone who steps even a centimetre out of line—it's still pretty frightening to be up in front of a cop, even for us city dwellers. Who knows if they really understand the laws they are supposed to enforce . . .'

'Tell me about it!' said Guan Buyu with a sigh. 'My ex-wife is threatening to use the new laws about women's rights to stir up trouble for me. Three years ago, when we divorced, her share of the property was much bigger than mine, but still she treats me like a bank! I don't know, marriage is like getting onto a pirate ship: once you're aboard there's no way back. And these divorce laws are never ending.

Yesterday she was after me for money to buy an air conditioner. I had to go into hiding . . .'

Guan Buyu continued talking as he followed Manager Shui into the house. 'How lucky you are to be free and single. When you eat, the whole family's fed. Plus you live in a mansion. Do you plan to stay single all your life? . . . Come in all of you,' he said, turning to the three sisters and their uncle. 'Welcome to Manager Shui's Palace!'

Three, Five and Six gazed in awe at the glorious spectacle that greeted them. They were standing in a huge reception room decorated in the European style, with a sumptuously upholstered purple and gold five-piece suite occupying pride of place in the centre. Against the walls were numerous tables, desks, cabinets and shelves all displaying a host of interesting ornaments: there were carved wooden animals, antique curios and a selection of artfully arranged house plants. At the windows hung opulent red and gold velvet curtains, and from the ceiling five magnificent crystal chandeliers glinted with light and colour. Scottish wool rugs, woven with designs of knights and bagpipers lay on the floor, while the corridor leading to the dining room and bedrooms allowed glimpses of elaborately carved chairs and gorgeous silk bedspreads.

Guan Buyu and Shu Tian propelled the three gaping girls to the sofa on which Uncle

Two had already taken a seat.

'Please, sit down,' said Manager Shui. 'I've got some preprepared food in the fridge and I think we should all have a bit to eat before Guan Buyu and I go to our meetings.' He went off into the kitchen, stomach swaying, and the sisters soon heard the hum of a microwave oven, and detected the delicious smell of fermented tofu and pork—a southern favourite. 'Here we go,' said Manager Shui coming back with a tray. 'One bowl each. We know each other well enough to take pot-luck so don't worry about which one to choose. There's a city saying that the best way to get out of a bad place is to go through a "good door"—or in other words, "find yourself a protector". Let me be your door . . . Now, hurry. Eat.'

Uncle Two held the bowl of food in his hands and looked at his three nieces. He felt overwhelmed by conflicting emotions. If he hadn't been worried about them, he wouldn't have taken his trip to Hell, and yet here they all were, safe and sound, and enjoying a meal in beautiful surroundings. How was it possible to travel from Hell to Heaven in the space of a single day?

'Eat Uncle Two,' said Three gently, 'otherwise we'll all worry about you.'

As the meal drew to a close, they discussed what Uncle Two should do next.

'I think I'd better go home at once,' said

302

Uncle Two, who was gazing into the distance, an unreadable expression in his eyes.

Guan Buyu thought for a while then made a suggestion. 'How about I send someone to the Happy Fool with Three and Uncle Two to explain everything to my sister-in-law and ask permission for Three to go home for Spring Festival today with Uncle Two. As for Five, I think she should stay on until after the Kitchen God Festival. Manager Shui tells me she's one of his most valued workers, so he'll need her during the busy period before the Festival. Ah, Six, I can see your clever brain trying to work out how city people can have a festival when they don't have a Kitchen God. Well, stay for the festival and you'll see. Every family has a fire for cooking. We pay our respects to that fire and that counts as worshipping the Kitchen God.'

'Thank you, kind sir. That will reassure their parents,' said Uncle Two, overwhelmed with relief that one of the sisters would be able to return with him. Not only was he afraid of losing his nieces again, but he felt in need of company after his experiences of the previous night. Even now he was finding it difficult to know whether he was awake or dreaming.

'I should've thought of it before,' said Guan Buyu. 'Without computers and telephones in your village, and with most people unable to read letters, you rely on word of mouth for news of each other. But I guess that, even

303

then, it's hard for the girls' parents to believe they are well without actually seeing them. If you hadn't seen them with your own eyes, I doubt you'd believe us either, right?' Guan Buyu's eyes lit up as he had an idea. 'Shu Tian, didn't you say you had a digital camera in your car? When you deliver the girls to their workplaces, take some photographs so that Uncle Two can take them back to the village. There's still time if you hurry. The bus doesn't leave for four hours.' He took a red envelope from his inside pocket and placed it in Uncle Two's hand. 'Take this too. It's a little something from me to their mother.'

'You Nanjingers are much kinder than the people down south,' said Uncle Two gratefully. 'You think of everything.'

As they were getting ready to part and both cars were starting up, Manager Shui stuck his head out of his window to ask Guan Buyu whom he had contacted at the police station to get Uncle Two out. 'You never told me! Was it Deputy Head Han or Officer Huang?'

'Neither,' shouted Guan Buyu over the roar of the Xiali's engine. 'A document came through today saying that the law against vagrancy has been abolished. Apparently, from now on, country people won't need papers from their local government when they go away from home. Uncle Two's a lucky man!'

'He sure is,' said Manager Shui in amazement. 'I can't believe they've finally scrapped restrictions on movement!'

'So it would seem,' said Shu Tian. 'Some of the older policemen at the station were saying that, what with the discontinuation of the laws against cohabitation as well, they might have to lay off staff, and the prisons will be a lot emptier!'

'That's a bloody Cultural Revolution!' exclaimed Manager Shui. 'Great stuff! They should have taken this step ages ago. If the population doesn't move around, information can't either and society stays static. Well, gotta go. See you soon!'

'I'd better go too,' said Guan Buyu to Shu Tian. 'My ex-wife has someone tailing me, taking down number plates. Don't worry, I'll get a taxi. I don't want to drag you into this. You take the girls back by yourself.' And, with this, he was gone, leaving the three sisters and their uncle sitting in the back of Shu Tian's car feeling as if they had just been caught up in a whirlwind.

12

HOMECOMING

For days after Uncle Two returned home for Spring Festival, the inhabitants of the village could talk of nothing but how changed he was. Instead of his usual, put-upon expression, he wore a constant smile on his face and was full of affection towards everyone and everything. He hugged and kissed all the snotty-nosed children playing in the mud and even stroked the family pig after it had spent the day wallowing in the cesspit. As for his family . . . his daughters and wife had never known him to laugh so much, or make such a fuss of them. He picked out choice morsels of food to put into his children's bowls and bewildered his wife by revealing a passion she hadn't known he possessed.

In fact Auntie Two was so concerned about what might have happened to her husband that she went to talk privately to Three, who answered as her uncle had instructed her: 'Uncle Two had a terrible dream about visiting the underworld that changed him. He has decided he wants to live well from now on, otherwise he will have lost his soul for nothing.'

The villagers were also extremely impressed

by the photographs that Uncle Two had brought back from the city. A constant flow of curious visitors had the Li household in a state of continual uproar late into the night. Li Zhongguo grumbled from time to time about the waste of good lamp oil, but even he couldn't stop looking at the picture of a gorgeously illuminated dragon's mouth with Five standing smiling in front of it, her face glowing with health and vigour. Who would have believed that his stupidest, ugliest daughter could have become so capable! Three saw her father admiring the photograph of Five and thought to herself that it had been worth almost missing the bus in order to take it. They had waited until it was dark so that they could get a photograph of the Dragon Water-Culture Centre in its full glory.

However, there was one person who wasn't happy. Three's mother had noticed a change in her daughter and was worried. No matter how much the villagers showered Three with admiration, her motherly intuition could sense that there was something seriously wrong. Although she did not know who or what had stolen her daughter's spirit away, her thoughts turned instinctively to the secret and bitter agony she herself had once suffered, without ever telling a soul. As a girl she had fallen desperately in love with a young man in her village. They had grown up side by side, calling each other brother and sister, and it had never

307

occurred to her that she would lose him. Only when this young man had excitedly told his 'little sister' that he was getting a wife, did she awake with a shock to the realisation that she was not the bride of his dreams. There was no one in whom she could confide, and no one to pity her. It was the firm belief of those around her that it was a man's world, and only a man could select his partner for life. A peasant girl's desires would be mocked as a mere infatuation. They might even think she was not 'right in the head'.

Only she would know how many times she had soaked her quilt with tears, how many stars she had counted, how many insoles she had embroidered for him in secret, then secretly torn to pieces. It was not until her parents married her off to the Li family's eldest son in exchange for a wife for one of her brothers that she understood it was her fate to live a life that so many millions of other women had not been able to avoid, regardless of their wishes.

Yet, although Three's mother suspected what was destroying her daughter, it didn't occur to her to talk to Three about it. She had never been to school and therefore her only example in life had been her own mother. Since her mother had never expressed a wish to know about her daughter's joys or sorrows, but had simply taught her what men considered to be bad or good in a woman,

Three's mother had no idea how to share her daughter's pain. Never in her life had she seen or heard of a mother and daughter who could open their hearts to each other and talk freely. Instead she watched helplessly as Three became thinner and thinner, and worried also for the safety of her other daughters. If this was what the city had done to Three, were Five and Six truly as happy as in the photographs? And why hadn't they come home for the Kitchen God sacrifices? Although Three reassured her mother that her sisters were well, how could Three know? She worked in a different place to them, and didn't see them often . . . Three's mother, who had never even been to the local town, had no idea how easily information was exchanged in the city. For her, communication could only take place if you met someone face to face. She lived a mere twenty or thirty miles from the village where she grew up, but, since her marriage, the only news she had received from her birthplace came from travellers or visiting relatives.

It was not until Five and Six arrived home, two days before the start of the Spring Festival celebrations that their mother began to smile a little. Though Three continued to look sad and wan, her two other daughters were so smartly dressed and cheerful that she could see for herself that all was well with them. For the first time ever, the Li family home was filled with the sound of happy conversation and laughter. Five and Six told stories of city life and all the village girls, wives, and their mothers-in-law gathered at the house to listen to them, too excited to blink, looking over and over again at the photographs of city streets and smiling city people. The older generation saw things there that they could never have imagined in a million years.

Before their New Year's Eve dinner, Three, Five and Six wrapped up the gifts they had brought for their family in newspaper. They had agreed that they would put everything in a big parcel and give it to their mother to open, so that she could know how much her chopstick girls loved her, and how they understood what she had endured during her hard and difficult life. But when they handed her the gift, their mother immediately passed it respectfully to their father, the head of the family.

'You open it,' said Li Zhongguo quietly. 'The girls gave it to you.'

'To me?' said their mother in bewilderment. In over twenty years of marriage, she had never heard her husband say that anything in the house belonged to her.

'Go on, open it!' he said in a voice that made clear he didn't expect any further questions.

Slowly, and with trembling hands, she peeled away the layers of newspaper.

Although the wrapping was not the fashionably glossy paper that city people used for their gifts, it was precious nevertheless. It came from the English newspapers that Six read to practise her language. She had thought long and hard before parting with these pages. Nobody in her village had even read a newspaper article to the end, let alone one in English. They wouldn't have a clue what the English letters meant. Nevertheless, they were Six's gift to the village: evidence of the wider world that existed beyond the confines of this tiny place.

Inside the newspapers was a Chinese-style jacket of reddish-purple brocade, with a beautifully embroidered border and elaborately knotted fastenings; a carved wooden pipe decorated with the face of Lao Shou Xing, God of Longevity; a big pink scarf; a pair of butterfly-shaped hair clips, one blue, one green; several envelopes and a cloth bundle.

Five unfolded the jacket and gestured to her mother to put it on. Blushing, she slipped her arms through the sleeves. It was a perfect fit. The whole family was astonished to see how lovely their mother looked in it, and Five noticed that, even her father, who had never once touched his wife in front of his children, went red in the face and put his arm round her shoulders.

'Who chose this jacket?' he said admiringly.

'Someone's got a good eye!'

'It was Five!' Three and Six said together.

'But how did you know it would fit me so well?' asked their mother, looking in surprise at the daughter everyone had written off as incapable of learning anything.

'I . . . I . . . Three, please help me explain!' Five begged her sister, blushing.

'Well, Mother, it was like this,' said Three, coming to the rescue. 'Ever since Five first arrived in the city, she spent all her free time looking at the shops. We couldn't drag her away from the windows of the city department stores and clothes shops. She stood for hours looking at the fake people inside, dressed up in samples of the clothes they sell. I had no idea why she was doing this until we went to take a photograph of the Dragon Water-Culture Centre just before coming home. Five's boss, Auntie Wang, told me that, whenever Five saw a female client who had your build, she would politely ask her dress size. When the clients found out that it was because she wanted to buy her mother a present, they were only too happy to give her the information, and many of them praised her as a good daughter, saying there weren't many girls like her in the city these days. As I said, Mother, Six and I had no idea Five was doing this. She worked it out all for herself . . .'

Everyone exclaimed with wonder at Five's cleverness, and then the other presents were distributed: the scarf to Four, the carved pipe with its beaming God of Longevity to their father, and the hairslides to their mother, to be given to One when she next saw her.

'Since Two isn't here,' said Three quietly, 'One will have to be beautiful on her behalf.'

'My poor ill-fated child,' moaned her mother.

Three saw her father take a sharp pull on his pipe. 'This is a box of sticky rice-balls from the Tofu Lady,' she continued, not wishing the family to dwell on the misery of the past, 'and these envelopes contain gifts from our bosses, and a letter from Six's foreign friends to the two of you.'

'Foreign? What do you mean foreign? Devils with yellow hair and blue eyes like the ones your uncle talks about?' asked their father, at a loss. Part of Six was secretly delighted to see how her father, who did not normally have much to say that wasn't a put-down, now needed her help to understand something.

'That's right,' she said proudly. 'I've met a lot of different people from different countries. They are extremely nice and have taught me a lot.'

'Do you work together?' said her mother, tugging at her hand with excitement.

Her father scoffed. 'Typical woman, making assumptions about a world you've never seen! Don't you listen to a word Uncle Two says?

313

Those foreigners come here to do desk jobs. How could a manual worker like our daughter work alongside them? Just learning their language would take a lifetime and more . . . Three, did you say just now they've written to us? What for? How do they know about me? Explain yourself! And don't try to bamboozle us with fancy city words either!'

'But Dad, they're Six's *friends*!' interrupted Five. 'It's like my friends know all about Mum and you.'

As soon as the words were out of her mouth, Five lowered her head instinctively. She had never interrupted anyone in her family, let alone her father. She waited for the inevitable scolding but nothing came.

'Humph,' said her father after a while. 'Five's got a point! Now read out this letter, Six, and let's hear what these foreigners have got to say for themselves.'

Five was so stunned by the fact that her father had listened to her opinion and treated it with respect, that she heard none of the letter Six was reading. But, even if she had been paying attention, it is unlikely that she could have made much sense of it. Her mother certainly couldn't.

'Child,' she said to Six, 'you know your mother has no education. I can't understand that educated letter of theirs. Couldn't you just tell me what it means?'

Their father, who had been sitting with

neck outstretched and brow furrowed with embarrassment, was flooded with relief when she said this, since it let him off the hook.

'Women are always sticking their noses in!' he complained. 'Six, go over it again slowly for your mother!'

Six and Three exchanged glances about the lengths their father would go to avoid losing face.

'Well, Dad,' said Six, 'you, Mum and Four have all been invited by my foreign friends and my employers, the Shu family, to spend two days with us in Nanjing during the Lantern Festival. We will all go to see the lion dances and stilt walkers, eat rice-balls, and look at the lanterns, and you won't have to pay a penny. My friends will take care of travelling expenses, including food and lodging, and you can come and see where we all work ...'

'That's fantastic,' said Five, jumping up and down. Even Four seemed to understand that she would be included in a treat and made inarticulate cries of excitement. Only their father remained stony-faced.

'We can't possibly go. Imagine what a laughing stock we'd be if we went about spending other people's money. We may have no sons, but we have our pride!'

'But, Dad,' said Three quietly, glancing at Five and Six, 'we don't need to spend other people's money.' When her two sisters nodded, she took the cloth bundle that still lay

315

amidst the newspaper and placed it in her mother's hands.

'Mum, this is for you.'

Their mother's hands trembled as she took the bundle. She recognised the cloth immediately. She had wrapped sweet-potato bread in it for her daughters when she had seen them off to the city eleven months before, but it didn't look as if it contained sweet-potato bread now. Once again she glanced nervously at her husband. He nodded and gestured, with his old pipe in one hand and his new one in the other, that she should open the package.

Carefully she unfolded the cloth. Inside were three neat bundles of hundred-yuan notes, as thick as bricks.

'But this is enough to build a new kitchen!' she gasped, tears coming to her eyes.

Her daughters said nothing, overcome by emotion. They all looked towards their father.

For a while Li Zhongguo said nothing, staring in wonder at the money in his wife's hands. But then his eyes too began to redden and he asked, in a weak voice, 'Is it possible that our chopstick girls will be able to hold up our roof?'

It was true that there was still doubt in his voice—that he had asked a question, rather than state a fact. But the three sisters didn't care. These were the words they had been waiting all their life to hear.

AFTERWORD: THE STORY AFTER THE STORY

As soon as I had finished this book, I sent it to my translator, Esther Tyldesley, who is always my first reader and, more importantly, a trusted friend. She is unusual among Westerners in having a deep knowledge of rural China. After studying Chinese at Cambridge University, she spent four years living in a small town in Guizhou, one of the less developed provinces of China, and her perspicacity when it comes to Chinese women's lives always surprises me. I was on tenterhooks to know what she would think.

I had to wait a while. Esther was busy marking exam papers at Edinburgh University, where she works, and I knew that she valued the importance of 'letting things settle', a quality to be cherished in this busy, frantic world of ours. But two weeks later an email arrived in my inbox that filled me with happiness. 'Someone should have told the world about China's "chopstick" girls long ago,' she said. 'Thank goodness that, now, you have.'

After that, we had a long telephone conversation about the book. As well as discussing how long the translation might take, we shared our opinions about young Chinese

317

female migrant workers. True to form, we saw eye to eye on many issues. And Esther had good news: she was going to marry her Chinese boyfriend, whom she had known for nearly ten years. The wedding would take place, as is traditional in China, in her husband-to-be's home town, on 1 August—the anniversary of the foundation of the People's Liberation Army. We talked for a long time about the marriage and then, just as we were about to say goodbye, Esther made a comment that stayed with me. 'I wish I knew what happened to the three sisters afterwards,' she said, 'and I suspect a lot of your readers will too.' This is Esther all over! She knows the Chinese art of quietly and gently suggesting how something might be made better.

*   *   *

To be honest, I don't know how the stories of the three sisters finish. Books end, and we can't see beyond their final sentences. However, I will tell you what I know.

In 2003 I interviewed a cleaner in the Bailuzhou Hotel near the Confucius Temple in Nanjing. She was from the north of Anhui Province, and she told me the story of her elder sister (the girl who is called 'Three' in this book). Her sister had tried hard to escape village life, she said. She had worked in the city for three years. However, she became very unhappy when she fell in love with a man who didn't love her back. When at the end of the third year she went home for Spring Festival, her parents had married her off to a village official who had never left his home because he was lame in one leg.

'What was it like for her to return to the poverty-stricken countryside after three years in the city?' I asked. 'It must have been very hard for her to go back to that way of life . . .'

'Who said it wasn't?' replied the young woman. 'But my sister was resigned. She had argued herself into a corner: she couldn't stay in the same place as the man she loved. I encouraged her to go and find a job in some other city, but she said all city men reminded her of the man who had rejected her.'

'Is her husband good to her?' I asked.

The young woman looked at me as if I were from outer space. 'What does good and bad mean to her there? You just go with whomever your parents marry you off to! That's been the fate of billions of Chinese women since time began . . .'

I was struck by her vehemence. 'Will you follow that fate?'

'No way! I'm not like my sister. She has a heart of stone: once something's in there, it's in for good—she can't change. Her three years in the city didn't teach her a thing about women's freedom and independence. She even warned me not to pick up bad ways from bad

319

women! You tell me, what's good and what's bad? How can she be so stubborn, so blind? The standards of good and bad in the country and the city are completely opposite in so many things. You've seen foreign countries . . . Do they have the same standards of good and bad as us? Even my mother and grandmother believe different things. I won't go back home so my parents can play games with my life. They can't even read, so they won't be able to find me.' As she spoke she clasped her hands together forcefully, as though she was swearing a vow to someone.

'But aren't you afraid that you will destroy your family's reputation?' I asked. 'Your sister must have a good name, surely?'

'Good name? What's the use of that? In our village women are always killing themselves for the sake of a good name. But what's the use of a good name if you're dead? No one will shed any tears over you. They'll just use your death as a rod to beat other women's backs. Country people's hearts have been soaked in poverty and bitterness for so long, there's not a hint of humanity left!'

With these words, the young woman went back to her work, leaving me feeling chilled to the bone even though it was the height of summer.

After our interview I went to see where her sister used to work. The whole place was a building site, with signs advertising Kentucky

Fried Chicken everywhere. There were some old people playing chess in the nearby lane, so I asked them what was going on. They'd heard that several buildings at the junction had been bought out by KFC for its expansion.

'Did you know the Happy Fool restaurant?' I asked.

They all nodded vigorously, and every one of them had something to say.

'That's right, a nice little restaurant it was . . . The foreigners destroyed it with their money!'

'Come off it! It was just a gimmick, and a ridiculous one at that. How can you make any money out of some country girl's tricks with vegetables?'

'Don't say that! It's better than stuffing cash into the pockets of the Yanks!'

'What does it matter who the money belongs to, as long as life is good and the country is at peace. Who knows, the Happy Fool may well have sold for a good price! You can still say they got their just deserts.'

'That's easy enough to say, but how would you feel if our Confucius Temple was converted into a Catholic church?'

'How could that happen?'

I left the elderly chess-players to continue their debate. I could see that these questions—which are on the lips of so many Chinese people at the moment—were going to occupy them for hours.

When I returned to Nanjing in 2005, the young cleaner had found a new job at the five-star hotel, Zhuang Yuan Lou. She told me that her elder sister had given birth to a baby girl and was already pregnant with a second child. Apparently the poor woman was desperately worried that it might be another girl, in which case she would repeat her mother's fate and be discriminated against for the rest of her life as a woman who couldn't 'lay eggs'. I asked the young woman to take two sets of 'Five Poisonous Creatures' clothes to her sister's children, in the hope that they would bring peace and help her wishes come true.

* * *

I met the girl whom I have called 'Six' in Beijing in 2002. She too came from a poor area in the north of Anhui Province and was actually the ninth child in a family of ten. She had a healthy younger brother, but four of her elder sisters had died young. When I asked her how, she said 'of natural causes', but it was hard to be sure whether she was being truthful. In the remote, poverty-stricken areas of China girls are of no more value than donkeys, horses, cattle or goats.

I had gone into a small teahouse to find out what had happened to a good vegetarian restaurant I remembered in the area. 'Six' was wearing a uniform in the traditional style, and had a piece of paper in front of her on which she was writing in English. She told me that lots of people came into the teahouse to ask questions about places they had known but could no longer find. She had heard her boss say that the vegetarian restaurant had been pulled down. Out of curiosity, I asked which university she was at, and praised her for using the quiet moments in the teahouse to study. When she replied that she had never been to university, and that actually she was a migrant worker who liked books and wanted to save money to go and study abroad, I was flabbergasted. I had talked to many young female migrant workers, but a 'chopstick' girl with such a deep love of books and the desire to study abroad was rarer than a phoenix or a unicorn. I was extremely eager to interview her, and to ask her more about herself.

I made a date with 'Six' to visit the bookshops in the Wangfujing shopping street with me on her free half-day. There I bought for her tapes and books that would help her prepare for the English exams she needed to take, and afterwards we went to a traditional Beijing restaurant for supper. Hoping to imprint on this young girl's heart good memories of her native land before she went abroad, I ordered dishes with a strong regional flavour: sliced cold beef with hot, pungent spices from Sichuan called Husband-and-Wife Lung Slices; Manchurian pickled vegetables;

deep-fried silver whitebait from the Yangzi delta; and a bowl of Cantonese 'Dragon and Tiger Fighting' (wanton and noodles). We talked as we ate, and by the time our plates were empty, I had written down her story.

In 2003 I went back to the teashop, full of excitement at the prospect of seeing her again. I had brought with me information packs from British universities. But both she and the teahouse had vanished. The neighbours said that that teahouse had been shut down for 'selling banned books'. I was not able to find the girl again. All I had was a telephone number for the teahouse which simply gave a 'number unobtainable' tone.

*   *   *

They say that 'out of blows, friendship grows', and that is how I got to know 'Five'.

In 2003, my English husband and I met an American man in Shanghai who was amazed at having discovered that a Chinese businessman he was dealing with held his meetings in a bathhouse. I wasn't quite so amazed. Ancient texts like the *Medical Canon of the Yellow Emperor* show how the nurturing of the body has been central to Chinese culture for centuries. But, while the American man's discovery made me feel patriotic, it simply made my husband curious. I could see the gleam in his eye: he was eager to visit one of Shanghai's 'Water-Culture Centres' to experience for himself this revived interest in the medicinal properties of water.

It was late afternoon when we arrived at the baths. We collected our tokens and towels from reception, and were given various health checks before separating to take a shower. It is important to be clean before entering medicinal pools. But when I got into one of the pale-blue shower cubicles and bolted the door, disaster struck. I turned on the cold tap only to find that the water was scalding hot. Thinking that perhaps the taps had been wrongly labelled, I tried the hot tap, only to find that hot water came out of that one too. I immediately tried to turn off the taps but the threads were so worn that they wouldn't turn. The shower head was set at such an angle that the water (which was getting hotter and hotter) sprayed in front of the door, making it impossible for me to unlock the cubicle without burning myself further. All I could do was squeeze myself into the corner furthest away from the jet of water, and call for help.

After a while an attendant heard my cries, but explained, extremely slowly, that she had no way to open the door from the outside. I would have to open it myself. On hearing this, I became frantic.

'If you don't find a way to get me out of here, I'm going to be seriously injured,' I said. 'I can't keep my body away from the water entirely, and it's scalding me. Hurry and find someone who can turn it off.'

'Really?' The voice outside still seemed not to sense the urgency of the situation.

'Listen to me!' I shouted, 'If you don't hurry up and find someone, you'll be blamed for my injuries!'

When I think back on it, my voice must have sounded terrifying. I heard the girl running away. While I waited, I tried to keep changing position so that different parts of my body took the pain. I had counted up to two hundred by the time I heard rushing footsteps and shouting:

'Which cubicle? Good heavens, didn't they seal that one off last night? How come it's open again? That's the one that doesn't work properly! Quickly, go and turn off the hot water! The other customers will just have to be cold for a moment. If there's trouble, I'll take responsibility. Now get a move on. Turn off the stopcock!'

There was another burst of running footsteps, and then the hot water stopped. I opened the door to find three women in uniforms standing open-mouthed outside the cubicle, staring at my bright red body.

'Sorry, we're sorry,' they apologised in chorus.

'I'm afraid that, although my brain understands you, my body doesn't,' I said resentfully.

At this, the youngest of the three women stepped forward and began to take charge in a very capable manner. Signalling to her colleagues that they should go and turn the hot water back on, she said that she would look after me. I recognised her voice: she was the one who had promised to take responsibility if any of the other customers complained about the cold water.

'My name's Mei,' she said. 'I'm going to take you to the Skin Treatment Room where they can look at your burns.' Without giving me a chance to object, she gently placed a big bath towel around my shoulders and led me to a treatment room. The towel was extremely painful wherever it came into contact with my skin, but the doctor in the treatment room promised that the salve he was using would get rid of the redness and pain in half an hour.

He was right: the pain did begin to ease, especially when Mei gave me a foot massage afterwards. While she was rubbing my feet we talked, and I found out that she too came from Anhui. By the time my husband and I left the Water-Culture Centre late that night, Mei and I had become firm friends. She is the 'Five' in this book, and really was her parents' fifth child.

Because Mei couldn't read, we were only able to keep in touch by telephone, which we did for nearly two years. Then, in September 2005, I was told by another employee of the

Water-Culture Centre that Mei had been sent on a course of advanced study, and that she did not have her new telephone number.

I was perplexed. How could a girl who couldn't read or write be sent on a course of 'advanced study'? But then I thought again: through sheer hard work, Chinese people have achieved many things that others have thought impossible.

*　　*　　*

I wrote this Afterword during a visit to Tasmania, where I was staying in a small wooden hut next to Cradle Mountain. February is the height of summer there, and there were days when the sun was so strong it could burn your skin. On other days, however, there would be snow flying outside my window. In Cradle Mountain, they call it the Sky Mother looking for her children who went out during the summer to play.

On the last night I spent in Tasmania, I was taken with a group of other people to see a colony of Little Penguins. It was a rainy, windy night and we walked through the dark down to the sea, chatting to each other in our excitement. When we got there, our guide told us to be quiet. 'Please don't use flashlights, and be careful where you put your feet. You are now in the penguins' territory.' As he spoke, he switched on a special torch, designed to give off a gentle light. Its beam revealed a huge crowd of tiny penguins standing right in front of us—not black and white, like the ones I had learned about in school, but dark-blue and white. The largest was barely twenty centimetres high, and they were all waving their tiny, soft wings, and calling out to each other as they searched for their mates. My companions and I were awed by the peaceful harmony in which these little creatures lived. Involuntarily I greeted them in Chinese. Who knows—I might have been the first person ever to speak Chinese to them. The guide asked us three questions: 'Why are the penguins waddling so awkwardly? Why do they make so light of having to spend five or six hours climbing from the sea to the top of the ridge? And why are they making so much noise?'

A long silence followed. We could hear nothing but the ocean and the penguins 'discussing' our ignorance.

Since no one in the group knew the answers to the questions, our guide provided them. As I listened to him, surrounded by the roar of the ocean and the cries of the penguins, my heart wept.

'Firstly, penguins can't bend their legs. Think how difficult it would be to climb a mountain with no knees! What would take us ten minutes to climb, takes them hours, with many rest-stops. Why do they do it every day?

Because their mates and babies are at the top of the ridge, and they must bring them food. And finally, the noise . . . The ocean is the place that gives them life and keeps enemies at bay; on dry land they and their offspring are far more exposed to predators. So when love drives them to climb the ridge for their family, they are worried, confused and lonely. They need the calls of their own kind to comfort them . . .'

The guide's words seem a fitting footnote to the story of Three, Five and Six, and all the peasant women who come to work in China's cities, or labour in the fields from dawn to dusk. They do not have the advantages we were born with—the knees that allow us to walk freely through our lives and our choices. Many of them have never been cuddled by their parents, never touched a book, never had warm clothes, never eaten their fill. But in conditions that we would consider 'impossible', they fight for their self-respect, their aspirations, their loves.

Just as I was humbled by the sight of the little Tasmanian penguins who had struggled up the ridge, I am full of admiration for the chopstick girls who, with their energy, give us so much.

Thank you.

MAPS

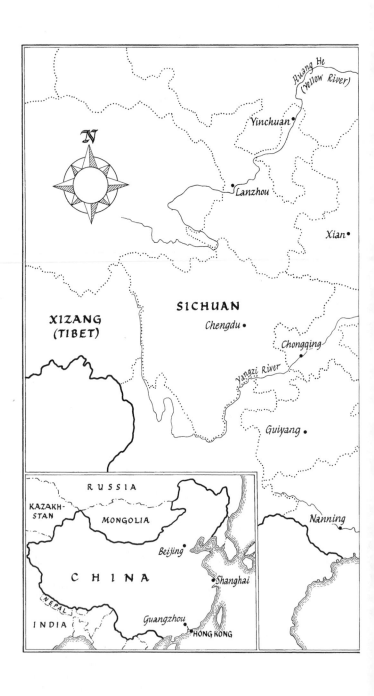

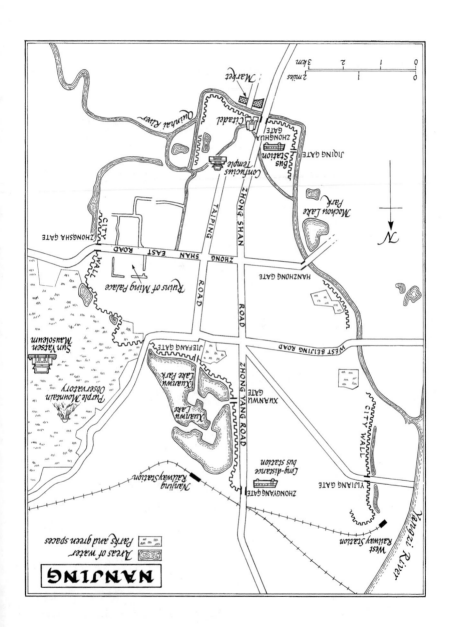

EDITOR'S NOTE: A LIST OF CHINESE FESTIVALS

There are many different festivals celebrated in the cities and villages of China, and the way in which they are marked varies from region to region. It is impossible to list them all, but here are the some of the most important ones:

Spring Festival, *also known as Chinese New Year* (last day of 12th lunar month and the first 5–15 days of 1st lunar month): This is the most important festival in the Chinese year. First preparation is made for New Year. Houses are cleaned, the family banquet is prepared and people paste pictures of the 'door gods' onto their front doors to protect the family. Relatives visit each other and there are fireworks.

Lantern Festival (15th day of 1st lunar month): Celebrated with the lighting of lanterns and lion dances.

Tomb Sweeping Day, *also known as the Festival of Pure Brightness* (12th day of 3rd lunar month): A day for honouring one's ancestors by cleaning their tomb and burning ceremonial paper money. Families go on outings.

Dragon Boat Festival (5th day of 5th lunar month): This festival commemorates the death of the great Chinese poet Qu Yuan, who committed suicide by drowning. Dragon boat races are held. People also eat Zong Zi, glutinous rice dumplings wrapped in bamboo leaves. It is also a time when people protect themselves against illness. It is thought that this period of the year is when the Five Poisonous Creatures (snakes, scorpions, spiders, lizards, toads) awake from hibernation and cause harm, particularly to small children. Parents protect their children by giving them special clothes to wear decorated with pictures of the Five Poisonous Creatures.

The Night of Sevens, *also known as Magpie Festival* (7th day of 7th lunar month): A day which celebrates lovers, this festival marks the night when the goddess Zhi Nü was allowed to meet the mortal cowherd Niu Lang with whom she had fallen in love. On the seventh night of the seventh moon, magpies would form a bridge for the two lovers to meet. The two lovers became stars (Vega and Altair), divided by the Milky Way.

Ghost Festival (15th day of 7th lunar month): a day when people burn paper money and making offerings to their dead ancestors so that restless spirits will not trouble the living.

Mid-Autumn Festival, *also known as Moon Festival* (15th day of 8th lunar month): Based on the legend of Chang Er, this is a festival where families come together to eat moon cakes.

Double Ninth Festival (9th day of 9th lunar month): A day for warding off evil, celebrated in many different ways. Traditions include climbing a mountain, drinking chrysanthemum wine and carrying sprays of dogwood.

Winter Solstice, *also known as Mid-Winter Festival* (day of winter solstice): A day for worshipping one's ancestors.

Laba Festival, *also known as Congee Festival* (8th day of 12th lunar month): The day Buddha attained enlightenment. People eat Laba congee which is made of mixed grains, meat and fruit.

Kitchen God Festival (23rd day of 12th lunar month): On this day the Kitchen god returns to heaven to give a report to the Jade Emperor (in Chinese mythology the Jade Emperor is the ruler of heaven) about the family's activities over the past year. Families therefore spend the day performing acts of appeasement to the Kitchen god so that he will give the Jade Emperor a favourable report.

ACKNOWLEDGEMENTS

My heartfelt thanks to my husband Toby Eady, whose cooking skills and exquisite literary knowledge sustain me; and to my son PanPan for his independence and indomitable hard work. Without all the help these two people have given me, I could not have finished writing this book whilst juggling my frantic activity with the charity the Mothers' Bridge of Love (MBL), and my talks, interviews and lectures all over the world.

Thanks to all the volunteers and supporters of MBL: their generosity and encouragement has helped me to understand the self-respect and will to become successful and strong that lie behind the achievements of China's chopstick girls.

Thanks to Esther Tyldesley. I feel lucky and honoured to have such a translator. Like me, she is proud of Chinese women, and wishes to help others love and understand them. I would like this book to be a wedding present for her.

Thanks to my editor Rebecca Carter—whose questions have helped me understand what Westerners do and don't know about China—and to everybody at Random House who has worked on this book. It is their professional knowledge that has made my stories into the book you are reading now.

Thanks to all my friends in publishing and the media all over the world. They have helped me to express in thirty different languages all the hopes for China I have described with my Chinese pen.

Thanks to Tantan's mother Liu Tong, MBL CEO Wendy Wu and Meiyee Lim, excellent Chinese women who have helped so many chopstick girls.

Thanks to you, the readers, for reading, and for your love and appreciation of the chopstick girls.

sharing chinese culture
helping chinese children

MBL's Heart to the World

Over fifty per cent of Chinese people live in poverty. Millions of Chinese children can only dream of a decent education. These children ask: 'How can I ever go to school?'

In 2004, the charity 'The Mothers' Bridge of Love' (MBL) was founded to help disadvantaged Chinese children, and to build a bridge of understanding between the West and China. The seeds of hope planted in 2004 for all those who have suffered and lost, have been watered by the charity's many volunteers in China, the UK and the twenty-seven other countries involved. They have now developed two buds: *Sharing Chinese Culture* and *Helping Chinese Children.* Our great thanks goes to all the volunteers and supporters who have allowed these two buds to reach out of the soil.

Before you close this book, and as you reflect on the story of *Miss Chopsticks*, we ask

341

you to take a little time to find out about the activities of MBL.

If you wish to support MBL charity activities, you can send a cheque to:

MBL 9 Orme Court
London W2 4RL UK

If you would like to make a bank transfer, please send funds to:

The Mothers' Bridge of Love (MBL)
Sort Code: 400607
Account Number: 11453130
HSBC Bank Russell Square Branch
1 Woburn Place, Russell Square
London WCIH 0LQ
SWIFT Code: MIDL GB2142E

If you would like to make an online donation please visit:
http://www.justgiving.com/mbl/donate

For further information please do visit our website: www.motherbridge.org.

Executive Director: Wendy Wu
Founder: Xinran
MBL—The Mothers' Bridge of Love: Charity Registration No. 1105543

Chivers Large Print Direct

If you have enjoyed this Large Print book and would like to build up your own collection of Large Print books and have them delivered direct to your door, please contact **Chivers Large Print Direct**.

Chivers Large Print Direct offers you a full service:

✧ **Created to support your local library**

✧ **Delivery direct to your door**

✧ **Easy-to-read type and attractively bound**

✧ **The very best authors**

✧ **Special low prices**

For further details either call Customer Services on 01225 443400 or write to us at

Chivers Large Print Direct
FREEPOST (BA 1686/1)
Bath
BA1 3QZ